The Chinese Catalog

To Ruthie and Charlie,
This is the only thing
we could find that we figured
you didn't get in China.
Best to you for the holidays.
Gaye and Ray
Xmas '84

The Chinese Catalog

Your source book for things Chinese in America

Compiled by Ed Laube and Craig Walker
Designed by Lauren Dong

HIPPOCRENE BOOKS
New York, New York

Printed in the United States of America

ISBN 0-58254-920-0

Contents

Chinese Art
in America

Chinese Chronology

Neolithic	ca. 5000 — ca. 1500 B.C.
Shang	ca. 1523 — ca. 1028 B.C.
Chou or Zhou	ca. 1027 — 256 B.C.
Ch'in	221 — 206 B.C.
Han	206 B.C. — A.D. 220
Three Kingdoms	221 — 265
Chin	265 — 420
Southern Dynasties	420-589
Northern Dynasties	386-581
Sui	581-618
T'ang	618-906
Five Dynasties	907-960
Song or Sung	960-1279
Yuan	1279-1368
Ming	1368-1644
Ch'ing (Manchu)	1644-1912
The Republic of China	1912 — (now on Taiwan)
The People's Republic of China	1949 —

THE BODHISATTVA, KUAN-YIN.
Polychromed wood. Eleventh to twelfth century. H: 95 in. W: 65 in.
Nelson Gallery of Art and Atkins Museum. Kansas City, Missouri

Introduction

Museum visitors in the United States are often surprised and puzzled by the oriental art collections they encounter. Surprised, because China is generally regarded as being rather isolated and it is almost shocking to see art from that country in such abundance here; puzzled, because so much of that art is unlike anything in the occidental world. China is on the other side of the world, but it has not always been all or partially closed to the West. For a long time, in fact, China and the West (particularly England and America) were very close trading partners. During the eighteenth and nineteenth centuries, trade with China grew to an almost unbelievable level of activity. In part, the trading fever was due to Western shippers taking unfair advantage of a China slowly falling to pieces under the progressively more corrupt Manchu dynasty. Nevertheless, today we can thank those years of intense trade relations for much of the splendid Chinese art we have in this country and Europe. And even though Chinese art is different and a bit hard to fully appreciate at first, a few basic guidelines help to explain a good deal about it.

To begin with, it is important to realize that Chinese art developed independently of the artistic traditions of Greece and Rome. Therefore, the attitudes about artistic expression that were established in the West simply did not exist in China. There is, for instance, very little attempt to capture reality in Chinese art. Recent archeological finds have shown us that early emperors were buried with representative statuary—guards, soldiers, horsemen—carved or molded of hard-fired clay. But this early sculpture did not begin an artistic tradition. Certainly verisimilitude never played a very important part in Chinese painting or bronze casting. The Chinese art aesthetic that emerged over the centuries was one of refinement and symbolic and idealistic representation of the natural and supernatural worlds. Chinese art attempts to create a kind of ultimate harmony—a harmony not found in reality but rather in a kind of constructed spiritual unity.

Secondly, it is important to modify the Western attitude towards the decorative arts when considering the Chinese forms. In Western minds, there is a decided difference between "high art" and the so-called "decorative arts." And there is a first and second class attitude at work when this distinction is made. The same distinction is not made in China. Certainly painting is held in highest regard in the Orient. It was, after all, the business of the scholar-poets and the ruling class or mandarins. But the difference between sculpture and jade carving or between bronze casting and ceramics is not so distinct. In the West, practical objects, no matter how beautifully made, are generally considered to be decorative arts. A carved jade brush holder, however, is no less a work of art than is a bronze ritual urn by Chinese standards. This difference in point of view is helpful when looking closely at Chinese art.

Finally, much of the art of the Orient seems unusual to us because it is based on religious and philosophical ideas that are unfamiliar in the West. Confucianism, Buddhism, and Taoism played important roles in establishing symbolic and intellectual references for Chinese arts. Even a brief study of these religions can be of great benefit in understanding Chinese art.

In this section, you'll find some enlightening information on each of the major Chinese art forms—bronze, jade, landscape painting, porcelain, and so forth. There is also a list of selected museums in the United States that hold quality collections of Chinese art. Some of the collections described are quite large; others are small but selective. Some were chosen because they represent the largest collection in a certain geographical area. Along with this information you'll find photographs of some of the interesting pieces of Chinese art in these American collections. Finally, at the end of this section, you'll find a group of books listed. These books either discuss Chinese art in general or take up one or two specific forms in detail. All of the books are recommended, and any one is bound to make your trip to one of the museums a great deal more enjoyable.

Chinese Landscape Painting

One of the unique and certainly one of the most characteristic of Chinese visual arts is landscape painting. Perhaps this is the case because the Chinese themselves held landscape painting in such high esteem. It was the art of the scholar and mandarin and was widely popular throughout the history of imperial China.

Few people realize that the first masters of Chinese landscape painting lived in the tenth and eleventh centuries. Ching Hao (900–960) and Li Ch'eng (940–967) are two celebrated masters of the tenth century. Tung Yuan and the brilliant Fan K'uan carried the art of landscape painting into the eleventh century. These, and a handful of other masters, set the standards for this genre that would endure into modern times. By contrast, it's interesting to note that there were no landscape painters at all in the West at that time and no *masters* of any type of painting. Giotto and the masters of the early Renaissance in Europe were still three to four centuries away.

Chinese landscape painting occupies a place all by itself in the history of art. It is unlike any other form of painting in several respects. It is done largely in inks—cool, bluish-black and warm, brownish-black. The inks are applied with special brushes, which, in the hands of the masters, provide an incredible range of tonal variations. Watercolor is sometimes added to enhance the landscape's prominent features. Except for a few murals in palaces and temples, almost all Chinese landscape paintings were done on silk or paper. Although some small round, oval, or rectangular paintings, called "album leaves," were done, the two most common formats are unknown in Western art. One is the vertical scroll—perhaps the most recognizably Chinese format. Meant to be hung vertically, it is longer and narrower than common Western painting shapes. This format is well known because it is so closely associated with mountain and waterfall landscape paintings. But another popular and perhaps more unusual format is the hand scroll. These paintings are done horizontally, sometimes on quite long rolls of paper or silk. The scrolls are made to be held, one in each hand, and unrolled slowly to reveal the painting. Dramatic panoramas open before the viewer with the effect that he feels as if he were actually traveling through the splendid and exotic landscapes depicted.

Another distinctive aspect of Chinese landscape painting is the inscription of poetic verses on the paintings themselves. These verses, done in strikingly beautiful Chinese calligraphy, sometimes comment on the painting, sometimes on the painter, the collector, or on the landscape itself.

The Chinese established a very close relationship between poetry and painting. No similar relationship has ever existed in Western art. It must be remembered that Chinese landscape artists were scholarly men. The combination of painting, calligraphy, and poetry was not only desirable but expected of these men. This aspect of scholarly devotion should be kept in mind when looking at Chinese landscape painting.

Most American museums have some examples of album leaf and scroll painting. Remember that the Chinese artist was not terribly concerned with representing nature or creating the illusion of reality. Instead, the painters tried to represent the spirit of nature and, in the process, create a kind of "unreal" reality within their illusion. The concepts of beauty, harmony, and even technique in Chinese landscape painting are matters more of philosophy than of artistic intent. And it is upon this point that Western and Oriental art differ so enormously. Although both artistic endeavors aspire towards perfection and the illumination of higher truths, Western art tends to look for a kind of mystical revelation of truth through the uninhibited expression of the human heart. Oriental art, on the other hand, strives to establish a philosophical discipline in which heart and mind work in harmony and thereby produce expressions very close to perfection and revelations very close to truth.

Museums with Exceptional Painting Collections

Boston Museum of Fine Arts
Boston, Massachusetts

The Cleveland Museum of Art
Cleveland, Ohio

The Nelson Gallery of Art
Kansas City, Missouri

Smithsonian Institution
Freer Gallery of Art
Washington, D.C.

CHU-JAN: BUDDHIST RETREAT BY STREAM AND MOUNTAIN. Hanging scroll, ink on silk. Northern Sung dynasty, later tenth century.
The Cleveland Museum of Art, Gift of Katherine Holden Thayer. Cleveland, Ohio

Chinese Porcelain

Scholars are not certain when the word "china" first started being used with reference to the beautiful pottery produced in China. It was probably during the eighteenth century, when it began appearing in the homes of wealthy Europeans. Nowadays it is more accurately known as "porcelain," a sonorous, vitrified, translucent ware made of kaolin clay combined with quartz and feldspar, and coated with a durable shimmering glaze.

The potter's art in China is ancient. Neolithic ancestors of the Chinese were producing a primitive earthenware around 3000 B.C.. Of course, the Minoans and Egyptians had successfully produced it a thousand years before, but the Chinese can be credited with first refining the art.

Household utensils—bowls, cups, plates, and vessels—are among the practical results of developing the art of making pottery. But refining and perfecting the process for artistic expression was probably the result of another application of the potter's skill. Like the Egyptians, the Chinese used ceramic reproductions of men, animals, houses, and other worldly goods in the ritualistic entombment of the dead. Ceramic representations of relatives and servants replaced the human sacrifices made during more primitive times. Ceramic miniatures of animals, soldiers, furniture, and the like were also buried with the deceased for use in the afterlife. The Chinese potters evidently took great pride in these burial pieces. Ceramic horses of the T'ang dynasty (A.D. 618–907) in particular provide a stunning example of the early development of Chinese ceramic techniques.

By the tenth century, during the period known as the Five Dynasties (A.D. 907–960), Chinese potters began developing the white porcelain that would set a new standard for ceramic ware. They also developed a unique glazing process destined to make Chinese porcelain the most valued in the world.

From the tenth to the fourteenth centuries, great refinements in the clay used for porcelain were made. Elegance of design and precision of execution also became hallmarks of Chinese ceramic ware. It was during this period that the thick, jadelike green and blue-green glazes known as celadon glazes were perfected. Kuan (Imperial) ware, also developed during the Five Dynasties period, featured a controlled crackle glaze that has since become synonymous with refined Chinese porcelain.

This refined and subtle tradition in porcelain might have continued to develop in China had it not been for the invasion of the Mongols and the establishment of the Yuan dynasty (A.D. 1279–1368) under Kublai Khan. The Mongol emperors desired a more decorative porcelain. It was during the Yuan dynasty that the first illustrative designs in cobalt blue were painted on pure white backgrounds and then covered with a transparent glaze. The result, now regarded as the very typification of Chinese porcelain, was later perfected during the Ming dynasty. So significant was this development that it would influence world porcelain for five centuries after Kublai Khan. Descendants and copies of this traditional ceramic style are still being made today.

PORCELAIN PLATE. Cobalt blue underglaze on white ground. K'ang Hsi, Ch'ing dynasty (1662–1722). *The Duke University Museum of Art. Durham, North Carolina*

The Ming dynasty (1368–1644) is very closely associated with fine porcelain. The "Ming vase" is certainly part of the vernacular. When the Mings forced the Mongols from China, it meant the return of home rule in China. But the artistic innovations made during the Mongolian experience were not cast off. The blue-and-white porcelain techniques were improved, and a new degree of refinement and delicacy was brought to the production of all porcelain. The Mings also introduced fabulous monochrome ware with the famous "Imperial yellow" and "sacrificial red" glazes.

The Ch'ing (Qing) dynasty (1644–1912), the last dynasty in China, carried the art of Chinese porcelain into the modern age. It perfected a technique known as "five color" decoration, which is essentially the art of suspending colors in various "layers" of underglaze. Also new were some magnificent monochrome glazes such as "peach blossom" and "mirror black." One of the very last and perhaps one of the most beautiful developments in the porcelain of imperial China is known in the West as *"blanc de chine."* The pieces most representative of *blanc de chine* are figurines and tableware of intricate molding and delicate openwork. Most pieces of high quality *blanc de chine* are covered with a thin, creamy white glaze.

For hundreds of years the Chinese have exported porcelain. As a result, you'll find that most museums have a good deal of it to display. In fact, porcelain is often the core of an oriental collection. Since so much Ming and Ch'ing (Qing) dynasty porcelain has been copied, you may feel at times that you're looking in a department store window instead of a museum display case. But these later pieces need close examination to be appreciated. Up close you'll see that the shapes, patterns, and glazes for this porcelain could not be mechanically produced. You'll see the skill and the art of the individual craftsman on each piece. Early porcelain is even more enjoyable to study. The celadon glazes are exquisite, and you will be surprised by the timeless design of these early pieces. Ancient Chinese potters set standards for the development of porcelain, and many of their original ceramic shapes and glazes became classic styles that are still produced today.

Museums with Exceptional Collections of Porcelain

Asian Art Museum of San Francisco
San Francisco, California

The Cleveland Museum of Art
Cleveland, Ohio

Jacksonville Art Museum
Jacksonville, Florida

Los Angeles County Museum of Art
Los Angeles, California

Philadelphia Museum of Art
Philadelphia, Pennsylvania

Sculpture in China

For one reason or another, sculpture in China was never given the dignity or the attention that painting, calligraphy, or the decorative arts were accorded. Early sculpture through the era of the Han dynasty (206 B.C.–A.D. 220) is certainly unremarkable. Most of the smaller pieces are fashioned in the style of bronze art— poor stone copies of fine bronze pieces. They are often decorated with incised geometric patterns or undercut in very low relief. There is very little sense of movement, grace or beauty of shape in this sculpture. Larger pieces, in wood or clay, of this period are generally life-size models of soldiers and horses similar to those found in Han tombs and in particular the tomb of China's first emperor, Ch'in Shih Huang-ti (250–210 B.C.). But these figures hardly represent the emergence of a tradition in sculpture. They are, in fact, merely portraits made with factory-like precision by skilled artisans.

The fall of the Han dynasty was a turning point in Chinese history. After the Han, the Chinese suffered a long period of instability. The period is known historically as the Northern and Southern Dynasties. It amounted to a collective nervous breakdown in Chinese society. Anarchy and factional strife became a way of life. Faith in the old ways and in the Confucian tradition faltered. It was at this point that the Buddhism of India began making inroads into Chinese culture. And Buddhism, with its tradition of icons and graven images, brought with it the only genuine sculptural tradition China has ever known.

By the fifth century Chinese sculptors were turning out images of Buddha in both ritualistic and monumental sizes. Although they were following many of the sculptural traditions established by Indian artisans, a linear and geometric Chinese style soon began to emerge. Taking advantage of the traditional garments and ornaments worn by Buddha and bodhisattva (divine intermediary) images, the Chinese developed a decorative motif reminiscent of the low-relief designs on earlier Han sculpture.

It is interesting to note that unlike Western sculpture, which developed a more and more three-dimensional and realistic appearance, Chinese sculpture was treated as if it was a linear drawing carved in stone. Even the free-standing statues of the later sixth-century sculptors are rarely fully rounded, much less meant to be viewed from all angles. Furthermore, the garments, jewelry, and headdresses represented in Chinese sculpture tend to become design motifs themselves rather than suggesting the movement or shape of the body beneath. Folds in a robe, for instance, may become an intricate pattern of ovoidal lines with very little relation to reality or meaning in the sculpture. Despite these limitations, however, some of the sculpture of the sixth and seventh centuries exhibits an incredibly graceful and inspirational quality. Facial expression in particular is often very evocative of a peaceful or enlightened meditation.

Most Chinese sculpture in American museums is Buddhist. The frequent religius upheavals in China have made religious statuary easy to come by. It is interesting to look at, but most Westerners find it rather repetitious. After the beautiful sculpture of the sixth and seventh centuries, the art of sculpture in China seems to have run out of creative steam. Technically, of course, the sculpture improved. But innovation never seems to have taken hold. Exquisite detailing, especially in wood, reached a peak in the twelfth and thirteenth centuries. Even some degree of realism was attained during this period, and provincial sculpture of small figures called "Louhans" (devoted followers of Buddha) thrived. All of these pieces are interesting to the Western eye, but they are not artistically very important.

Chinese sculpture, as an art, became locked into a repetitive rendering of familiar icons. What is more, sculpture in China remained closely tied to the two-dimensional world of painting. So closely tied, in fact, that it never really managed to break free and become a full-blown art form of its own.

ELEVEN-HEADED KUAN-YIN. Sandstone. T'ang dynasty, late eighth century. H: 51 in. W: 25 in.
The Cleveland Museum of Art, Mr. & Mrs. Severance A. Millikin Collection, Cleveland, Ohio

Museums with Exceptional Sculpture Collections

The Cleveland Museum of Art
Cleveland, Ohio

The Metropolitan Museum of Art
New York, New York

The Nelson Gallery of Art
Kansas City, Missouri

Smithsonian Institution
Freer Gallery of Art
Washington, D.C.

The Bronze Age in China

The art of bronze metallurgy in China has always been something of a mystery to art historians. Although it appears that work in bronze began in China some 2,000 years after it first appeared in the West, early Chinese bronzes display an unusually high degree of artistic and technical skill. It seems almost as if a period of primitive bronze metallurgy never existed in China.

Much is yet to be discovered about ancient Chinese civilization, but recent archeological excavations help explain some of the mysteries surrounding the Chinese Bronze Age. The opening of ancient tombs in recent years has revealed two important things about the early cultures of the Shang and Zhou dynasties (approximately 1500–250 B.C.). First of all, it appears that bronze was held in extremely high esteem in early China. It seems to have been given the same sacred significance given to jade. It was believed to have a power against evil and was thought to be a key to immortality. Like jade, it was also a material used primarily to make objects used in religious rituals. That probably explains why the earliest bronze pieces discovered in China are ceremonial wine containers, urns, cauldrons, and sacrificial axes.

Also significant is the discovery of a very early porcelain or "near porcelain" technology in ancient China. It is now believed that an early form of porcelain was being produced during the Shang dynasty (1523–1028 B.C.). That might explain the high degree of skill exemplified in the earliest known Chinese bronze work. To cast bronze objects, the Chinese used a process called "piece molding." This process requires a highly developed ceramic technology, because the molten bronze is poured into carefully designed clay molds. The more elaborate the shape of the piece, and the more intricate its surface design, the more perfectly made and fired must be the clay mold. Since ceramic technique was so advanced in ancient China, the step to highly refined bronze castings was probably a fairly simple one.

Ornamentation and surface design are probably the most interesting characteristics of Chinese bronzes. Although there are many beautifully shaped pieces of ancient Chinese bronze, many of the ritualistic pieces and those related to the governmental ceremonies are large and rather clumsy by Western standards. They frequently lack the grace and delicacy found in their Western counterparts. But the surface designing, with its abstract animal and spiritual shapes, certainly lifts Chinese bronze work to the level of important art.

There are many striking collections of Chinese Bronze Age pieces in the United

DEEP FOOTED BOWL WITH "ANIMAL MASK" MOTIF. Bronze: Shang dynasty (1523–1028 B.C.). *The Detroit Institute of Arts, Gift of Allan Gerdau. Detroit, Michigan*

States. The high point in Chinese bronze work was attained during the Shang dynasty (1523–1028 B.C.) and was carried into the early years of the Chou dynasty (1027–256 B.C.). Look for pieces with dates in this time period in order to see examples of true Chinese Bronze Age castings.

One of the most interesting things to look for in these early bronzes is the ornamental "animal mask" motif worked into the surface designing. This is a recurring motif found most often on urns, wine and food containers, and axes. It represents the face of an animal, although the eyes are usually the only recognizable feature. To spot the mask, look first for the two eyes. The nose, jaws, ears, and sometimes even the body are represented by a complex network of geometric shapes. The line and character of these early abstract animal shapes represent the beginning of what we now recognize as a particularly Chinese style.

These designs established patterns that were to be used in calligraphic and architectural designing in China for many centuries. Also apparent in these Chinese bronzes is one of the very basic differences in Western and Eastern art traditions. From very early in Chinese history there seems to have been no aspiration towards representational art. Realism, as we know it in the West, does not seem to have influenced the direction of Chinese art at all.

Museums with Exceptional Bronze Collections

The Art Institute of Chicago
Chicago, Illinois

The Minneapolis Institute of Arts
Minneapolis, Minnesota

The Nelson Gallery of Art
Kansas City, Missouri

Chinese Furniture

It is interesting to Westerners to find that the Chinese never seem to have held furniture or furniture makers in very high regard. There is very little written about the development of the style of Chinese furniture despite exhaustive histories written about other forms of Chinese art. There are no "great men" of Chinese furniture—no Chippendales or Hepplewhites—and, even more surprising, practically no pre-Ming (pre-1368) furniture even exists today, either in China or elsewhere.

All this leads us to believe that the furniture so many Westerners stand in awe of was simply not considered that important to the Chinese. It was obviously not saved and passed down from generation to generation, and it must not have been considered suitable to export in any significant way either. It is true that Chinese furniture tends to be very plainly practical, and that is probably why so much of it appeals to modern tastes. But in its functional simplicity, it achieves a kind of beauty that can only be judged in relation to high art.

What little has been learned about the history of Chinese furniture has been gathered from representations found in ancient paintings or woodcuts, and in the miniature models made of clay or ceramics that have been found in the tombs of royalty. From these facsimiles, a few interesting conclusions can be drawn.

To begin with, Chinese furniture, up to and including the time of the T'ang dynasty (A.D. 618–906), seems to have been designed for a society that lived close to the floor. Furniture of this early period seems very similar to what we now think of as traditional Japanese pieces. During the period of the T'ang, however, a Western-style chair also came into use. It was probably originally reserved as a place of honor, but it was soon adapted to general use. The chair changed the perspective of all Chinese furniture—tables, beds, settees and the like, were all raised from floor level, and cabinetry was built taller in order to stay in proportion.

In addition, from what we can see in early representations, it appears that Chinese furniture has not been subject to the major style modifications so common in the West. There appears to be no equivalent of the great changes in style such as occured between 18th century (Louis XIV) and 19th century (Empire) French furniture, for instance. Rather, the Chinese seem to have held fairly strictly to basic designs, modifying only simple aspects of ornamentation and improving the techniques of construction.

Certainly the woods used in Chinese furniture add to the interest and the beauty of the pieces. Much is made of the "purple sandalwood" used in construc-

CH'UANG (COUCH). Yellow rose wood. Ming dynasty, early seventeenth century.
The Portland Art Museum. Portland, Oregon

tion of some of the most elegant pieces. It is a beautiful, almost black, tropical wood from southern India. But Burmese or East Indian rosewood is probably the most prized and certainly one of the most beautiful of Chinese furniture woods. Redwood, satinwood, cedar, and camphorwood are also frequently found in fine Chinese furniture. Unlike Western furniture, Chinese furniture often has a distinctive fragrance as a result of the woods chosen for its construction.

Despite its stepchild status in China, Chinese furniture is much prized and collected in the museums of the West. Most Chinese furniture in American museums is from the Ch'ing dynasty (A.D. 1644–1912). Most pieces are readily recognizable because counterparts exist in the West. One group of pieces, however, is unusual and particularly Chinese. These pieces are associated with the Chinese living platform called the *k'ang*. The *k'ang*, as it first existed in North China, was a built-in platform heated by an underground or contained fire. This type of *k'ang* still exists in some homes of North China. The platform is covered with thin mats for sitting and sleeping, and it is equipped with small pieces of furniture, quilts, rugs, cushions, etc. A *k'ang* table is a low table that looks much like a Western coffee table. It is used primarily for tea service on the *k'ang*. Low *k'ang* chests are built to hold tea things and linen. A wooden *k'ang* is a piece of furniture itself. To the Western eye it looks something like a very wide, flat couch with short railings around three of its sides. But the Chinese sit facing one another in a kneeling or cross-legged position on top of it. A small *k'ang* table is often placed in the center of the wooden *k'ang*. In South China, there was no need for a heated platform, but the *k'ang* way of life was introduced in the south with the use of the wooden *k'ang* and by constructing large, wooden canopied beds that could be used like *k'angs*. Some beds are large enough to accommodate *k'ang* tables and chests in addition to the sleepers.

Of all oriental furniture of museum quality, the *k'angs* are probably the most interesting. *K'angs* are very closely associated with leisure and with the intimate brand of hospitality that has become a tradition of Chinese life.

Museums with Exceptional Collections of Chinese Furniture

Metropolitan Museum of Art
New York, New York

The Nelson Gallery of Art
Kansas City, Missouri

Portland Art Museum
Portland, Oregon

Chinese Jades

Certainly no stone or metal is as closely associated with Chinese art as is jade. Believed to possess spiritual powers, and regarded as an extremely precious stone, jade has been quarried and worked since the very earliest days of Chinese civilization. The uninitiated westerner tends to think of jade as the milky or dark green stone used for jewelry. Actually those stones are probably not jade at all, but are jadeite—a silicate stone something like true jade but with a different crystalline structure. True jade, as worked by the Chinese, is the mineral nephrite, an extremely hard silicate stone found through out Asia.

An ancient Chinese book described jade's five basic characteristics in this way. True jade is ice-cold to the touch; it is translucent when cut thin; it cannot be marred or scratched by metal; it emits a musical note when struck; and it may be polished to a very high gloss. True jade, or nephrite, is found in a variety of colors. Yellow, green, red, black, and white are the five colors traditionally used in Chinese jade carving. Of these, white jade has always been most prized.

Jade carving before the Han dynasty (206 B.C.-A.D. 220) was primarily limited to the production of what are now called "ritual jades." Very little is known about how these early jades were used. Most of them have been found in the tombs of nobles and are believed to be funerary representations of common implements or weapons. Jade axes, daggers, and spearheads have been found. But it is generally agreed that jade objects such as these were never actually used. Rather they were sacred or ritualistic totems meant for the tomb alone.

Along with the representational items, two mysterious symbolic objects are also commonly found at ancient gravesites. These two objects are often found in the coffin with the deceased. One is a perfectly round disc with a large hole pierced

RITUAL DISC, *Pl.* Pale greenish-yellow nephrite (jade). Eastern Chou dynasty, fifth to third century B.C.
Nelson Gallery of Art and Atkins Museum. Kansas City, Missouri

through its center. This disc is called *pi*. The other object is a rectangular block, square in section, sometimes tall and sometimes squat, with a circular bore drilled through it from top to bottom. This object is called *ts'ung*. Very little is known about either of these objects, but the Chinese believe that the *pi* represents the deity of heaven, and the *ts'nung* represents the deity of earth. How these forms symbolize those deities, and whether or not the objects themselves were ever used in any practical way, is not known. Their representation in jade, however, is obviously meant to make them objects of the highest reverence.

Jade is a very difficult stone to work because it can be cut only with substances harder than itself. Quartz sand and crushed garnet were probably used by the ancients with primitive lathes and drilling tools. Still, the early craftsmen were able to make delicate decorative items for the wealthy in addition to the ritual objects.

During the Han dynasty, ritual jades began to disappear. Decorative items such as amulets and pendants representing birds, turtles, and other animals, now became the primary focus of jade carving. This secular application of the art of working jade led to the objects we now most closely associate with Chinese craftsmen.

It is extremely difficult to date Chinese jades, especially those produced between the Han dynasty and the Ming dynasty. Few records were kept pertaining to archeological discoveries prior to the Ming, and jades are almost never inscribed with dates or names. Therefore, jades are generally dated by a "best guess" method which takes into account design motifs and technical skills employed.

Chinese collections in America usually have very interesting and varied jade pieces on display. Few collections lack an array of ritual jades with a *pi* and a *ts'ung* thrown in for good measure. But the miniature carvings of birds, fish, dogs, cats and exotic or mythological animals are by far the most common jade objects.

Figures, especially of old men or young boys with animals, are also popular in old and relatively modern jades. Jade implements for the Chinese scholar's desk such as paper weights, brush rests, and water pots are common because a great number of them were made during the Ming dynasty. More recent jades have been effectively carved into mountain landscapes or rockeries. They are incredibly detailed and are fascinating to examine closely. Certainly a look at Chinese jade carving supports the view that these objects represent perhaps the most refined of the sculptural arts.

Museums with Exceptional Jade Collections

Art Institute of Chicago
Chicago, Illinois

Asian Art Museum of San Francisco
San Francisco, California

Metropolitan Museum of Art
New York, New York

DRAGON ROBE. Embroidered blue silk gauze. Ch'ing dynasty, early nineteenth century. *The Denver Art Museum. Denver, Colorado*

The Silk and Embroidery of Imperial China

Of all the arts and crafts in China, embroidery and silk weaving are perhaps the oldest. In North China, tribes of Mesolithic men (8000–4000 B.C.) are known to have worn fitted clothing decorated with sewn-on shells, beads, and pieces of mother-of-pearl. As early as 3000 B.C., silk was being cultivated and woven into fabric, and silk embroidery probably started around the same time. Unfortunately very few pieces of actual fabric or embroidery work from the early dynasties are still in existence. But important fragments of material and needles made of bone, ivory, and bronze have been found in ancient tombs. These findings indicate that silk weaving and embroidery were highly developed arts very early in Chinese history.

During the Han dynasty (206 B.C.–A.D. 220), the production of silk and embroidered textiles grew rapidly. When Han silks, damask, and embroidered fabrics hit the Near Eastern and Western markets, they were an immediate sensation. No Middle Eastern or European fabrics of the period could compare with them. The "silk road" trade route was established during this period, and it led Chinese merchants as far west as the Roman Empire. Romans, in fact, paid staggering prices in pure gold and silver for the exquisite fabrics. For a time, in the markets of India, Syria, and Parthia, silk was actually used as a medium of exchange in place of gold or silver. As a result of this tremendously profitable trade, the Han Empire grew in wealth and power. In many ways, this silk trade laid the financial foundations that were to support the expansion and the glory of imperial China for centuries to come.

Not only were the silk and Chinese embroidery technically superior to most Western textiles, but the colors and patterning motifs were much more imaginative. Han fabrics displayed a wide variety of damask and polychrome weaves that were unknown in the West. And the embroidered designs representing the Chinese animals of myth and fable—dragons, phoenixes, unicorns, etc.—were engagingly exotic to Western customers.

Textiles are, sadly, one of the most perishable of artifacts. Not only are they often used until they are worn or weakened, but they disintegrate naturally over time and are very often discarded or destroyed by fire. Few examples of Chinese textiles made before the Ming dynasty (A.D. 1368–1644) exist today. Most examples of Chinese silk and embroidery in American museums are from the pe-riod of the Manchu or Ch'ing dynasty (A.D. 1644–1912).

Although silk and embroidered tapestries and wall hangings were made in China, the most interesting examples of Chinese textile art can be seen in the tunics and robes made for the emperors and nobles of the Ming and Ch'ing dynasties. Of these garments, the most interesting are the famous "dragon robes" of the emperors. In China, the dragon came to be associated with power and authority. The five-clawed dragon was considered an imperial symbol. Only the emperor and his immediate family were allowed to wear robes decorated with the five-clawed dragon. In 1759, twelve additional symbols were added to the imperial dragon robe. This robe became known as the Twelve Symbol Robe. Again, only the emperor and his family could wear this robe. The twelve symbols included the dragon, the moon, the sun, stars, mountains, grain, grasses, fire and so forth. Each stood for a particular quality or duty of the emperor, and the robe itself represented the universe.

There are many other interesting symbols to look for in Chinese embroidered textiles. A common symbol is the bat, which the Chinese regard as a symbol of good luck. The peach is a longevity symbol. The flaming pearl (a disc with abstract flames shooting from it) is usually found near the dragon on dragon robes. It was the symbol of the power of authority for the emperor. The phoenix was used as a symbol of goodness and benevolence and eventually came to be associated with the empress. Cranes, peacocks, egrets, pheasants, lions, panthers, tigers and the like were used as symbols of rank among the mandarins (the military and civil service classes) of imperial China. Each rank was assigned an animal by the emperor. The animal symbol was then embroidered onto a square of fabric. The squares are known as "mandarin squares" and they were meant to be worn on informal robes by the mandarins as an indication of rank.

Museums with Exceptional Collections of Chinese Silk and Embroidery

The Denver Art Museum
Denver, Colorado

The Newark Museum
Newark, New Jersey

University of Oregon Museum of Art
Eugene, Oregon

Metropolitan Museum of Art
New York, New York

Chinese Craft and Trade Items

A number of the artifacts in many Chinese collections in the U.S. are what might be called craft and trade items. Craft items from China are often of very high quality and exhibit an interesting tradition in Chinese arts. China trade items are of more historical than artistic interest. Many craft items became trade items as the export business grew in China. In many ways this spelled the end of excellence in the crafts.

Craft pieces, for the most part, are often made in quantity and most, though not all, are strikingly similar in style. Silver and gold work, cloisonné, lacquerware, ivory carving, and snuff bottles are the most often seen craft artifacts. Many of these items were made for the emperors or for noble families in China and are of exquisite quality. Other pieces were made specifically for trade with the West. These pieces are interesting, but of noticeably inferior quality.

We know that Chinese porcelain and silk were being traded in the West long before the days of the famous harbor trade at Shanghai, Hong Kong, Macao, and Canton. Silk got to Europe during the Roman period, and porcelain was being exported from China in great quantities by the seventeenth century. It was tea, however, that set the stage for the enormous export business China was to do in the eighteenth and nineteenth centuries. The great desire for tea sent ships of all nations to the shores of China. This trade established, the Chinese began to offer a number of decorative items for trade—items based on ancient Chinese crafts but made for mass market export.

LACQUERWARE

Lacquer as an artistic medium probably began as early as the Shang dynasty (1523–1028 B.C.). Essentially it is the art of applying a number of very thin coats of lacquer to the surface of carved or finished wood. The surface of the object is then smoothed with charcoal dust. Gold, silver, mother-of-pearl, and opaque paint colors can be suspended in the layers of clear lacquer much as color is suspended in the glaze of fine porcelain. The resulting finish is extremely hard and quite beautiful. Lacquer ware was prized in China, especially by the imperial household. Lightness and durability made lacquered products a natural export commodity.

INCENSE BURNER. Cloisonné. Ming dynasty, sixteenth century. H: 5½ in.
Smithsonian Institution, The Freer Gallery of Art. Washington, D.C.

CLOISONNÉ

Cloisonné is the art of firing brightly colored enamel pastes that are held inside small cells made by placing silver or gold wire on a flat metallic surface. The resulting piece has a surface of multicolored enamels that look as if they are inlaid with gold or silver. The technique was used both in Europe and the Orient, but Chinese cloisonné items became very popular export items.

IVORY CARVING

Ivory, of course, was an exotic material to most Westerners, and the great skill of the Chinese ivory carvers was remarkable. Medicine balls, pagodas, and intricate landscapes became enormously popular as export items. Ivory carvings are still prevalent in Far Eastern markets despite the fact that, for conservation reasons, it is now illegal to bring ivory of any kind into the U.S.

GOLD AND SILVER

One of the most unusual things from a Western point of view is the fact that gold and silver were never held in quite the esteem in China that they were in other parts of the world. Gold and silver were particularly fashioned to suit the European and American markets. Tea sets, trays, bowls, utensils, boxes, and covered jars were very popular objects worked in precious metals for both Chinese nobility and export.

SNUFF BOTTLES

Snuff bottles are perhaps the most unique craft items on display in American museums. Snuff, pulverized tobacco, became very popular in nineteenth century China, and Chinese artisans found the decorative snuff bottles to be a perfect outlet for their creative talents. As a result, snuff bottles present some stunning examples of Chinese craftsmanship. They were not really an export item, but they appealed to collectors in the West and a number of famous snuff bottle collections are now on display in American museums.

Most museums have a good number of these craft and export items on display, and in many ways they provide an insight into the lives of the Chinese that the standard or "classic" forms do not give us. These things were, after all, used by a people very attuned to the beautiful, and very dedicated to the idea of bringing a refined and artistic grace to everyday life. Chinese craft items seem to capture the essence of this rarefied way of life.

Museums with Exceptional Collections of Chinese Craft and Trade Items

Asian Art Museum of San Francisco
San Francisco, California

Farnsworth Library and Art Museum
Rockland, Maine

Los Angeles County Museum of Art
Los Angeles, California

The Minneapolis Institute of Art
Minneapolis, Minnesota

Museum of the American China Trade
Milton, Massachusetts

Seattle Art Museum
Seattle, Washington

PAGODA. Ivory. Ch'ing dynasty, eighteenth century. H: 17 in.
University Art Gallery, Rodnay A. Horne Collection. State University of New York. Binghamton, New York

Museums

THE ART INSTITUTE OF CHICAGO
Michigan Avenue at Adams Street
Chicago, IL 60603
(312) 443-3600

The Art Institute has a collection of Chinese art that includes all periods and mediums, including bronze, wood, stone, lacquer, painting, pottery, porcelain, jade, silver, and textiles. The pieces themselves represent all aspects of life, religious and secular.

Due to limited space, the entire collection cannot be displayed at one time. The exhibit is rotated periodically, however, to provide exposure of as many items as possible. Ancient bronzes and archaic jades are two areas of particular interest in the Art Institute's collection.

THE ASIA SOCIETY GALLERY
The Asia Society
725 Park Avenue
New York, NY 10021
(212) 288-6400

The Chinese holdings at the gallery are part of a larger collection of Asian art assembled by Mr. and Mrs. John D. Rockefeller over a period of thirty years. About ninety of the pieces are Chinese, a majority of them ceramics. There are ritual bronzes and Buddhist and tomb sculptures along with some paintings and lacquer pieces.

Gallery hours are Tuesday–Saturday, 10:00–5:00; Sunday, 12:00–5:00; Thursday 10:00–8:30. Closed Monday. Admission is $2 for non-members, $1 for students and senior citizens.

ASIAN ART MUSEUM OF SAN FRANCISCO
Golden Gate Park
San Francisco, CA 94118
(415) 558-2993

It is difficult to rank museums in terms of their Chinese holdings because different museums emphasize different aspects of Chinese art and because the quality of a collection often has nothing to do with the quantity. With that understood, it is still amazing that the Asian Art Museum's collection of Chinese art numbers 5,000 items. A good number of these items were a part of the Asian art collection of the late Avery Brundage and the collection bears his name. There are about 750 ancient bronzes and close to 2,000 ceramic objects covering all periods and styles. The jade collection of 1,200 pieces is one of the most extensive in the world. The jades are housed in a special

DISH WITH LANDSCAPE DESIGN. Carved cinnabar lacquer on wood or cloth. 13⅝ in. diameter. Ming dynasty, fifteenth century.
The Asia Society, Mr. & Mrs. John D. Rockefeller III Collection. New York, New York

gallery and are regularly rotated—about 300 displayed at any one time. A gilt bronze Buddha, one of about 250 sculptures, is internationally famous as the earliest dated Buddha image from China in the world. An inscription dates it at 338 A.D. The museum also has lots of paintings. Finally, the museum has about 350 pieces of cloisonné, lacquer, ivory, tortoise shell, and rhinoceros horn—exotic craft items that add a colorful touch to the collection.

The museum is open every day, 10:00–5:00. Admission for adults is $1.50. On the first Wednesday of every month, admission is free.

SEATED BUDDHA. Gilt bronze. Later Chao dynasty (dated 338 A.D.). H: 15½ in. W: 9⅝ in. *Asian Art Museum of San Francisco, Avery Brundage Collection. San Francisco, California*

Yao T'ing-mei: LEISURE ENOUGH TO SPARE. Hand scroll, ink on paper. Yuan dynasty, fourteenth century. *The Cleveland Museum of Art, John L. Severance Fund Purchase. Cleveland, Ohio*

BOSTON MUSEUM OF FINE ARTS
465 Huntington Avenue
Boston, MA 02115
(617) 267-9300

The Chinese art collection here is one of the most significant in the world in terms of its completeness and the quality of the pieces. It represents all media and periods, starting with ceramics from the third millennium B.C. There is a small but outstanding collection of archaic bronzes. Painting and sculpture are the major media representing the T'ang and Song periods. In recent years the museum has taken interest in 19th and 20th century Chinese painting and has acquired one of the nation's most important collections.

The museum is open Tuesday–Sunday, 10:00–5:00; Wednesday, 10:00–10:00. Closed Monday. Admission is $3.

THE CHRYSLER MUSEUM
Olney Road and Mowbray Arch
Norfolk, VA 23510
(804) 622-1211

The Chrysler Museum's collection of Chinese art comprises over 400 pieces dating from Neolithic times to this century. Ceramic arts are well represented, ranging from Han dynasty tomb pieces to export porcelain of the last century. The museum also has archaic bronzes and Manchu (Ch'ing dynasty) robes from the 19th century.

The Chrysler is open Tuesday–Saturday, 10:00–4:00; Sunday, 1:00–5:00. Closed Monday. Admission is free, but a voluntary contribution of $1 is appreciated.

CINCINNATI ART MUSEUM
Cincinnati, OH 45202
(513) 721-5204

The Cincinnati Art Museum has a small but first-rate collection of Chinese art. Principal areas represented include archaic bronzes, ceramics from all periods, sculpture in stone, wood, and metal dating from the Han to the Ming, and paintings from the late Song.

The museum is open Tuesday–Saturday, 10:00–5:00; Sunday, 1:00–5:00. Closed Monday. Admission is $2 for adults, $1 for children 12–18. Free on Saturday.

THE CLEVELAND MUSEUM OF ART
11150 East Boulevard
Cleveland, OH 44106
(216) 421-7340

The Cleveland Museum houses one of the country's most extensive collections of Chinese art. There is a very large group of Buddhist sculptures from roughly 300 A.D. to 1600 A.D. There is also an important collection of paintings spanning the years from 1300 to 1900; the works of major masters of this collection are rotated on a regular basis. The large ceramic collection dates from pre-history through the Ch'ing period. Funerary art includes bronzes, jades, tomb tiles, and wood sculptures.

The museum is open Tuesday–Friday, 10:00–6:00; Wednesday 10:00–10:00; Saturday, 9:00–5:00; Sunday 1:00–6:00. Closed Monday. Admission is free.

COLUMBUS MUSEUM OF ART
480 East Broad Street
Columbus, OH 43215
(614) 221-6801

The Columbus Museum of Art's collection of Chinese art includes: Chinese ceramics from the T'ang dynasty; Chichou ceramics dating from the Sung dynasty, Yuan dynasty, and Ming dynasty; Sung white-glazed Ting ware, Ming blue-and-white porcelain; and a number of Chinese paintings from various periods.

CINNABAR JAR. Ch'ing dynasty, eighteenth century. de Saisset Gallery and Museum. *University of Santa Clara. Santa Clara, California*

THE DAYTON ART INSTITUTE
Forest and Riverview Avenues
P.O. Box 941
Dayton, OH 45401
(513) 223-5277

The Patterson-Kettering Gallery of Asian Art was named in honor of two well-known Daytonians who played crucial roles in the establishment and development of the Asian collection. The museum collection includes paintings, sculpture, ceramics, and decorative objects, including China trade porcelain and snuff bottles.

The museum is open Tuesday–Friday, 12:00–5:00; Saturday, 9:00–5:00. Closed Monday. Admission is free. A gallery guide and checklist are available from the museum.

DE SAISSET ART GALLERY AND MUSEUM
University of Santa Clara
Santa Clara, CA 95053
(408) 984-4528

The de Saisset Museum's permanent collection includes a number of Chinese pieces which encompass painting, textiles, jewelry, and sculpture. The two-dimensional works vary in period from the 16th century to contemporary work and are in watercolor and pen and ink on both paper and silk. The textiles are predominantly 19th century. The museum also has some interesting 19th century jewelry with an emphasis on jade works. The largest part of the museum's Chinese collection is made up of jade sculpture and porcelain.

EQUESTRIAN FIGURE. Terra-cotta with traces of pigment. T'ang dynasty.
Columbus Museum of Art. Columbus, Ohio

BURIAL URN. Painted earthenware. Neolithic period, Yang-Shao culture, c. 2200 B.C.. H: 14 in.
The Dayton Institute of Art, Gift of the Estate of Mrs. Harrie G. Carnell. Dayton, Ohio

POCKET. Multicolored silk thread on black satin. Ch'ing dynasty.
The Denver Art Museum. Denver, Colorado

THE DENVER ART MUSEUM
100 W. 14th Avenue Parkway
Denver, CO 80204
(303) 575-2793

The Denver has a permanent gallery of Asian art. About 200 objects are from China. This collection includes a range of pieces in the areas of painting, jades, lacquers, and furniture. Among the most interesting of the museum's holdings is the Grant collection of Chinese court costumes. Most of the items are from the 18th and 19th centuries, and their quality is considered to be outstanding. The Grant collection is one of the largest of its kind. In the words of one of the museums spokesmen, the pieces "simply have to be seen to be believed."

The book shop sells books on China as well as a number of handicraft items made in China. A handbook, *Denver Art Museum: Major Works in the Collection* (1981) has information about many of the Chinese pieces.

The museum is open Tuesday–Saturday 9:00–5:00; Wednesday, 9:00–9:00; Sunday, 1:00–5:00. Closed Monday. There is a suggested $2 contribution for adults.

15

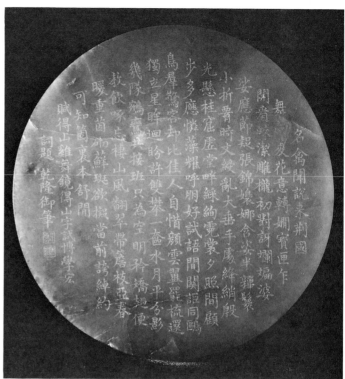

Ch'ien Lung: CIRCULAR TABLE SCREEN WITH PHOENIX AND PEONY DESIGN, AND INSCRIBED POEM ON REVERSE. Pale green jadite. Ch'ing dynasty, later eighteenth century. 7½ in. diameter.
The Duke University Museum of Art. Durham, North Carolina

MANDARIN SQUARE (WITH MANDARIN DUCK DESIGN).
Satin stitch on blue satin. Ch'ing dynasty, eighteenth century.
The Denver Art Museum. Denver, Colorado

SEWING BOX MADE FOR AMERICAN AND EUROPEAN EXPORT MARKET. Lacquer over cedar with cast bronze feet and ivory fitttings. Ch'ing dynasty, mid-nineteenth century.
William A. Farnsworth Library and Art Museum. Rockland, Maine

Unknown Chinese Artist—School of Chinery: CANTON HARBOR. Oil on canvas.
Ch'ing dynasty, mid-nineteenth century.
William A. Farnsworth Library and Art Museum. Rockland, Maine

THE DUKE UNIVERSITY MUSEUM OF ART
Durham, NC 27708
(919) 684-5135

Colonel Van R. White was a member of the Marshall Mission, which tried to arbitrate between the Nationalist and Communist forces after World War II. Colonel White became interested in Chinese art and began to collect it. His collection of 120 pieces, covering a period of 3,500 years, is now on display at the Duke Museum. The collection consists of mostly porcelain and jade pieces with some ancient bronzes and a few ivory items.

FARNSWORTH LIBRARY AND ART MUSEUM
Box 466
19 Elm Street
Rockland, ME 04841
(207) 596-6457

The museum is on the shores of Penobscot Bay, a center for clipper ship trade with the Orient during the 19th century. Opened in 1948, the museum has developed a small but very select collection of Chinese art, including textiles, lacquerware, ivory, and porcelain. There are models of the old clipper ships and exhibits of items connected with the China trade.

The museum is open Tuesday–Saturday, 10:00–5:00; Sunday, 1:00–5:00. Closed Monday. Admission is free.

FOGG ART MUSEUM
Harvard University
Cambridge, MA 02138
(617) 495-7768

The Fogg is one of those special museums that has representative pieces from a variety of media and dynastic periods. One of the strengths of the collection is in early art. The ritual bronzes cover a great range of styles and shapes, from about 1500 B.C. to the Han dynasty. Complementing the bronzes are many ceremonial jade pieces from roughly the same period, as well as bronze and jade weaponry. In religious art, there is Buddhist stone sculpture in addition to a notable collection of gilt bronzes. Paintings cover a wide range of schools and periods, from T'ang to the present. Finally, the museum has a large collection of ceramics roughly dating from the period 1000 to 1600 A.D.

The museum is open Monday–Friday, 9:00–5:00; Saturday, 10:00–5:00; and Sunday 2:00–5:00. Admission is free.

BUDDHA. Gilt bronze. Six Dynasties period, fourth century. H: 12½ in.
Fogg Art Museum, Harvard University. Cambridge, Massachusetts

Lu Chi: LANDSCAPE AND MOUNTAIN PAVILION. Hanging scroll, ink and light color on paper. Ming dynasty, 1572.
Kimbell Art Museum. Fort Worth, Texas

KUANG (BRONZE VESSEL). Bronze. Shang dynasty, twelfth to eleventh century B.C.. H: 8¼ in. L: 9 in.
Indianapolis Museum of Art, Gift of Mr. & Mrs. Eli Lilly. Indianapolis, Indiana

INDIANAPOLIS MUSEUM OF ART
1200 West Thirty-Eighth Street
Indianapolis, IN 46208
(317) 923-1331

The collection of Chinese art at the IMA boasts a number of pieces which may be counted among the finest of their types in the world. Major objects of different media and time are supplemented by a large number of good secondary quality works so that the collection presents a remarkably representative panorama of the development of Chinese art from the earliest days to the present.

The scope of the collection and its strengths may be listed as follows.

Ceramics: Neolithic to Ch'ing, particularly representative of Sung traditions; **Jades:** Shang to Ch'ing, rich with Ch'ing objects; **Metalwork:** Shang to Ming, with emphasis on early ceremonial vessels and small Buddhist figures; **Painting and Calligraphy:** Sung to present, with major works of the Yuan and Ming; **Textiles:** comprehensive Ch'ing items.

JACKSONVILLE ART MUSEUM
4160 Boulevard Center Drive
Jacksonville, FL 32207
(904) 398-8336

The eight-year-old Koger Gallery of the Jacksonville Art Museum houses oriental porcelain, almost 500 pieces of which are from China. And these represent only about one-fourth of the Koger Collection. This marvelous collection of Chinese ceramics, the largest in the southeastern U.S., has examples dating from the Neolithic period to the end of the Ch'ing dynasty. The heart of the collection is white porcelain from Fukien province and the monochrome-glazed wares, brilliantly colored in cobalt blue, turquoise, purple, yellow, and red. There are two earthenware urns from about 2500 B.C., lead-glazed pieces from the Han dynasty, and a number of pieces from the T'ang. But most of the pieces are wares of the Sung, Ming, and Ch'ing dynasties.

The museum is open Tuesday, Wednesday, and Friday, 10:00–4:00; Thursday, 10:00–10:00; Saturday and Sunday, 1:00–5:00. Closed Monday.

HERBERT F. JOHNSON MUSEUM OF ART

Cornell University
Ithaca, NY 14853
(607) 256-6464

The university's Chinese art collection is housed in a modern building designed by I. M. Pei. Six of the nine galleries are devoted to Chinese art, the majority of which is several hundred pieces of ceramics representing all periods. The museum has about 100 paintings, several dozen archaic bronzes, some ancient jades, and several tomb figurines.

The Asian galleries are on the fifth floor of the museum, affording patrons a beautiful view of Lake Cayuga and the Finger Lakes. Except for a short period in January, the museum is open Tuesday–Sunday, 10:00–5:00. All visitors are welcome. Admission is free.

KIMBELL ART MUSEUM

Will Rogers Road West
P.O. Box 9440
Fort Worth, TX 76107
(817) 332-8451

The Chinese collection at the Kimbell is small, but it represents a major body of Chinese art in the area. There are a few well-chosen paintings dating from the 14th to 18th centuries. There is also a collection of ceramics, including some earthenware from the 7th, 8th, and 9th centuries, and celadon and blue-and-white wares from later periods.

The museum book store carries a number of books and exhibition catalogues on Chinese art.

The museum is open Tuesday–Saturday, 10:00–5:00; Sunday, 1:00–5:00. Closed Monday. Admission is free.

OFFICIAL (ONE OF A PAIR). White pottery with three-color glaze. T'ang dynasty. H: 47½ in. W: 12 in. by 11 in.
Los Angeles County Museum of Art, Gift of Leon Lidow. Los Angeles, California

LOS ANGELES COUNTY MUSEUM OF ART

5905 Wilshire Boulevard
Los Angeles, CA 90036
(213) 857-6111

The museum has a comprehensive Chinese collection representing all media and periods from the third millennium B.C. to the Ch'ing dynasty. The ceramics collection includes such pieces as typify the most elegant styles of the Sung, Ming, and Ch'ing dynasties. Jade pieces from Neolithic times to the present are also represented. The lacquer collection at L.A. County is extensive, including woven lacquers as well as carved and painted pieces.

The gift shop has items for sale in conjunction with current exhibitions. On a regular basis there is available some Chinese cloisonné jewelry and a unique selection of authentic Chinese ethnic amulets and necklaces with astrological motifs, priced from $150 to $1,000.

The museum is open Tuesday–Friday, 10:00–5:00; Saturday and Sunday, 10:00–6:00. Closed Monday. Admission is $1 for nonmembers.

THE LOWE ART MUSEUM

The University of Miami
1301 Miller Drive
Coral Gables, FL 32234
(305) 284-3535

The strength of the Lowe collection is ceramics, which has representative pieces from all the major dynastic periods. The museum also has an array of archaic jades and bronzes, as well as some very fine jades from the 18th century. Paintings include works of some of China's most famous painters from the Ming and Ch'ing dynasties.

The museum store stocks a number of books related to the art, history and culture of China as well as a selection of handicraft items produced in China.

The museum is open Tuesday–Friday, 12:00–5:00; Saturday, 10:00–5:00; Sunday, 2:00–5:00. Admission contribution is voluntary.

THE METROPOLITAN MUSEUM OF ART

Fifth Avenue at 82nd Street
New York, NY 10028
(212) 879-5500

The Metropolitan Museum of Art in New York City is, without a doubt, the greatest "encyclopedic" museum of art in the U.S. It is also one of the most respected museums in the world. Its Chinese art collection is truly worthy of its superior reputation. The collection was begun in 1879 with the purchase of a collection of Chinese ceramics. Since that time a Far East Department has been established as a curatorial entity and the collection has been added to year by year. Most noteworthy among the holdings is a sculpture group ranging from the Six Dynasties to the Ming dynasty. Chinese ceramics are also well represented from the Neolithic period through the Ch'ing dynasty. Major additions to the Chinese painting group have been made recently and the Douglas Dillon Galleries reflect these important additions. The Astor Court is a re-creation of a typical Ming dynasty courtyard, constructed with elements made in the People's Republic of China and put in place in the museum by a team of twenty-seven craftsmen from the PRC. The collection also includes a large group of Chinese costumes and textiles, as well as jades, early bronzes, and furniture.

The museum is open Tuesday, 10:00–8:45; Wednesday–Saturday, 10:00–4:45; Sunday, 11:00–4:45. Closed Monday. Suggested contribution $4; children and seniors $2.

THE MINNEAPOLIS INSTITUTE OF ARTS

2400 Third Avenue South
Minneapolis, MN 55404
(612) 870-3046

The department of Asian art at the Minneapolis Institute of Arts was established as recently as 1976. Due to the specialized interests and generosity of a few local collectors, however, certain aspects of Chinese art are already well represented.

The areas best represented include ancient Chinese bronzes (the Alfred F. Pillsbury Collection), Chinese jade (the Pillsbury, Searle, and Walker Collections), Chinese gold and silver, monochrome porcelains, carved rhinoceros horn, snuff bottles, and Chinese silk textiles.

In addition, there are some Chinese paintings, a few good works of early Buddhist sculpture, an excellent collection of T'ang ceramics, and representative works of lacquer and cloisonné. The ceramic collection is fairly comprehensive from the Neolithic period through the 18th century. Due to space limitations the ceramics, textiles, paintings, and snuff bottles are rotated in exhibit.

The museum is open Tuesday–Saturday, 10:00–5:00; Thursday, 10:00–9:00; Sunday, 12:00–5:00. Closed Monday. Admission is $2 for adults, $1 for children.

TEAPOT MADE FOR ENGLISH TRADE MARKET. Silver with mercury gilding. Ch'ing dynasty, early eighteenth century.
Museum of the American China Trade. Milton, Massachusetts

MUSEUM OF THE AMERICAN CHINA TRADE

215 Adams Street
Milton, MA 02186
(617) 696-1815

The Museum of the American China Trade was founded in 1964. It specializes in the history and art connected with early American contacts with China. It is the only museum in the world devoted solely to the collection and display of China trade decorative arts and to the study and interpretation of their histories.

Now housing over 10,000 objects, the museum has comprehensive collections of porcelain, paintings, textiles, furniture, lacquer, and silver. There is an archive and library for students as well.

The museum is open Tuesday-Sunday, 1:00–4:00. Closed Monday and holidays. Admission is $3 for adults, $1.50 for senior citizens.

MUSEUM OF FINE ARTS
255 Beach Drive North
St. Petersburg, FL 33701
(813) 896-2667

The museum has a large collection of ceramics dating from the earliest period to the 19th century. Wood and stone sculpture, mostly Buddhist, date from the 4th to the 10th century. From the Ch'ing period are scroll paintings, textiles, and a few items of furniture.

The gift shop carries jewelry, prints, and small decorative objects from China.

The museum is open Tuesday–Saturday, 1:00–5:00; Sunday, 1:00–5:00. Closed Monday. Admission is free, but a $1 contribution is suggested.

MUSEUM OF FINE ARTS
49 Chestnut Street
Springfield, MA 01103
(413) 732-6092

The museum has an internationally recognized collection of Chinese fine and decorative arts. A number of pieces, such as incense burners, knives, mirrors, and kitchenwares, afford glimpses into the lives of ancient peoples.

The museum shop carries a large number of Chinese products, including pieces in soapstone, celedon, and porcelain. Also available are antiques, lacquered chests, opera puppets, cloisonné jewelry, straw products, and kites.

The MFA is open Tuesday, 12:00–9:00; Wednesday–Sunday, 12:00–5:00. Closed Monday. Admission is free.

MUSEUM OF RHODE ISLAND HISTORY
110 Benevolent Street
Providence, RI 02906
(401) 421-6567

Edward Carrington, an 18th century native of Providence, was the first American consul in China. A majority of the items in the museum are from his collection. They include porcelains, textiles and works of art on paper. The museum has a number of silver pieces made in China for the American market. Finally, there are several portraits of Rhode Island sea captains painted by Chinese artists between about 1800 and 1820.

The museum is open weekends only during much of the winter. Starting in March it is open every day, 11:00–4:00. Admission is $2.50 for individuals, $7 for families.

HORSE. Glazed pottery. T'ang dynasty. H: 20 in.
Museum of Fine Arts. Springfield, Massachusetts

Hsu Tao-ning: FISHERMEN (detail). Hand scroll, ink on silk. Early Northern Sung dynasty, eleventh century. 82 in. long, 19 in. high.
Nelson Gallery and Atkins Museum. Kansas City, Missouri

NELSON GALLERY—ATKINS MUSEUM
4525 Oak Street
Kansas City, MO 64111
(816) 561-4000

The Nelson's magnificent Chinese art collection is one of the largest and most complete in this country. Represented are the major mediums from all periods of Chinese art. For example, the Bronze Age from about 1200–500 B.C. has ceremonial vessels, weapons, and chariot fittings. There are a number of jades from the 5th through the 3rd centuries B.C. The Chinese temple room has several larger-than-life wood sculptures of Buddhist deities. The ceramics include some brilliantly glazed funerary art of horses, camels, attendants, and guards. Finally, the Nelson's collection of Chinese paintings is among the best outside Asia. Pictures are rotated throughout the year, so as to provide maximum exposure.

The museum shop has a number of books on Chinese art and sells a very informative handbook about the Nelson's own collection.

The museum is open Tuesday–Saturday, 10:00–5:00; Sunday, 2:00–6:00. Closed Monday. Admission is $1.50 for adults. Free on Sunday.

ZOOMORPHIC SPIRAL. Bronze. Western Chou dynasty, probably earth ninth century B.C. H: 13½ in. W: 9¼ in.
Nelson Gallery and Atkins Museum. Kansas City, Missouri

THE NEWARK MUSEUM

49 Washington Street
Newark, NJ 07002
(201) 733-6600

Numbering several thousand objects, the Newark's Chinese collection includes bronzes from the Chou and Han periods; ceramics from Han through Ch'ing; textiles and costumes, lacquers and enameled bronzes of the Ming and Ch'ing. Paintings are represented on both silk and paper in hand scroll, hanging scroll, and panel formats and are primarily of the 18th and 19th centuries.

Forty-five important pieces from the collection were published by China Institute in America (New York City) in 1980. This catalogue is available from the Newark Museum for $10 plus $1 mailing charge. A catalogue of the ceramics alone (including export porcelains) is available for $4 (plus $1 mailing).

Newark Museum is open every day from 12:00–5:00. Admission is free.

TEMPLE OF WISDOM, PEKING.
Ming dynasty, c. 1444 A.D.
Philadelphia Museum of Art.
Philadelphia, Pennsylvania

PEABODY MUSEUM OF SALEM

East India Square
Salem, MA 01970
(617) 745-1876

The opening of trade with China in 1784 was the beginning of a gentle revolution that touched many American households. Scarcely any facet of American decorative art—painting, porcelain, silver, ivory, and furniture—was untouched by the influence of the new imports. The Peabody Museum houses a vast store of such object. Porcelains, paintings, furniture, silver, and lacquerware items make up most of the Peabody's extensive collection of China trade articles.

Admission is $1.50 for adults, 75¢ for senior citizens, students, and children 6–16.

PHILADELPHIA MUSEUM OF ART

26th Street and Ben Franklin Parkway
Box 7646
Philadelphia, PA 19101
(215) 763-8100

The museum's Far Eastern wing houses art from India and central Asia, China, and Japan. The six Chinese galleries have on exhibit a total of thirty-five pieces of wood, marble, and stone sculpture; thirty paintings; about thirty-five pieces of Ming furniture; jades, rock crystals, lacquerware, cloisonné, and snuff bottles. The museum also has about 250 pieces of Chinese ceramics ranging from the Neolithic period through the Ch'ing dynasty.

The museum also has some rather unusual exhibits in the form of entire Chinese buildings. Originating in China, they were dismantled, brought to the U.S., and reassembled here. They are a Ming palace hall, the interior of a temple, and a scholar's study. The hall was designed to serve as the chief reception room of a palace built in the early 1600's by an important eunuch. The room measures about thirty-four feet by thirty feet, and is over thirty feet high at the peak of the roof. Except for the plaster walls and tile floor, the room is original, from the marble bases of the great red lacquered columns to the peak of the intricately made ceiling.

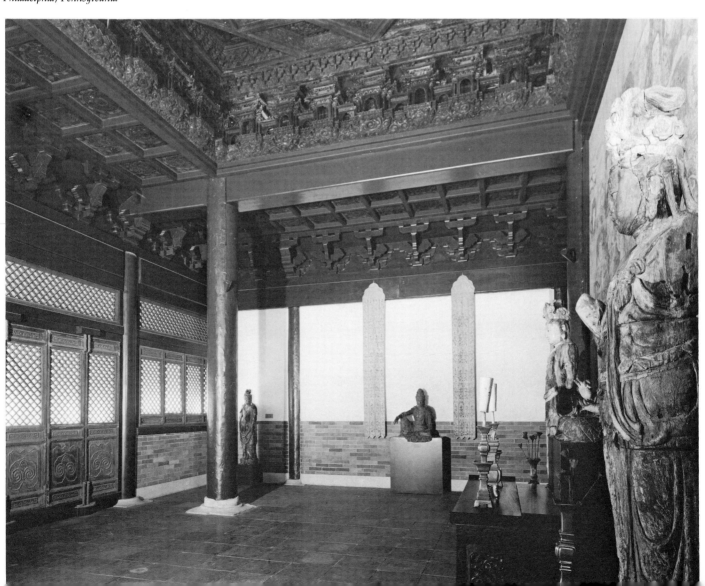

PHOENIX ART MUSEUM

1625 North Central Avenue
Phoenix, AZ 85004
(602) 257-1222

The Phoenix Art Museum has a small but growing collection of Chinese art. The collection now includes a small number of Shang and Chou bronzes, Buddhist sculptures, later Chinese paintings, and a fairly large collection of Chinese ceramics and decorative arts. The strength of the ceramics collection lies in the area of late Ming to early Ch'ing porcelain, especially Transitional Style blue-and-white. On long-term loan to the museum is a large group of Chinese ivories from the Sir Victor Sassoon collection.

Hsuan-Tsung: BIRDS AND RABBITS IN SNOW (detail). Ink on silk with color. Ming dynasty, 1427. *San Diego Museum of Art. San Diego, California*

PORTLAND ART MUSEUM

1219 Southwest Park Avenue
Portland, OR 97205
(503) 226-2811

The Portland Museum has, over the years, chosen to emphasize certain areas of Chinese art and give limited emphasis to others. It has a significant group of tomb figurines and early ceramics. Furniture of the Ming and Ch'ing periods is the great strength of the collection. There are also significant groups of snuff bottles and textiles. More limited are the holdings in Buddhist sculpture, Ming painting, and bronze.

The museum is open Tuesday–Sunday, 12:00–5:00; Friday, 12:00–10:00. Closed Monday. There is no admission fee, but the museum appreciates a $1 contribution; less if you're a junior or senior citizen.

CHUNG (BELL). Bronze. Early Chou dynasty, eleventh or tenth century B.C.. H: 19¾ in. *The Portland Art Museum. Portland, Oregon*

24

BUFFALO AND HERDSBOY IN LANDSCAPE. Style of Li T'ang (c. 1050– after 1130). Album leaf, color on silk. Sung dynasty, eleventh to twelfth century.
Seattle Art Museum. Seattle, Washington

THE ART MUSEUM
Princeton University
Princeton, NJ 08544
(609) 452-3788

The museum has a fine, though moderate-sized, collection of Chinese bronze ceremonial vessels, sculpture, paintings, and some examples of minor arts such as bronze mirrors, clay tomb figures, and a collection of snuff bottles.

The museum is open Tuesday–Saturday, 10:00–4:00; Sunday, 1:00–5:00. Closed Monday and some holidays.

SAN DIEGO MUSEUM OF ART
Balboa Park
San Diego, CA 92112
(714) 232-7931

All of the Chinese art in the museum is in the Asian Court. The museum houses a good general collection of Chinese art, from virtually all periods, and in all the major media: porcelain, bronze, jade, sculpture, and painting.

The museum is open Tuesday–Sunday, 10:00–5:00. closed Monday. Admission is $2 for adults, $1.50 for senior citizens, and $1 for students.

SANTA BARBARA MUSEUM OF ART
1130 State Street
Santa Barbara, CA 93101
(805) 963-4364

The museum has a range of Chinese art covering most major periods and media. Among the most rare pieces are a bronze bell from about 300 B.C., a pair of stone guardian lions from about 400 A.D., and a number of Buddhist sculptures covering a period of a thousand years up to about 1300 A.D. Probably the best represented medium in the Chinese art holdings at Santa Barbara is ceramics, which range from the Han through Song dynasties.

The museum is open Tuesday–Saturday, 11:00–5:00; Sunday, 12:00–5:00. Closed Monday. Admission is free.

Chuang Che: AUTUMNAL FEELING. Collage and oil on canvas. 1965.
Helen Foresman Spencer Museum of Art, University of Kansas. Lawrence, Kansas

SEATTLE ART MUSEUM

Volunteer Park
Seattle, WA 98112
(206) 447-4710

There are a number of outstanding examples of Chinese painting housed in the Seattle museum. The museum's well-known collection of snuff bottles comprises more than 300 objects. There are representative pieces covering the full range of the development of ceramics. Arts from the Bronze Age include ritual vessels, fine jades, and lacquers. And the museum has a number of Buddhist paintings and sculptures dating from about 400–1600 A.D.

The museum is open Tuesday–Saturday, 10:00–5:00; Thursday, 10:00–9:00; Sunday, 12:00–5:00. Closed Monday. Admission is $2, $1 for seniors and students.

SPENCER MUSEUM OF ART

The University of Kansas
Lawrence, KS 66045
(913) 864-4710

The Spencer's Chinese holdings, while rather modest, do include a number of ancient bronzes and representative porcelains from roughly the year 1000 A.D. to the present. There are also a number of examples of lacquerware, jades, snuff bottles, and a small assortment of textiles. Paintings include a small group of comparatively recent date, from about 1600 through the last dynasty (1912), and a number of modern works.

The museum is open Tuesday–Saturday, 9:30–4:30; Sunday, 1:00–4:30. Closed Monday. Admission is free.

SMITHSONIAN INSTITUTION

Freer Gallery of Art
Washington, D.C. 20560
(202) 357-2104

Charles Lang Freer (1856–1919) of Detroit, Michigan, began collecting art after a successful business career with American Car and Foundry Company. His interests in collecting soon turned to the classic arts of China. When he died, his will provided that his collection be given to the Smithsonian. The Freer Gallery was built to display the collection and was formally opened in 1923.

Since that time, a great deal of art has been added to the original collection. All periods and all media of Chinese art are represented at the Freer. The quality of the work sets a standard of excellence by which other collections can be judged. The Freer also makes special provisions for students to study the collection, especially those pieces that cannot be put on permanent display.

The Freer Gallery of Art publishes an excellent sales catalogue that offers color

SAKYA-MUNI AND TWO BODHISATTVA. Bronze, gilded. Sui dynasty. c. A.D. 597. *Smithsonian Institute, The Freer Gallery of Art. Washington, D.C.*

TERMINAL ORNAMENT: BIRD IN PROFILE. Stone. Shang dynasty, late Anyang period, eleventh century B.C.. H: 4⅝ in. *Smithsonian Institution, The Freer Gallery of Art. Washington, D.C.*

reproductions, cards and notes, jewelry, and the like. Another book, *Masterpieces of Chinese and Japanese Art*, is essentially a guide to the Freer collection. It is a beautiful and informative book and can be ordered from the Smithsonian, as can the sales catalogue.

The Gallery is open every day from 10:00–5:30. Closed Christmas Day. Admission is free.

THE FOUR SEASONS. Ivory, carved. Ch'ing dynasty, nineteenth century. H: 8 in. University Art Gallery, Rodnay A. Horne Collection. *State University of New York. Binghamton, New York*

UNIVERSITY ART GALLERY
Rodnay A. Horne Collection
State University of New York
Binghamton, NY 13901
(607) 798-2634

The Rodnay A. Horne Collection of Chinese Art can be generally described as an assemblage of decorative arts—objects that would have been found in temples and the houses of the Chinese upper class. The collection covers a wide range of media: ivory carving, ceramics, wood carving, bronzes, and textiles. It includes objects dating from the 7th or 8th to the 20th centuries, originating from Tibet, Mongolia and Manchuria, as well as China proper.

The earliest works in the collection, and among the most important, are the T'ang dynasty ceramics. The largest part of the Horne Collection, however, dates from the late Ming and Ch'ing dynasties. As this collection deals with works intended for domestic or decorative uses, it provides an interesting insight into the lives and aspirations of those people for whom these objects were made.

INDIANA UNIVERSITY MUSEUM OF ART
Bloomington, IN 47405
(812) 335-5445

The Chinese portion of the museum's Asian collection numbers about 100 objects from the bronze, pottery, jade, lacquer, and painting art forms. Areas of particular significance are the Shang and Chou bronzes and pottery figurines from the 3rd to the 8th century.

MUSEUM OF ART AND ARCHAEOLOGY
University of Missouri
1 Pickard Hall
Columbia, MO 65211
(314) 882-3591

The museum has a modest collection of about 150 objects of Chinese art. Most of the museum's pieces are decorative arts of later periods including ivory figurines, decorated porcelains, and embroidered robes. Among the most notable pieces are two bronze wine vessels from the Shang dynasty and a pair of terra-cotta horse heads of ancient origin.

The museum is open Tuesday–Sunday, 12:00–5:00. Closed Monday and national holidays. Admission is free.

TRIPTYCH. Ivory and rosewood. Ch'ing dynasty, nineteenth century. H: 16¾ in. W: 11¾ in. University Art Gallery, Rodnay A. Horne Collection. *State University of New York. Binghamton, New York*

MUSEUM OF ART

University of Oregon
Eugene, OR 97403
(503) 686-3027

Ch'ing dynasty court textiles and garments are a special area of focus at this museum. Jade, porcelain, and jewelry of the same period also make up a good portion of its holdings. From earlier periods, there are some archaic bronzes and jades. Figurines, primarily of people and horses, constitute the bulk of ceramic mortuary items from the Han through T'ang dynasties.

The museum is open Tuesday–Sunday from 12:00–5:00. Closed Monday. Admission is $1.50.

THE UNIVERSITY MUSEUM

University of Pennsylvania
33rd and Spruce Streets
Philadelphia, PA 19104
(215) 243-4000

The museum's Chinese collection is not large, but is considered remarkable for its quality and rarity, especially in the area of sculpture. The most important of the sculpture collection are two stone reliefs of horses from the tomb of the first emperor of the T'ang, who ruled in the early 7th century. There is a small but very select collection of ritual bronzes and jades from both very early and later periods.

The museum is open Tuesday–Saturday, 10:00–4:30; Sunday, 1:00–5:00. Closed Monday. A contribution of $2 is suggested.

DRAGON ROBE FOR A YOUNG BOY OF HIGH RANK. Red satin, embroidered. Ch'ing dynasty, early nineteenth century.
University of Oregon Museum of Art. Eugene, Oregon

THE VANDERBILT MUSEUM

180 Little Neck Road
Centerport, NY 11721
(516) 261-5656

The museum is the former estate of William K. Vanderbilt II known as "Eagle's Nest." Much of its collection are pieces from the China trade—porcelains, rosewood furniture, lacquer screens, ivory, and carved stone and wood figurines made for sale in the U.S. The collection does include some archaic objects, however, including bronze vessels from the Shang and Chou periods.

The museum is open from May 1 through October, Tuesday–Saturday, 10:00–4:00; Sunday and holidays, 12:00–5:00. Closed Monday. There is a 75¢ admission charge for adults.

UTAH MUSEUM OF FINE ARTS

The University of Utah
Salt Lake City, UT 84112
(801) 581-7049

The museum houses the Bert G. Clift collection of Chinese ceramics. The collection is composed mostly of items from the Ch'ing dynasty and is primarily porcelains. It is fairly representative of Ch'ing dynasty porcelains, and includes a number of the much sought after "imperial" pieces.

Although the collection is small, about sixty-two pieces, each item is thoroughly annotated in a handout available at the museum.

WORCESTER ART MUSEUM

55 Salisbury Street
Worcester, MA 01608
(617) 799-4406

The museum has a small but first-rate collection of Chinese art including ancient bronzes, jades, and other archeological material. There are a number of Ming and Ch'ing paintings, including works by Tao Chi and Wen Cheng-ming. Also on view are ceramics exemplifying major types from the T'ang through the Ch'ing dynasty.

Selected Books on Chinese Art

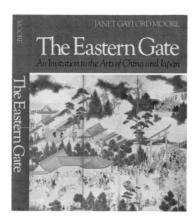

THE ART AND ARCHITECTURE OF CHINA
Laurence Sickman
Alexander Soper
Penguin Books 1971
527 pp.

This is one of the Pelican History of Art series, which is planned to cover the history of art and architecture of all ages in over fifty volumes. Sickman deals only with sculpture and painting, Soper with architecture. Both authors are internationally known in their fields, and this book can be considered one of the standard authoritative guides to Chinese art.

Although this book might be a rather large undertaking for the pleasure reader, it rewards with a great deal of insight and information. It is not a book which readily entertains the eye either. The illustrations in this soft-cover edition are black-and-white and rather small. But it does provide a good basic outline of the progress of painting, sculpture, and architecture in China.

THE EASTERN GATE
An Invitation to the Arts of China and Japan
Janet Gaylord Moore
William Collins Publishers, Inc. 1979
296 pp. $24.95

This book might very well be one of the best and most enjoyable introductions to Far Eastern art on the market. The approach is unique in that Ms. Moore concentrates on specific arts and artists and on certain representative cultural influences in order to provide an overall introduction to the arts of China and Japan.

For the most part, the book deals with painting and porcelain as the two most revealing Chinese art forms. She pays particular attention to the influences of nature and religion on these and other arts. There is also some interesting information on calligraphy and the progress of

archeology in China. As a bonus, she throws in a very enjoyable "Literary Interlude," which presents poems and stories from the sixth century to the present. The book is beautifully and informatively illustrated.

THE ARTS OF CHINA
Hugo Munsterberg
Charles E. Tuttle Co. 1972
243 pp. $29.50

This is a general introduction to the major arts of China: ceramics, bronze, painting, sculpture, and architecture. The author, a scholar and professor of oriental art, treats the arts in chronological fashion, interweaving information about social structure, changes in philosophy, literature, and technical and governmental changes. Each age seems, in retrospect, to have had one dominant artistic form, and this chronological approach is helpful in making that tendency clear. The text is illustrated with 115 plates, ten of which are in color.

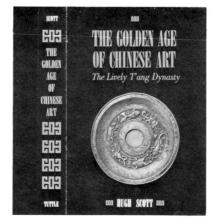

OUTLINES OF CHINESE SYMBOLISM AND ART MOTIVES
Charles Alfred Speed Williams
Charles E. Tuttle Co. 1974
(reprint of 3rd revised edition, 1941)
472 pp. $20

Mr. Williams described his book as, ". . . a practical handbook of the science of Chinese symbolism as based on the early folklore." It's not only practical, it's complete. The book is a gold mine of material on many individual subjects, presented together with aspects of the topics that are relevant to understanding Chinese culture: history, customs, philosophies, and values. A sampling of the subjects covered includes such diverse subjects as conch shells, Confucius, rats, mosquitoes, unicorns, pagodas, pomegranates, and gods. They are arranged in alphabetical order for easy reference.

This book is a valuable guide for virtually anyone interested in any facet of Chinese art.

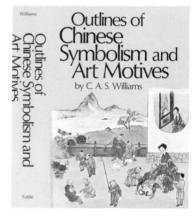

THE GOLDEN AGE OF CHINESE ART
Hugh Scott
Charles E. Tuttle Co. 1982
191 pp. $33.50

During the seventh and eighth centuries, the T'ang emperors of China controlled an international empire far greater than that of the contemporary, Charlemagne. Hugh Scott, former U.S. senator from Pennsylvania, has been collecting Chinese art for over forty-five years. He is an acknowledged expert in the area of T'ang art, and the objects pictured in the 124 illustrations in this book come from his collection. Metalwork is the dominant medium in the collection—mirrors, boxes, bowls, and the like—but there are also ceramics and lacquers. It is an attractive book and one that adopts an interesting approach to a very significant period in the art of China.

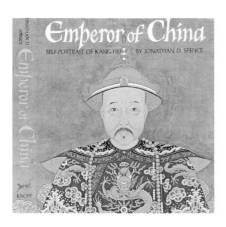

THE EMPERORS OF CHINA
Christopher Hibbert
Stonehenge Press Inc. 1981
176 pp. $21.95

This book isn't really about Chinese emperors, but rather the evolution of Chinese culture from early times until the last dynasty. It provides a view of the culture through its art and artifacts. Many of these pieces were commissioned by various emperors, and some of the paintings were actually done by the emperors themselves.

The strength of this book is its color photos. There are about 100 color plates, many of which are two-page spreads. Jewelry, sculpture, bronzes, jades, and paintings are all wonderfully reproduced. The captions and descriptive material for the plates, however, leave a lot to be desired. What there is seems incomplete and there is, for instance, no indication of the sizes of any of the pieces illustrated. There is some interesting and relevant historical information accompanying the plates, but this book can be enjoyed primarily for its excellent reproductions of classic Chinese art.

THE ART TREASURES OF DUNHUANG
Ten Centuries of Chinese Art from the Mogao Grottoes
Edited by the Dunhuang Institute for Cultural Relics, PRC
Lee Publishers Group, Inc. 1981
254 pp. $85

The Mogao Grottoes at Dunhuang are one of the richest troves of Buddhist art in the world. Though distant from the centers of Chinese civilization, Dunhuang was an important station on the Silk Route that linked China with western Asia. It was along this route that Indian Buddhism originally came to China. In an arid climate relatively isolated from the destruction that accompanies civilization, the massive works of artists and artisans have managed to survive down to the present.

This beautiful book, bound in yellow silk, was limited to a printing of 2,000 copies. There are 200 color plates, each accompanied by detailed information about the works of art pictured.

TREASURES FROM THE BRONZE AGE OF CHINA
The Metropolitan Museum of Art, New York
Ballantine Books 1980
192 pp. $12.95

The development of bronze metallurgy in ancient civilizations marked an important step forward because it assured the creation of better tools and better weapons. In China, bronze technology found a third important role, the casting of ceremonial food and drinking vessels. Bronze objects became symbols of power for the nobility. This book is a collection of photographs from the bronze exhibition from the People's Republic of China that toured the U.S. in 1980 and 1981. It provides an overview of the brilliant achievements of the later Bronze Age in China. The 105 color plates are remarkable for their clarity and vivid color. About thirty pages of introductory text chronicles the political and artistic developments of the Bronze Age. Extensive notes describing each plate are found at the back. It is an attractive exhibition book, reasonably priced and very informative.

EIGHT DYNASTIES OF CHINESE PAINTING
Sherman E. Lee, Wai-Kan Ho, Laurence Sickman and Marc F. Wilson
Indiana University Press
408 pp. $60

The Nelson Gallery in Kansas City and the Cleveland Art Museum, with two of the finest collections of Chinese paintings outside China, collaborated on this panoramic survey of Chinese painting. All the major schools and periods are represented in 282 photos, eight of which are in color.

By far the most important feature of this book is the attention given to each of the reproductions. Biographical information on the artists, signatures, seals, and complete bibliographic information accompany every painting. The explanations act as a guide to viewing the plates, and stimulate the reader's sensitivity to a wealth of detail that might otherwise go unnoticed. It is unfortunate that so few of the plates are in color.

CHINESE PAINTING
James Cahill
Rizzoli International Publications Inc. 1977
216 pp. $14.95

The author, a noted expert on Chinese painting, has succeeded here in doing something that specialists often have difficulty with—presenting material in a general way for the reader with little background. He covers the entire sweep of traditional Chinese painting, from Han figure painting to the classic work of the eighteenth century masters. The text presents the paintings (many of which have never before been reproduced in a book) against the background of the aesthetic and critical ideas prevalent at the time.

This book achieves a pleasing balance of visual beauty and scholarly narrative. The 100 color plates are beautifully reproduced. This is a highly recommended introduction to the fascinating world of Chinese painting.

PARTING AT THE SHORE
Chinese Painting of the Early and Middle Ming Dynasty, 1368–1580
James Cahill
Weatherhill 1978
281 pp. $32.50

This is the second in a projected five book series Mr. Cahill intends to write about later Chinese painting. This book highlights the lives and work of almost fifty artists. It tells of the Ming continuation of major features already evident in the earlier Yuan period. This is a bigger, more complex book than the first; there is more information about the artists and more of their works have survived. The result is that Mr. Cahill is able to be more precise in discussing local schools and traditions and in drawing correlations between the situations of individual artists and their works. In short, Ming painters find representation as artistic personalities rather than as remote masters. As in the first book, the text is predominant with the illustrations serving only to support various theories and observations.

HILLS BEYOND A RIVER
James Cahill
Weatherhill 1976
198 pp. $25

James Cahill is one of today's eminent historians of Chinese art. He has written a number of books, both scholarly and of a general nature. This book is the first of a projected series of five volumes intended to introduce the history of later Chinese painting.

He begins with the Yuan dynasty (1279–1368) because, as he states, "Understanding the achievements of the Yuan masters . . . is as crucial to the study of later Chinese painting as is understanding the Renaissance to the study of European painting." It is a combination of historical analysis and aesthetic insight that makes this book interesting. In each chapter the format is the same: the author outlines his observations and theories concerning certain periods or certain painters, then illustrates his points with examples of paintings chosen from museums around the world. The book is not, however, aimed exclusively at the China scholar. It is a detailed book, but very readable and extremely informative.

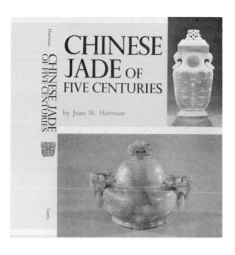

CHINESE JADE OF FIVE CENTURIES
Joan M. Hartman
Charles E. Tuttle Co. 1969
172 pp. $27.50

Ms. Hartman has brought together a collection of jade pieces exclusively from museums in this country. She limits the dates of the pieces to the Ming and Ch'ing periods, roughly the last 500 years. The author points out that most of the truly superb jade carvings were executed during this period. Besides the ten color and forty-five black-and-white plates, the book provides a good deal of information about the carving of jade, the differences in each carving, methods of attribution, and the function and symbolism in the various pieces.

There is clearly a sense of "mission" in this book. The author is out to prove that jade carving is truly a high art. She believes that it was the "supreme achievement" of the Chinese earlier years and was "invested with genuine affection, the highest expectations, and unalterable immovable faith."

CHINESE JADE THROUGHOUT THE AGES
Stanley Charles Nott
Charles E. Tuttle Co. 1962
193 pp. $47.50

First published in 1936, this book had become a collector's item by the time the Tuttle Company got around to republishing it in a new edition. It is a comprehensive history of jade, a standard work on the subject. Here is a full, descriptive account of the significance of jade carving in China from the earliest times, around 1500 B.C., down to the twentieth century. It includes an explanation of the different types of jade, its decoration, folklore, and symbolism. Included are thirty-nine color plates, 110 black-and-white plates, and seventy-three line drawings taken from pieces in collections from all over the world. For those interested in learning about jade, this book may be the best place to start. For jade aficionados, this book is a must.

THE ART OF ORIENTAL EMBROIDERY
History, Aesthetics, and Techniques
Young Y. Chung
Charles Scribner's Sons 1979
183 pp. $25

The purpose of this book is to show the importance of embroidery as a major traditional art form in Asia, to describe its development, and to provide some idea of the rich cultural heritage that surrounds it. The author relates the history of embroidery in China, Japan, and Korea and explains the techniques in each country. She has included examples from public and private collections all over the world. She describes scrolls, screens, banners, and home accessories. One chapter is devoted to each of the ultimate examples of the art—the Chinese dragon robe, the Japanese kimono, and the Korean bridal robe. Ms. Chung also pays a great deal of attention to design and its symbolism.

DRAGONS AND OTHER CREATURES
Chinese Embroidery
Katherine Westphal
Lancaster-Miller 1979
72 pp. $8.95

When the Manchus came from the north and became the ruling power in China in 1644, they brought along a style of dress characteristic of a nomadic people. The most unique piece of Manchu clothing was a heavily decorated long robe, known as the "dragon robe." Almost completely covered with embroidery, many of these robes are now treasured museum pieces.

This book has about fifteen pages of text explaining the many aspects of fine embroidery, followed by twenty-five color plates. On the page facing each plate is a drawing and analysis of the pattern pictured. The plates themselves are done in rich color; the explanation greatly enhances the reader's understanding of these truly remarkable garments.

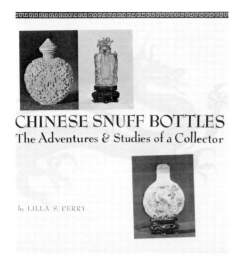

CHINESE SNUFF BOTTLES
The Adventures and Studies of a Collector
Lilla S. Perry
Charles E. Tuttle Co. 1960
158 pp. $35

Snuff is a preparation of pulverized tobacco that is inhaled through the nostrils. The practice gained currency in China in the eighteenth century, roughly 100 years after the introduction of tobacco by Westerners. This coincided with the final flowering of artisanship in the "minor arts." Consequently, all the skills and ingenuity of Chinese artisans were lavished on these tiny bottles.

The author is a long-time collector of snuff bottles. Coupled with her personal tales about bargaining for snuff bottles is a great deal of material about the history, production and merchandising of the bottles.

The book has ninety color and seventy black-and-white plates, all of excellent quality. This was the first full account of snuff bottles in any language. The author knows and loves her subject, and her enthusiasm is infectious.

THE CHINESE GARDEN
Maggie Keswick
Rizzoli International Publications Inc.
216 pp. $35

The classic Chinese garden was a place of repose deliberately engineered to nourish the spirit by appealing to the senses. This English author first went to China when she was four and has visited the country repeatedly since 1961. Educated in Shanghai, Hong Kong, and Oxford, she is in a unique position to interpret the Chinese garden to western readers. The text is a mixture of description and interpretation together with cultural anecdotes and selections from Chinese literature. The book has over 250 illustrations, mostly photos, with reproductions of traditional paintings of Chinese gardens.

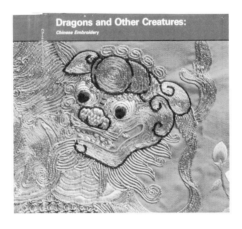

OUT OF CHINA'S EARTH
Qian Hao, Chen Heyi, Ru Suichu
Harry N. Abrams 1981
208 pp. $50

This book is essentially a picture book documenting ten archeological sites and the objects they have yielded. The oversize volume contains 226 color plates and 60 black-and-white photos. It is beautifully laid out, and the quality of the photos is excellent. The text, written by three Chinese scholars, is also very informative.

The book represents the first full account of the digs that have been undertaken in China in the past thirty years. Besides the now familiar terra-cotta army of the first emperor of China and the lady with the jade burial suit, the book describes the finds of digs along the old Silk Road and those investigating Han culture in Inner Mongolia.

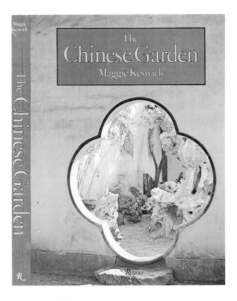

ART AND ARCHEOLOGY IN CHINA
Edmund Capon
The MIT Press, dis't. 1977
196 pp. $9.95

Subject matter in this book is confined to the objects comprising the Chinese exhibitions that toured Europe and America in the late 1970's. The author's aim is to provide an historical and cultural background to the arts of early China and to introduce some of the recent finds which thrilled so many people in the West.

After the initial chapter on China and the West, there are chapters on archeology in China and on the pre-historic period and the Bronze Age. Thereafter, beginning in the third century B.C., the author adopts a dynastic approach, covering the five major periods, ending with the Yuan dynasty. The organization is clear and the 118 color plates are beautiful. The scope of the book is limited, but it is very well done and sensibly priced.

Chinese
Kaleidoscope

Museums
American Museum of Natural History
Wing Luke Memorial Museum
Oroville Chinese Temple
Pacific Asia Museum

Crafts and Collectibles
Chinese Crafts
Stamps
Coins
Glass
Carpets
Antiques & Collectibles

Health, Sports, and Hobbies
Acupuncture
Ginseng
Secrets of Chinese Herbalists
Ping Pong
Boxing
   T'ai-chi Ch'uan
   Pa-kua
   Hsing-I
Kites
Mah-Jongg
Gardens

Religion and the Occult
Confucianism
Taoism
I Ching
Chinese Horoscope
Signs of the Zodiac
   (12 signs)

Language, Literature, and Performing Arts
Chinese Poetry
Fiction
Shadow Puppetry
The Peking Opera
Speaking and Writing Chinese

"The Gift of a Thousand Flowers"

Early in the history of Chinese literature, there was a particularly rich period of achievement that was called "the time of a thousand flowers." We in America have been the recipients of many of the finest achievements of the Chinese. To the United States the Chinese have brought a legacy of at least "a thousand flowers."

Trade and immigration between the U.S. and China have been taking place now for almost two centuries. In the process, many things Chinese have found their way into the American culture. Some, such as Chinese cookery, have taken root here and become an integral part of the American way of life. Many others are still remote and even rather exotic in our predominantly occidental society.

The recent improvement in the political relationship between the United States and the People's Republic of China has been a great boon to the rebirth of interest in many of the less well-known aspects of Chinese civilization. With continued interest on both sides in strengthening our cultural ties, both societies should reap some rich rewards. This section of *The Chinese Catalog* presents a number of areas of interest that seem to be growing in the U.S. today. It is a varied section reflecting some of the variety of Chinese civilization itself. No matter where your interests lie, you're sure to find something fascinating in this Chinese kaleidoscope.

Museums of Chinese Civilization

While Chinese fine art is widely represented in museums across the United States, there are only a few museums that offer good collections of historical and anthropological artifacts from the Chinese. As relations improve with the People's Republic of China, we may see more and better representations of the Chinese civilization in American museums of history and science. Interest in archeological digs in China has expanded dramatically in the last few years. The result of this work should be an increased availability of high quality Chinese artifacts. These will be a welcome and unique addition to many museums in the U.S.

Though few in number, the following museums offer extensive and very interesting collections of Chinese historical and anthropological relics.

This lion mask, used for celebrating Chinese New Year and other special festivals, is one of the many artifacts on display at the American Museum of Natural History, Gardner D. Stout Hall of Asian Peoples in New York City.

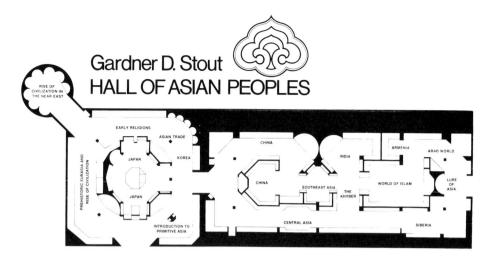

Gardner D. Stout
HALL OF ASIAN PEOPLES

The museum was founded in 1966, dedicated to the first person of Chinese ancestry to hold public office in the Northwest. Wing Luke was active in many public causes, and it was his idea to collect, preserve, exhibit and interpret Asian culture to the American public. The sole purpose of the museum is to bridge the cultural gap between Asian and non-Asian people. It is the only museum of predominantly Asian folk arts on the west coast.

The museum houses a large collection of Chinese and Asian textiles and artifacts. It also has a resource center containing histories and photos to document the record of Asian people in the Pacific Northwest. The center has materials available for loan, including narrative slide files and textile catalogs.

Each November the museum sponsors a CHINESE FLOATING ART AUCTION. Some 200 of the most talented artists in the area contribute their work. The proceeds from the auction provide the major share of the funding to operate the museum for the following year.

The Wing Luke Museum is a community center as well. It sponsors programs, lectures, offers translation and referral services and provides a meeting place for many diverse groups.

AMERICAN MUSEUM OF NATURAL HISTORY
Central Park West at 79th Street
New York, New York 10024
Tel. (212) 873-1300

The Gardner D. Stout Hall of Asian Peoples at the American Museum of Natural History was completed in 1980. It was perhaps the most ambitious project the museum had ever undertaken. Its 20,000 square feet of display area contain the largest and finest collection of Asian ethnographic materials in the Western Hemisphere. Incredibly, only five percent of the museum's Asian collection is actually on display, about 3,000 objects. The artifacts cover a time span from Peking Man, about 600,000 years ago, to the beginning of the nineteenth century when Western influences began to erode the traditional ways of life in Asia. Although many purely artistic pieces are included in the displays, the hall is basically aimed at anthropological study. Its goal is to give the visitor a deeper understanding of the cultures, value systems, cycles of life, and social organizations on the continent of Asia.

The arrangement of the artifacts is unique. Two routes may be taken through the hall; each route follows a major geographical route through Asia. One route begins in the ancient city of Samarkand and moves through the Near East, India, Southeast Asia, China, and Japan. The other begins in Siberia and traverses Central Asia and Buddhist High Asia. There are also special areas devoted to Primitive Asia, Prehistoric Eurasia, and the Rise of Civilization, World of Islam, and Asian Trade. There are ten classical dioramas, thirteen smaller dioramas, and twelve life-sized displays. The attention to detail and historical authenticity is, of course, expert in every way. It would be hard to imagine a collection that so beautifully reflects the diversity and significance of Asian civilization in a finite space.

The Chinese collection in the Hall of Asian Peoples is outstanding. There is a colorful diorama of a Chinese village wedding scene, a small diorama depicting ancient Peking, and a rare collection of Tibetan religious tapestries. There are interesting masks and costumes from Chinese theater as well as an outstanding collection of Chinese shadow puppets. The museum also houses the Drummond Collection of Chinese jades, and the Whitney Collection of Tibetan religious objects.

The American Museum of Natural History is open from 10:00 to 5:45 on Wednesday; and from 10:00 to 9:00 Friday through Sunday. The museum requests a contribution of $3 for adults and $1.50 for children.

Pacific Asia Museum. Pasadena, California.

OROVILLE CHINESE TEMPLE
1500 Broderick Street
Oroville, CA 95965
(916) 533-1496

The Oroville Chinese Temple was built in 1863 to serve a community of some 10,000 Chinese laborers. It includes three chapels, one for each of the three major strains of religious and ethical thought in China. The Chan room, Confucian, is dedicated to reverence for the ancestors. Taoism is represented in the Sanctuary of the Gods. The Moon Temple is dedicated to Buddhism. In addition, a Council Room was built to serve a variety of civil and cultural needs for the laborers—banking, letter writing, burial of the dead, and the like.

The Tapestry Hall is a new addition to the temple. In it is an extensive collection of embroidered tapestries, parasols, and other fabric craft items. Other folk arts such as pottery and lacquerware, typical of the things used by the Chinese during the heyday of the community in Oroville, are on display in an adjacent hall. The grounds also include an authentic Chinese garden, a quiet retreat designed for meditation and reflection. All of the flora in the garden came originally from China.

A major flood in 1907 inundated the Chinese community at Oroville, and most of the immigrants moved to other parts of California or went back to China. A private family assumed responsibility for the grounds for some thirty years. Then, in 1937, the area was deeded to the City of Oroville. The temple was opened to visitors in 1949.

PACIFIC ASIA MUSEUM
46 N. Los Robles Avenue
Pasadena, CA 91101
(213) 499-2742

Designed in the traditional "Imperial Palace" style, the Pacific Asia Museum features authentic Chinese architecture and decorative details. A work of art itself, the building houses an important collection of Asian and Pacific artifacts. The building surrounds a courtyard garden, the only authentic Chinese courtyard garden in the western U.S.

Pacific Asia is as much a cultural center as a museum. A library has 3,500 volumes devoted to oriental art. Two different shops sell works of oriental art. The Gourmet Gallery has items related to all aspects of preparing and serving oriental foods, in addition to a tea room. Additionally, the museum offers a variety of programs to further cultural understanding. There are classes open to the public in subjects such as Chinese brush painting and calligraphy, "shadow boxing," and Chinese cooking.

Chinese Collectibles

Although Chinese crafts are among the most popular items collected by Americans, there are lots of other things—old and new, cheap and expensive—that collectors might want to consider. In addition to the old reliables such as stamps and coins, Peking glass, carpets, antique jades, and porcelain make fascinating collections. All of these things are becoming more and more available in the United States as China seeks to draw foreign currency into its economy. Here are a number of favorite Chinese collectibles.

Chinese Crafts

With trade between the United States and the People's Republic of China officially open for some years now, everything from kites to canned tuna is being shipped from the PRC to test its marketability in the U.S. In addition to ordinary trade items, China is also attempting to reestablish itself as a source for the craft items that proved so popular in the nineteenth century. And along with the old standbys—lacquerware, porcelain, jade, and silk—some new crafts for trade are beginning to appear in the American marketplace. What are some of these items, and how does the quality compare with other craft items, foreign and domestic?

EMBROIDERY AND APPLIQUÉ

Silk embroidery and appliqué work have long been specialities of the Chinese. Ancient embroidered materials have been discovered in Han tombs. Chinese style in embroidery work has always emphasized the satin stitch. It is used most commonly to produce the wide, flat petals of flowers, leaves, clouds, and the like. Also gold and silver thread, used extensively in the T'ang and Ming dynasties, are making a comeback in some of the new export embroidery work. A new style of embroidery is coming out of Hunan Province. In this work hair-thin threads are used to produce realistic animal design—mainly cats. Appliqué work is done in the embroidery style with embroidery designing sometimes done on the appliqué itself. Pastel and bold colored patches are used to create floral spray decorations for tablecloths, dresser scarves, handkerchiefs, and the like. Both the appliqué and embroidery work seem to be steadily improving in China. Some early things that arrived in the U.S. were available only in Chinese curio shops or museum folk art shops. Now some of the finer tablecloths and household linens are available in better department stores. It would be foolish to compare the current products with the exquisite fancywork of imperial China. But those things were not made to be sold at all, much less mass marketed in the U.S.! Both the embroidery and appliqué work available in the United States are very reasonably priced.

LACQUERWARE

A tree native to southern China produces an unusual sap that can be made into a very hard, protective varnish known as lacquer. Over the past two thousand years, the Chinese have enhanced the use of this glossy preservative. Originally intended to coat boats, weapons, and food utensils, the results were so beauti-

ful that it was soon put to use as a decorative technique. We call the result "lacquerware." When China's internal chaos put an end to most of her export industries, Japan and Korea were quick to fill the vacuum. But China has been trying to regain some of the lost ground in the lacquerware trade. China never lost the technique for making superior lacquerware, and some of it is beginning to appear in the U.S. once again. Korea's lacquerware is largely imitative—of Japanese. And Japanese lacquerware is so perfectly manufactured as to almost be mistaken for extruded plastic. China will probably regain her dominance in lacquerware because the designing is original (the Chinese never copy anyone but themselves). And the production techniques have not become so intensely industrialized as to eliminate the input of the individual artisan from the work entirely. As a whole, Chinese lacquerware is highly decorative. Often several techniques such as painting, incising, carving, and inlay are combined on the same piece. This gives Chinese lacquerware a distinctively rich and luxurious appearance.

CLOISONNÉ

The art of fusing precious metals with fired enamels is certainly not Chinese. The ancient Chinese were never very impressed with gold or silver. And bright, enamel painting was popular in the Middle East, but not in China. Not, that is, until Kublai Khan came along with his gaudy Mongol tastes and his love of gold and silver. The Khans brought precious-metal workers and enamel painting artisans from the Middle East together, and cloisonné suddenly became a Chinese decorative art!

Imperial cloisonné was perfected in Peking during the first part of the Ch'ing dynasty. But like other highly developed imperial crafts, it went to pot around 1900. It deteriorated under Western pressure to export, and under the increasing corruptibility of the Manchus. It then further deteriorated during the years of political and social upheaval in the twentieth century. It still isn't what it was under the early Ch'ing, but new colors, and new, improved equipment for working the metal and firing the enamels have helped regenerate the industry. No other country took China's place in the cloisonné business while the factories were down. It has become a welcome export product once again in both America and Europe.

REGIONAL FOLK ARTS

In the nineteenth century not much thought was given to exporting the products of Chinese folk arts and crafts. The export business was aimed at the well-to-do, with porcelain, brocade, lacquerware, and other up-scale pieces of chinoiserie being the major export items. Now, things are quite different. There is a large market in the U.S. for inexpensive craft items of both domestic and foreign origin. China hopes to tap this market with some of its unusual regional craft items.

Most folk crafts develop originally to fulfill the needs of common people. They use materials that are easily and cheaply obtainable. Patchwork quilting in America, for instance, developed initially as a practical way to make use of scrap fabric. Chinese folk crafts developed in much the same way.

Papercuts are intricately cut paper designs originally made to be used as window decorations during the celebration of the Chinese New Year and Spring Festival. Papercuts were also used as embroidery patterns and as dyeing stencils for fabric decoration. Designs often became family heirlooms and were handed down from generation to generation. Export papercuts are often done with colored paper. The subject matter and technique usually reflect the regional background of the artist.

Bamboo weaving makes use of one of China's most abundant native plants. Almost every region in China has a special bamboo product or a unique style of plaiting bamboo strips. Chinese bamboo baskets are now available all over the U.S. Sturdy construction and unique weaving designs make Chinese baskets an attractive item to Western consumers. Bamboo animals have also shown up in many retail outlets in the United States. These animals look almost sculpted. Tiny bamboo threads are woven around lacquer animal molds. Then the bamboo "sculptures" are coated with lacquer to create a strong and durable surface. Rugs, hats, and bags of Chinese bamboo are also widely available.

Chinese lanterns became quite popular in America during the 1920's. The brightly colored, decorative kind have always had an appealing "partytime" quality. In fact, decorative and "palace" lanterns were used in the "Lantern Festival" which came just after Spring Festival and was quite widely celebrated throughout all of China. Nowadays lanterns are hung at Spring Festival in China, but they are really sort of nostalgic items only. And, as one might imagine, they are predominantly red. Japan has exported cheap, paper lanterns for some time, but more elaborate Chinese silk lanterns with fancy rosewood frames and such are appearing in specialty "import" stores.

Carvings in bamboo, wood, and soapstone are ancient folk crafts. Some of these products are showing up in American stores, too. Although the carvings are often rather crude, they have an attractive ethnic quality that is very appealing. In addition, the Chinese carver always cleverly uses the distinctive characteristics of the medium to emphasize some aspect of the design. A flaw in a stone, for instance, will be utilized in such a way as to appear necessary to the finished product. Carvings of animals and landscapes are particularly appealing to American customers.

New Year pictures are another decorative craft fairly new to most Americans. These pictures have a long history. In imperial China they were used to decorate windows and doorways at the Chinese New Year. The door posters were sometimes called "door guards." They depicted Chinese gods and heroes and were believed to ward off ghosts and evil spirits. Families made their own designs and carved them on wood blocks so that the designs could be printed year after year. A lot of hand coloring of the prints often added extra dash. The tradition has stayed alive, and some of the designs are so unique that they are now sold as folk art prints. They are easier to get in China than in America, but if they prove popular here, we'll see a lot more of them in the future.

Batik is not a folk craft native to China alone. It is a technique that has many variations and has been used in many areas of the world to produce interesting patterns in dyed textiles. Several of the minority nationalities in China make handsome batik articles. The process is essentially a resist-dye operation. The design is stenciled onto white cloth, design areas are then covered with wax and the article is dyed—traditionally a very deep indigo color. The wax is then boiled off and the design appears in striking contrast to the deep blue dyed areas of the fabric. Different areas in China use different subject matter in their batik articles. Nationalities from southwestern regions use elephants and peacocks as design motifs, while others may use fish and fruit, or birds and flowers. The delicacy and exotic beauty of these designed textiles make them a very attractive folk art item.

Collecting Chinese Stamps

Until 1972, when President Nixon made his historic trip to China, it was illegal for Americans to collect stamps issued in the PRC. Now it is not only legal but perhaps the fastest growing area of philately in the United States. Although the number of dealers specializing in stamps from China is relatively limited, individual and organizational interest is very widespread.

Postage stamps, as we know them in the West, did not appear in China until Western trade demanded their issuance late in the nineteenth century. Private message couriers operated for profit throughout Imperial China, but stamps were not used until 1878 when an American customs worker in Shanghai, H. B. Morse, designed a group of Chinese stamps now known as the "large dragons." The first set of commemorative stamps printed in China marked the sixtieth birthday of the Dowager Empress Tz'u Hsi of the Manchu (Ch'ing) dynasty. In 1896, the Chinese Imperial Post came into existence and a true postal service was initiated in China. Throughout the waning days of imperial rule it is interesting that the members of the royal household were never portrayed on postage stamps. It would have been considered an affront to the dignity of the imperial family. Of course, it was just that sort of "out-of-touch" eccentricity that finally did in the Manchus.

In 1911, dynastic rule ended forever in China and the Republic of China was born. A number of interesting stamps come from this period including stamps that picture Dr. Sun Yat-sen and China's first airmail stamp showing a biplane flying above the Great Wall. Later stamps from the days of the Republic commemorate the achievements of Chiang Kaishek.

Stamps from the imperial and republican periods of Chinese history are available, but it is now easier to collect the formerly "uncollectible" PRC stamps. Many early stamps from the PRC (1940's and 1950's) have been reprinted to facilitate collection. Most PRC stamps are sold in canceled-to-order sets. These stamps are canceled but unused and can be resold at a lower cost.

New collectors of PRC stamps can subscribe to new issue subscription services. These work a bit like book clubs except

This stamp portraying Chairman Mao and Lin Piao was officially printed for issue in 1968. Serious political differences arising between the two caused it to be withdrawn almost immediately. The stamp is now very rare and valued at about $10,000.
Photo courtesy Sun Philatelic Center, Inc.

This rare 1938 stamp commemorates "The Soldier of the Resistance Against Japan." It is valued at about $1,500 today.
Photo courtesy Sun Philatelic Center, Inc.

"A Dream of Red Mansions." Series of stamps depicting favorite characters from the famous Chinese novel of the eighteenth century. Issued November 20, 1981 and April 24, 1982.
Photo courtesy The China Stamp Agency in North America.

"Chinese Palace Lanterns." A series of six stamps issued February 19, 1981. The series depicts the popular hanging lanterns that date back to the sixth century.
Photo courtesy The China Stamp Agency in North America.

that you're sent all new issues whether you want them or not. They are generally sold at face value, so we're not talking about tons of money, but you can't send them back. You must cancel your subscription to stop the stamps. The China Stamp Agency in North America, One Unicover Center, Cheyenne, WY 82008, (307) 634-5911, serves as the official North American agency for distribution of stamps and other philatelic products from the PRC. The organization offers basically all new issues at face value or official selling price in the PRC.

Other dealers that specialize in Chinese stamps are:

Sun Philatelic Center, Inc.
1 Sutter Street, Suite 705
San Francisco, CA 94104
(415) 433-5020
[Specializes in large lots, auctions, and rare stamps]

Fidelity Trading Company
P.O. Box 353
Cypress, CA 90620
[Varied info on PRC stamps]

Peter Kovacs
14507 Draycott
Houston, TX 77045
[Publishes "Pandagram" collectors' list]

Washington Stamp Company
P.O. Box 34430
Bethesda, MD 20817
(301) 493-4982
[Publishes Pruitt China Pricelist]

Stamps for Collectors
Margie Roll
R.D. #1, Box 52-1A
Englishtown, NJ 07726
[Access to many kinds of Chinese stamps]

Although stamp collecting in China all but died out after reorganization under Chairman Mao, it is beginning to revive. Once considered a bourgeois, waste-of-time activity, the government has significantly changed its attitude toward philatelic endeavors. Foreign stamps are still hard to get in the PRC, however, and a Chinese pen pal will be happy to exchange stamps with an American collector if contact can be made.

Finally, the China Stamp Society, Inc., 7207 Thirteenth Place, Takoma Park, MD 20012, is an international philatelic society organized in 1936 to promote the study of the postal history of China. Six times a year it publishes "The China Clipper," the most authoritative journal in its field. For serious collectors, membership in this organization is highly recommended.

Chinese Coin Collecting

Modern archeological digs in China continue to add to our knowledge of ancient Chinese life. At present, however, it seems that coinage in China probably began during the Warring States period of Chinese history, about 480–221 B.C. The early coins from this period are interesting because they were minted in shapes that seem to imitate the shapes of ancient knives and spades. Knife and spade coins, as they are called, are widely collected today, and though they are somewhat hard to date and to attribute to a definite location, more is being learned about them every day.

As Chinese coinage progressed, round coins began to appear as standard tender in China. These round coins (cash) from the early dynasties to the last are often recognized by the square hole in the center. This pattern lasted for some time in China and precluded the impression of faces or other pictorial representations on the faces of the coins. Markings on Chinese coins are generally limited to the Chinese characters arranged around the square hole. Early coins of this type were cast rather than struck. In other words, inscribed molds were made and molten metal was poured into them to form the coins. In most Western minting operations, plain metal is "struck" or imprinted to make the coin. Chinese coins from Han through Manchu are widely available for collection.

One of the most popular Chinese coins collected today is the so-called "Dragon Dollar." These were among the first silver coins ever struck in China. They were first produced in the late nineteenth century and were used extensively in the China Trade. Though all provinces produced these large silver coins, the dragon symbol was common as the unifying symbol for imperial China. The subtle variations between the dragon dollars of the various provinces make them attractive collector's items.

Since trade and travel restrictions with the People's Republic of China have eased, numismatic interests have been enlivened in the U.S. The PRC has begun to produce commemorative coins. In 1980, for instance, the PRC produced an extraordinary set of Olympic coins. The coins were struck to commemorate the 1980 Winter Olympics at Lake Placid, New York. Further exchange with the PRC promises to revitalize Chinese coin collecting all over the world.

A number of coin dealers in the U.S. specialize in Chinese coins:

Scott Semans, P.O. Box 13007, New Orleans, LA 70185, publishes a list of world coins, paper money, books, and primitive money. An order form comes with the list. Scott Semans is the largest dealer in ancient Chinese coins outside of the Orient.

Lester D. Snell, Box 261, Sonoma, CA 95476, deals in all sorts of coins, but has an extensive list of rare Chinese coins. Mr. Snell publishes three lists a year. The list itself is the order form. You may call Mr. Snell at (707) 938-4958.

The Money Company, 19900 Ventura Blvd., Suite 200, Woodland Hills, CA 91364, specializes in Chinese modern series or struck coinage.

There are also a number of books that are valuable to the Chinese coin collector. Durst Publications specializes in books about coin collecting and offers a number of titles related to Chinese numismatics. Included on the Durst list are the famous volumes that make up the *Encyclopedia of Chinese Coins* by Arthur B. Coole; the F. Schjoth book, *Chinese Currency;* and the Yu-Ch'uan classic reference book, *Early Chinese Coinage.* For the Durst catalogue write: Sanford J. Durst, 170 E. 61st St., New York, NY 10021.

There are also many coin collecting periodicals available. "World Coin News," Iola, WI 54990 is recommended. Numismatics International, P.O. Box 30013, Dallas, TX 75230, publishes an interesting periodical called the *Numismatics International Bulletin.*

Peking Glass

Glassmaking has been to the West what porcelain manufacturing was to China. For this reason Chinese glassware has always been considered somewhat inferior as a collectible item. Certainly there is nothing in Chinese glass that can compare to Venetian art glass, Bohemian cut glass, or English and Irish crystal. Nevertheless, in the past few years new interest in Chinese glass has developed among some collectors. And this is a good opportunity to begin a collection of Chinese glass, "Peking Glass" as many collectors call it, because it has not yet begun to fetch the astronomical prices common in some areas of the collectible glass market.

There is not much ancient Chinese glass around. The first glass in China was probably imported from the Near East in large ingot-like chunks. It was then carved into amulets and ritual items that imitated those carved in jade. Some recently excavated tombs have revealed glass cicadas (locust-like insects, the Chinese symbols of regeneration), glass beads, and glass *pi*'s buried with the dead. But not much ancient glass has been found, and certainly very little is available to the average collector.

Perhaps because porcelain developed so early, glassmaking was never really considered an important craft in old China. It was not until 1680 in the early years of the last dynasty (Manchu or Ch'ing) that an actual glass factory was established at the palace in Peking. Even then, the major concentration at the glassworks was the imitation of porcelain and jade items. As skill developed, however, the Chinese craftsmen began to add their own distinctive touch to glass objects.

One of the most striking features in Chinese glass from the eighteenth century on is the incredible color achieved. Of course, from early on the Chinese glassmakers had achieved the subtle milky colors that imitated jade and white porcelain. But by using pure mineral colors and enhancing the glass with pure barium, the Chinese were able to produce some pieces of great beauty. It is odd, though, that not much attention was ever paid to refining the actual process of glassmaking. Chinese glass is known, and usually can be easily authenticated, by detecting the bubbles and pieces of clay in the final products.

It is from the work done in these early factories around the imperial palace that Chinese glass came to be called Peking glass. Actually, Chinese glass available today was often made in Poshan in Shantung Province and in Canton as well as Peking. Formerly, the bulk of antique Chinese glass in the U.S. was either

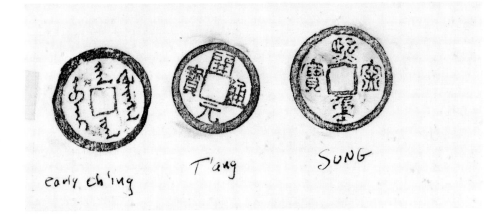

early ch'ing   T'ang   SUNG

brought over by Chinese immigrants or made-for-export glass from the nineteenth and early twentieth centuries. Since relations with the People's Republic of China have been established, a good deal more old glass should become available in America.

Several types of glass objects are very popular with American collectors these days. Probably the most popular items are the glass snuff and medicine bottles (often called "opium bottles" probably because it sounds mysterious and exotic). Occasionally one may run across very old snuff bottles, but the commonly collected medicine bottles often date from early this century. The technique of painting tiny pictures on the inside of narrow-necked bottles facinates the American collector. It is a technique that was perfected in Peking and although it is still going on, the modern examples are noticeably inferior to the older ones.

Another popular item is the glass flower arrangement. These were made for export primarily in the 1920's. They are sometimes framed and sometimes placed in tiny pots. The true Chinese glass flowers can usually be spotted because of their bright colors and the angular, sharply cut look of their leaves and flower petals. Also, the stems of Chinese flowers were usually made of iron wire and are often rusty. Since European glass flowers were made for export to America at about the same time, it pays to take special care in examining the item for sale.

Some older and more expensive items are vases and bowls made to look like Ming porcelain. There are also later glass containers made in the Chinese "layered" style. Layers of glass molded over one another are reminiscent of the porcelain glazes that hold suspended colors between them.

Finally, glass jewelry, especially beaded jewelry is becoming a more popular collectible item in the U.S. Again, color and brilliance are the striking characteristics of these items. Authenticity can often be verified by the obvious clay particles left in the beads themselves. Glass bead making in China was truly a cottage industry.

The wives and daughters of many Chinese families made jewelry for domestic and foreign sale. Backyard furnaces could be easily made to melt chunks of manufactured glass. Then wires or thin sticks were covered with clay and spun as drops of molten glass were poured onto them. Naturally, beads made in this crude fashion were far from perfect. Yet the quality of the glass colors and the imagination used, make these pieces interesting to collect. Finer pieces of Chinese glass jewelry—mandarin necklaces and the like—are quite a bit more expensive, but are also popular with American collectors.

Books about glass collecting are numerous. Some that include information on Chinese glass are:

Glass: A Guide for Collectors by Gabriella Gros-Galliner. Stein and Day, New York. 1970.

The Collector's Pocket Book of Glass by Geoffrey Wills. Hawthorn Books, Inc., New York. 1966.

Chinese Carpets

Certainly one of the happiest consequences of reestablishing relations with China has been the reintroduction of Chinese products to the U.S. market. And of these products, some of the finest and most welcome are the beautiful Chinese carpets. Of all oriental carpets, Chinese carpets are unique. In fact, it is almost impossible to speak of them in connection with the famous orientals of Persia (Iran) and India because they are so very different.

Although there is no real proof, it is generally considered probable that Chinese carpets developed on their own, that is to say independent of the carpet weaving techniques of India or the Near and Middle East. One reason for believing this is that a few ancient Chinese carpets from the eighth century and earlier have been found to have been made by a process called "felting" rather than by the standard knotting process used in ancient Persia. There is considerable evidence, however, that there were significant exchanges of rug weavers between China and Persia during the reign of Kublai Khan. This period of exchange may have resulted in the few similarities between Persian and Chinese rugs that we can see today.

Chinese rugs themselves can be divided into two very distinct styles as well. Old Chinese rugs, Ming and Ch'ing primarily, exhibit a fairly full field of design in a number of color schemes. Blue, beige, and brown have always been popular with Chinese rug makers, but old Chinese rugs used cherry, apricot, and yellow in ways that are reminiscent of their Persian counterparts. Many of these rugs were considered coarser and less beautiful than the Persians. Very few exist today. The best U.S. collection is probably the one at the Metropolitan Museum of Art in New York.

About 1850, as the Manchus began to lose control of China to Western influences, the rug export business began to flourish. Western markets were developed by catering to Western tastes, and the Chinese carpet began to change in appearance. For one thing, the field became less crowded. Designs began to be placed in the corners and in the center of plain fields of soft color. The carpets became very popular in the U.S. After the fall of the Manchu dynasty in 1912, the carpet industry grew in China. During the 1920's a new Chinese carpet of very thick, tight pile began to appear in America and elsewhere. These were the first of the truly fine quality Chinese carpets made for export. In the early 1930's the bottom dropped out of the carpet business in America as a result of the Depression. The result in China was to thin out the carpet weavers, leaving only the quality craftsmen in business. The long war with Japan that followed, however, practically wiped out the Chinese carpet industry. It did not begin to rebuild until after the tumult of the Communist revolution. It is once again a thriving industry in China, producing some of the finest carpets ever made for export.

There are many qualities associated with Chinese rugs that make them very attractive to the American consumer. For one thing, the colors and the spare, impressionistic designs tend to enhance antique, traditional, and modern furniture groupings. In addition, the Chinese have perfected a technique called "sculpting" which simply means cutting the thick pile in certain places to enhance the design elements. The result is a very luxurious appearance.

If you are interested in old Chinese carpets, you can just about forget any pre-Mings because very, very few exist. Even Ming and Ch'ing rugs are rare and extraordinarily expensive. You are more likely to find rugs made for export between 1890 and 1935. Of these, the rugs of the 1930's are perhaps the best. They were made with improved chemical dyes which have retained their brilliant color; the workmanship is excellent; and the quality of the materials used is greatly improved from that of the earlier rugs.

Some valuable books to look into before you go shopping for Chinese rugs are:

Chinese Rugs, the classic work by - Gordon B. Leitch. Still the most complete work on the subject. Dodd Mead, & Co., New York. 1928.

Antique Chinese Rugs, Tiffany Studios. A wonderful picture book. Charles E. Tuttle Co., Tokyo, Japan. 1969.

Oriental Rugs/A Complete Guide by Charles W. Jacobsen. Charles E. Tuttle Co., Tokyo, Japan. 1962.

45

FURNITURE AND DECORATIVE WOOD OBJECTS

There are a good many fine pieces of Chinese furniture floating around U.S. antique markets. Not all of them are truly Chinese, of course, because at one time Japan decided to make its own Chinese furniture to export to America. The real pieces from China fall into two categories: those made for use in China, and those made for export to Europe and America. There have been periods in Western trade history when both Europe and America went crazy over "chinoiserie"—things Chinese.

It's fairly easy to tell chinoiserie from the other type made for use in China, because chinoiserie is usually very decorative—carved dragons, marble inlay, mother-of-pearl gewgaws, and what have you. Pieces made for the Chinese market are classic, angular, simple, and very uncomfortable if made for sitting. Not everyone prefers Chinese classic, so there is a big business in chinoiserie. Chairs, camphor chests, curio stands, small tables, and, rarely, cabinets and wardrobes, are the basic pieces most often seen. Good pieces are not cheap. They are often made of teak or another heavy hardwood stained to look like teak. This is particularly true of chinoiserie because Westerners associated teak with the Chinese even though the wood itself came from India.

There are a number of decorative pieces also made of wood. Chinese table screens, lanterns, boxes, trays, and fans are fairly easy to come by in stores that deal in Chinese antiques. The inventive design motifs in these pieces, and the clever and varied use of woods make these items a lot of fun to collect.

Most antiques made of wood date from 1850 to 1920. Older items are very rare and not generally available to the average collector.

PORCELAIN

Of all things Chinese that are collected, Chinese porcelain is by far the most popular. Unfortunately, the porcelain trade is also the most notorious. The "Ming vase" is practically a shibboleth for high-brow antiquing. Needless to say, Ming porcelain is quite expensive and imitations are abundant. If you seriously shop for Ming or early Ch'ing porcelain, make sure you know and trust the dealer.

Nineteenth and twentieth century porcelain is also fun to collect. It can also be expensive, but it's more widely available and very lovely. Even a great deal of the porcelain made for export is superb. After all, the first blue-and-white porcelain was a terrific export item for China.

JADE

Next to porcelain, jade is the most popular Chinese collectible. Surprisingly, very old jade is fairly easy to get hold of in the antique circuit. Unfortunately, old jade is often pretty crumby looking. Little jade ritual cicadas and so forth used in ancient burial rites are really not that well done. Most jade lovers collect jade from the eighteenth to the twentieth century. That's probably why ancient jade is not so hot an item as one would think.

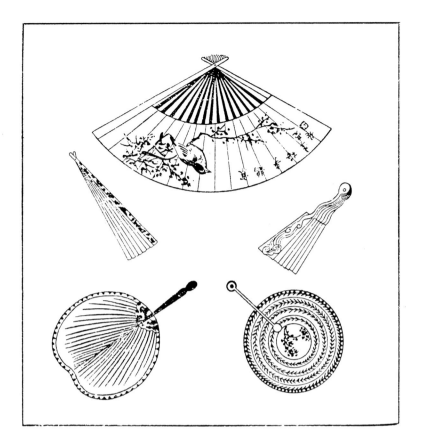

The techniques used to carve jade improved enormously during the Ch'ing dynasty. It became a big deal with the Ch'ing emperors and most of the monumental works were done during this period. Jade figurines, amulets, jewelry, and pots and boxes are popular collector's items. The only thing to watch for is to make sure that the object is true jade—nephrite or jadeite. Again, a reliable dealer is the best insurance.

OTHER COLLECTIBLES

More unusual Chinese items to collect are: fans, cork pictures, seals and calligraphy tools, puppets, and dolls. Both souvenir and export fans of rosewood and ivory made with painted silk and paper are interesting, if fragile, collectibles. Cork pictures are a South China specialty. Tiny slivers of cork are glued together to build up a three-dimensional picture (usually a landscape) in a shadow box frame. Seals and calligraphic items such as inkstones and brushes are a fairly inexpensive way of collecting something very old and very much a part of Chinese history. Puppets are still a bit rare, but seem to be showing up more and more on the Chinese antique scene. Shadow puppets are particularly Chinese but antique ones are not easy to find. And, of course, America's number one collectible—dolls—were made in China for both domestic and foreign markets. Chinese dolls, new and antique, are great collector's items right now.

An invaluable book for collectors:

Oriental Antiques and Collectibles
by Arthur and Grace Chu

This book was published by Crown Publishers, Inc., New York in 1973. It is certainly the best book of its kind on the market. In it you will find lots of valuable information about the most popular Chinese collectibles—porcelain, jade, silk, and so forth. Plus there are informative chapters that deal with less well known collectible items such as Chinese painting and calligraphy, carpets, folk crafts, glass, and furniture. If you are a serious lover of chinoiserie or have a specialized interest in some aspect of oriental collectibles, you need this book!

ORIENTAL ANTIQUES AND COLLECTIBLES
A Guide
by ARTHUR AND GRACE CHU

OVER 250 ILLUSTRATIONS

Health, Sports, and Hobbies

Very much like the fine arts, medicine and leisure time activities in China developed wholly apart from their counterparts in the west. Even today, the practice of medicine in China is vastly different from what we know in the U.S. And even general health considerations—exercise, nutrition, and hygiene—are based on very different assumptions. Similarly, games, sports, and hobbies developed quite differently in China. It is hard for us in the west to imagine, for instance, sports that are not directly competitive. But differences have not led to disinterest. Both the Chinese and westerners have enjoyed a fascination with alternative medical practices and leisure time activities. As you will see on the following pages, some Chinese games, sports, and hobbies have been popular in the U.S. for many years. Others are relatively new on the contemporary scene. All of them are interesting, and many are gathering devoted fans in the U.S. and elsewhere.

Acupuncture

The art of acupuncture is ancient and unique to the Chinese branch of oriental medicine. Essentially it involves stimulating designated points on the body by inserting needles a few millimeters into the skin. Stimulation may also be achieved by application of heat or pressure to the area. No one knows exactly when acupuncture began. The oldest text on the subject is called the *Nei Ching* which still exists in its "revised" version first published around A.D. 1200. The original *Nei Ching* is generally credited to Huang Ti, the legendary "Yellow Emperor" who ruled China sometime between 2697 and 2596 B.C. Amazingly, the *Nei Ching* is still the basic text and foundation for the study of acupuncture.

Although acupuncture was introduced in the West as early as the seventeenth century, it did not establish itself as a standard Western medical practice. One of the problems with acupuncture as practiced in earlier centuries was the problem of infection. Doctors, unaware of the presence of bacteria, did not practice under sterile conditions. Thus the needles they used were often unclean and infection was almost always the result.

Although the Chinese practiced acupuncture steadily through the centuries, it was given new impetus under Chairman Mao Tse-tung. Recognizing the shortage of doctors in China, Mao suggested that native doctors who successfully practiced acupuncture join modern, Western-style physicians in order to expand the medical force. Thus began a renewed interest in acupuncture in China that has lately been exported to the West.

No one knows exactly why acupuncture works. The ancient Chinese explained acupuncture as a means of restoring harmony within the body—the needles influenced the flow of *ch'i*, the

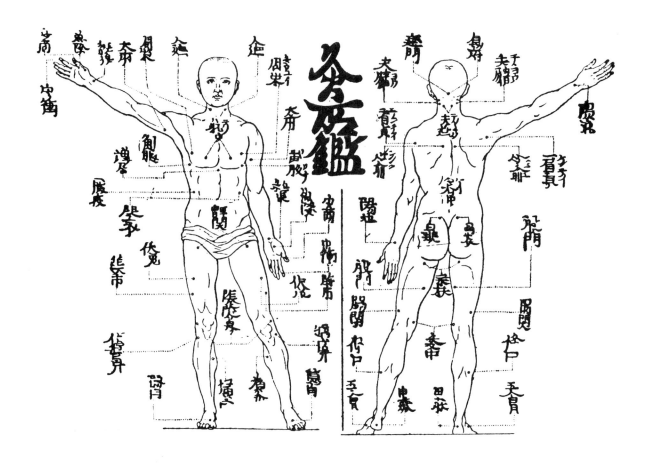

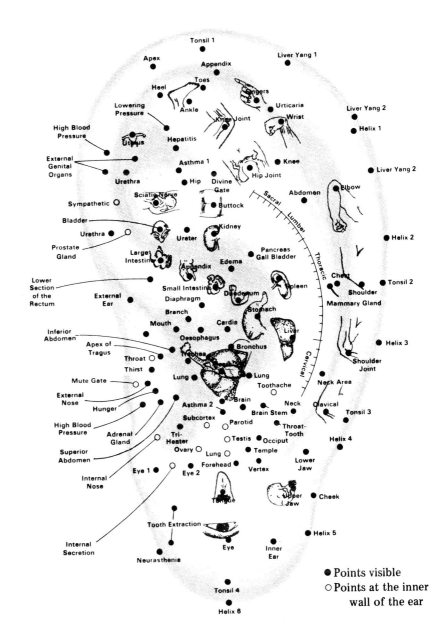

Distribution of ear points on the auricle.

(Courtesy of Chan's Corporation)

The "Divine Gate" point.

life energy force. Modern Chinese and Western physicians no longer accept the *ch'i* theory. But there is a striking similarity between *ch'i* and what modern science calls ATP (adenosine triphosphate). ATP is the main substance responsible for giving energy to living cells. *Ch'i* pathways, or "meridians" as they are called in acupuncture, seem to follow certain nerve networks. ATP powers nerve signals along these networks much as *ch'i* was thought to flow along the meridians by the ancients.

Acupuncture is not a mystical, witch-doctor procedure. There is much scientific substantiation for the practice and certainly a great deal of "case history" evidence of its efficacy. Major operations have been performed with acupuncture-anesthesia, both in China and in the U.S. Acupuncture is also frequently administered for the relief of chronic pain. Its effect on internal organs, however, is less well documented and much less understood. Generally, it is believed that acupuncture might have some salutary effect on organs with purely functional problems; this perhaps is achieved by mild electrical stimulation of those organs. In cases where organ disfunction is caused by an underlying degenerative disease or organic disorder, however, acupuncture can only relieve pain—it cannot restore an organ to normal organic health.

If you are interested in acupuncture, you should know that it is a licensed practice in many states. The American Medical Association (AMA) and the U.S. Food and Drug Administration (FDA) both suggest that the public rely on licensed physicians or dentists that regularly practice acupuncture. You may be referred to one by your own family physician or by a clinic or office of the AMA. It is best to beware of independent acupuncture technicians not associated with or recommended by licensed physicians.

For further reading you might investigate the following:

The Yellow Emperor's Classic of Internal Medicine, translated by Ilza Veith. University of California Press, Berkeley and Los Angeles.

The Layman's Guide to Acupuncture, by Yoshio Manaka, M.D., and Ian A. Urquhart, Ph.D. John Weatherhill, Inc. 1980

"Acupuncture: Myth or Medical Treatment?" by Theodore Berland. Public Affairs Pamphlet available by writing, Public Affairs Pamphlets, 381 Park Avenue, New York, NY 10016.

Ginseng—the Chinese Wonder Herb

Chinese medicine has a long tradition of herbal remedies for various ailments. Ginseng, also referred to as "Jenshen," is a root plant and is perhaps the most famous medicinal herb in the Orient. The name "ginseng" refers to the Chinese characters that represent "man," and the root is often called the "man plant." The name probably came about for two reasons. For one thing, the root itself sometimes resembles the figure of a man—the main root being the torso and offshoot roots the arms and legs. The other reason has to do with its application as an herbal tonic. It is believed to be an herb specifically suited to the longevity and overall health of the human being.

Herbal remedies have not, at least since the Middle Ages, made much of an impression on Western medicine. Ginseng is no exception. Only rather recently, probably as a result of the popularity of "health foods," has interest in ginseng been rekindled in the U.S. Recently, British and Russian medical teams have conducted studies of Chinese herbal remedies. In some instances their findings have shown that further investigation of herbal medicines might be of value to Western scientists.

Ginseng was not unknown to North American Indians and early settlers. The Penobscots and Cherokees used a decoction of ginseng to increase fertility and to prevent cramps and menstrual disorders in women. The Creeks used ginseng for shortness of breath and coughs. The Menominees believed ginseng was a useful tonic that helped increase mental powers. And many other tribes used ginseng remedies. Ginseng was discovered growing wild in North American forests by early pioneers. They often mixed the chopped root with rum as a tonic or tincture for relief of various symptoms—especially those related to colds and fatigue.

For the most part, ginseng is prepared by the process of decocting, that is putting the root in liquid and boiling it down. The thickest part of the root is considered to be the most beneficial. A small bit of it can be chopped, placed in water, and boiled until a tea-like liquor is rendered. This liquor can then be drunk like tea or mixed with other foods. Ginseng is also sold in other convenient forms; tea bags, prepared tonics, and dry bulk powder are fairly common in health stores.

At one time it was thought that ginseng could not be cultivated. It is a somewhat shy plant, growing best in undisturbed, shady patches deep in hardwood forests. But the Koreans have now been growing it commercially for many years. Chinese ginseng grown in Manchuria is still con-

sidered the highest grade of ginseng obtainable. But Korean ginseng is also a very high grade and it is the most widely available in the U.S. The roots must be between five and seven years old before they can be harvested for medicinal use. It is an old belief that the older the root the more beneficial it will be.

The claims for ginseng are much the same today as they were in ancient China. It is first and foremost a stimulating tonic. It is said to be especially good for the digestion and as a restorative in cases of fatigue or weakness, particularly in old people. Many also believe that it is valuable in preserving sexual vigor, which in turn helps increase longevity. And ginseng is often credited with improving mental acuity, eyesight, and hearing. Almost none of this has been scientifically proven, and it is important not to regard ginseng as a kind of cure-all. Even the Chinese don't believe that.

But it is not harmful, and, like many natural things, may be beneficial to our overall health.

Ginseng is available in most health food stores and in many Chinese grocery stores. If you can't find any in your area, you might try contacting one of these organizations.

Indiana Botanic Gardens, Inc.
P.O. Box 5
Hammond, IN 46325
(219) 931-2480
(Herbalist Almanac available)

K. D. Distributor, Ltd.
1038 South Grand Ave.
Los Angeles, CA 90015
(213) 747-7725

Nature's Herb Company
281 Ellis Street
San Francisco, CA 94102
(415) 474-2756
(Catalog available)

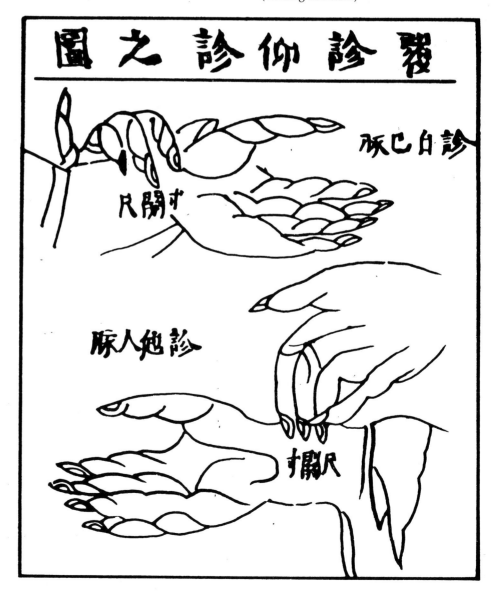

SECRETS OF THE CHINESE HERBALISTS
Richard Lucas
Simon and Schuster—Cornerstone Library
pp. 224 $3.95

This is an amazing little book. Richard Lucas spent years researching the history of herbal medicine in China. He translated a good deal of material from the original Chinese, and interviewed countless Chinese herbalists in order to come up with the information he passes along in this book. He has also included what little scientific information has been compiled on the subject. All in all, the book presents a fairly complete look at the Chinese herbalist. And it's put together in an intelligent and yet readable form.

Lucas begins the book by discussing the basic theories behind Chinese herbal medicine. He even gets into some of the yang-yin theory, which helps explain some aspects of the overall Chinese approach to health. After a general discussion of the subject, he gets into individual herbs and the tonics and remedies that can be made from them. Lucas devotes whole chapters of the book to specific types of ailments and how to deal with them herbally. There are chapters on stomach, respiratory, bowel, urinary, and circulatory disorders. Within each of these chapters he discusses relevant herbal remedies, some case histories, and preventative approaches facilitated by the use of herbs. He has special chapters set aside for male and female disorders and emphasizes building good health through diet, tonics and the like. Ginseng, the "wonder root," and Fo-Ti-Tieng, the "elixir of life," are given special treatment with chapters all their own. Both ginseng and Fo-Ti-Tieng are tonic herbs. Their availability and various forms are discussed thoroughly. The claims for both are similar. They supposedly bring about a mentally alert, revitalizing feeling of well being. Both are believed to aid in digestion and in improving strength after a debilitating injury or sickness. A number of case histories are given (not involving anyone you've ever heard of) but case histories just the same.

Probably the most interesting thing in the book is the collection of recipes for tonics and remedies. They are found within the chapters about various ailments. Most of the recipes are easy—no "eye of newt, and toe of frog" stuff. A typical remedy might be made by chopping up a certain root or herb, boiling it in one cup of water, and adding one teaspoon of honey. Nevertheless, the remedies and tonics sound interesting, and if you're into herbs, this book will probably be fun for you. Who knows, you may even discover your own personal "elixir of life."

Chinese Boxing

What people in the West call *kung fu* is an exaggerated, Hollywood version of *ch'uan shu*, Chinese boxing. In *kung fu* films, most of the stunts are faked by using trampolines, trick camera shots, and phony sound tracks. Real Chinese boxing has a number of forms, and three types are beginning to appear on the American self-defense and physical fitness scene. None requires the use of a trampoline.

All three forms of Chinese boxing are part of the *nei-chia* or "internal system" of boxing. In the U.S. these forms are called *T'ai-chi Ch'uan*, *Pa-kua*, and *Hsing-I*. They have much in common, but proponents of each make claims of superiority. There are still relatively few instructors in the U.S., but even with a limited offering, it is important to be alert to the possibility of "Kung Fu Fakers." The self-defense and exercise business in this country is hot! There's lots of money to be made, and lots of cheats are in the game. Probably the safest route to choosing an instructor is relying on references or on reliable institutions such as colleges, YMCA's and church affiliated organizations. Certainly one thing to be wary of is the "breaking bricks" type of come-on. Most genuine teachers of Chinese boxing will be less concerned with performing tricks than with teaching the basics.

All three forms of Chinese boxing seem to have roots in the *I Ching*, or *Book of Changes*. The *I Ching* is over 3,000 years old, and is the source of much of the philosophy of both Confucianism and Taoism. Both the book and Chinese boxing are based on the theory of constant change—flux and flow in the universe. And behind all boxing movements lies the theory of Yin and Yang. Yin represents the passive, soft, female aspect; Yang, the active, strong, male aspect. Both Yin and Yang must be utilized in the trained boxer's form and movement. Establishing proper balance between Yin and Yang is the philosophical basis for fitness through Chinese boxing. The three forms might almost be considered "schools" of the same art.

T'AI-CHI CH'UAN

Probably the most popular of the three types of internal boxing is T'ai-chi Ch'uan, which literally means "Great Ultimate Boxing." Its origins are believed to date back to the Sung dynasty (960–1279 A.D.). A famous boxer named Chang San-feng is generally credited with devising the method. Essentially it is a rhythmic exercise that is used to enhance physical stability and power. It is not so much a form of self-defense as it is a means to self-defense. T'ai-chi Ch'uan depends on the balance and emphasizes lowering the center of gravity in order to maintain stability. Many of the movements that typify T'ai-chi Ch'uan are executed in a semi-crouch because balance is enhanced by lowering the center of gravity of the body. Agility and coordination of continuous movements are two of the aims of T'ai-chi Ch'uan. Relaxed breathing and specific methods of preserving inner control must also be mas-

tered by the student. As exercise, T'ai-chi Ch'uan does not demand outward strength. Instead, it relies on inner concentration and controlled movement. This provides a kind of exercise unlike the common Western "muscle-straining" sort. As self-defense, T'ai-chi Ch'uan spurns muscular force and emphasizes movements that avoid an opponent's onrush of power and turns that power thrust back on the opponent. The theory is that a superior sense of movement dynamics will overwhelm the most powerful combatant.

HSING-I

Another of the three ancient internal boxing arts, Hsing-I Ch'uan (referred to commonly as Hsing-I) means "The Form of Mind Boxing." Again the emphasis is on a "moving meditation" form of exercise. Of course, it is derived from the same source as all Chinese boxing, but in this case a man named Chi Lung-feng who lived in Shanghai during the late Ming dynasty (seventeenth century) is credited with its development. There is no specific sparring method taught in this form either. Hsing-I is a method of boxing by one's self. Instructors in Hsing-I methods stress that competitive aspirations have nothing to do with mastering the art. In fact, a drive toward competitiveness will sometimes work against the Hsing-I student. Relaxation and a kind of "turning inward" is necessary to really understand internalized boxing

arts. Nor should self-defense be the primary reason for practicing Hsing-I. This is a difficult thing for Western sport enthusiasts to understand. There is as much to do with the mind, perhaps more, than the body in Hsing-I. And the results are not easily or quickly apparent as they are in muscle-building, competitive martial arts. One of the distinctive aspects of Hsing-I is the relation to animal forms in the five basic postures. These stances imitate aspects of the chicken, dragon, bear, eagle, and tiger.

PA-KUA

It is impossible to trace the exact origin of Pa-kua. It is known that a man named Tung Hai-ch'uan, active in the mid-nineteenth century, was an expert boxer and promoted the Pa-kua technique. Tung was supposedly able to defeat Hsing-I experts easily. Basically, Pa-kua is a variation on the classic Chinese boxing style. Again it relies on the meditative quality of mind and on the tenets of the Yin/Yang philosophy. There are a number of postures or positions in Pa-kua, some of which are modeled after animals much like in Hsing-I. Pa-kua emphasizes the importance of the palm of the hand as a weapon, however. The palm, being more flexible than a fist, can be used effectively in Pa-kua. Also, Pa-kua involves a circling movement. This fluid movement is essentially the basic difference between Hsing-I movements and those of Pa-kua. The circling, combined with the Pa-kua waist, arm, back, shoulder, and leg movements, makes Pa-kua one of the most complete exercise systems known to man. Pa-kua is rare in China and almost unknown in the West. It will, however, grow in popularity as it becomes better known.

The Chinese martial arts are still not as well known as Japanese Judo or Karate, or even as Korean Tae-Kwan-Do. There are, however, some books written in English about Chinese boxing. Some of the best are:

Hsing-I, Chinese Mind-Body Boxing, by Robert W. Smith.
Kodansha International Ltd. 1981
$6.95   112pp

Pa-kua Chinese Boxing for Fitness and Self-Defense, by Robert W. Smith.
Kodansha International, Ltd. 1980
$7.95   141pp

T'ai-Chi Ch'uan, A Simplified Method of Calisthenics for Health and Self Defense, by Chen Man-ch'ing.
North Atlantic Books, 1981
$8.95   135pp.

The Tao of Tai-Chi Chuan by Jou, Tsung Hwa
Charles E. Tuttle Co. 1980
$12.95   260pp.

Ping Pong

It will perhaps always be one of the curiosities of history that recognition of the People's Republic of China by the United States should be associated with ping pong. Yet that's how it all began. In April of 1971 a U.S. ping pong team was invited to Peking to play against the famed Chinese champions. But the game being played was not really ping pong, it was subtle and tentative diplomacy. Peking's startling invitation produced instant results. President Nixon immediately opened the doors to Chinese visitors and lifted some trade barriers. Shortly thereafter, full diplomatic recognition was extended to the PRC.

In a way, it was fitting that ping pong should have been the bridge between East and West. Introduced to China in 1916 by Western neo-colonialists, the sport was one of the few "decadent" pastimes allowed in China after the Communist revolution. Not only was it allowed to exist, but it was actually encouraged throughout China. Supposedly Mao said, "Promote physical education movements. Improve people's physical condition." It's not a quote that is likely to live forever, but it is often given as the basis and inspiration of the ping pong movement in China.

In 1953 the Chinese ping pong team entered international championships. Since then it has gone on to truly revolutionize (so to speak) the game throughout the world. What the Chinese did was to combine Japanese "loopspin" techniques with their own devastating "close-to-the-table-fast-attack" strategy. This plus a genuine dedication to the game make the Chinese the unchallenged leaders in the sport today.

A very interesting book has recently been released in the U.S. about Chinese table tennis. It was written and edited by Chinese experts from the PRC and translated into English for publication by Atheneum in 1981. The book is titled *The Chinese Book of Table Tennis* and is an excellent guide to Chinese technique.

The book also includes some rather blatant but amusing Red Flag waving. Here's an example: "The secret of how our players achieved such steady worldwide success is that coaches and athletes all followed the leadership of Chairman Mao in pursuing the teachings of Marx-Lenin-Mao as fundamental in training and strategy." Some games those three must have had!

Go Fly a Chinese Kite

No one is quite sure when the first kite soared into the air or first wrapped itself around a tree limb. But almost everyone agrees that these things probably first took place in China. Early kites were undoubtedly made of silk and bamboo. Silk was being cultivated and woven before 2000 B.C. in China; and, of course, bamboo has always been abundant there. So, it's not unlikely that the first kites were aloft in China by 1000 B.C.

Chinese legends and folklore recount many kite related events. One of the most interesting concerns a general named Huan Theng who opposed Liu Peng, founder of the Han dynasty, in his bid for power. Huan Theng, finding himself surrounded by Liu Peng's forces, sent a number of kites aloft one evening to hover above the opposing troops. He had fitted each kite with a sounding device made of thin strips of bamboo. He had also sent undercover messengers among Liu Peng's troops to spread rumors of evil spirits being released among them. The kites whistled and wailed menacingly above their heads. Soon the combination of eerie sounds and rampant rumors sent the troops scattering. Huan Theng's troops were then able to escape and regroup.

There are also a number of stories that tell about manned kite flights. The invention of paper in China around 200 B.C. led to the development of larger, sturdier, and more complex kite designs. Inevitably, the idea of sending men aloft on these kites was conceived. The results, of course, were mixed, as there could be very little control of a kite large enough to haul a man into the air. Many lost their lives in these early attempts at manned flight.

Today, kite flying is done mainly for pleasure and sport and is popular around the world. But the Chinese still put some kites to practical use. Fishing lines can be attached to kites and flown above water.

When a fish bites, the kite-flying fisherman pulls the kite (and the fish) in. Firecrackers with slow-burning incense fuses are also attached to kites in China. They're flown over crops or gardens and as the firecrackers are set off, they scare scavenging birds away.

Most Chinese kites, like their Western counterparts, are made just for fun. The Festival of Ascending on High is celebrated on the first through the ninth days of September—supposedly the most ideal days for flying kites. The ninth day of the festival is a holiday for schools throughout China. Pupils traditionally fly their kites all day on this last day of the festival, and finally let them go to be blown away by the wind. All bad luck, sickness, and evil are supposedly carried away with the free-flying kites. Kite

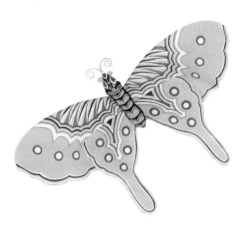

fighting is also popular in China. For these fights the kites must be designed for superior maneuverability. Several yards of the string closest to the kite are coated with a mixture of glue and powdered glass. The idea is to wrap your kite's string around the string of another's kite and slowly "saw" through the opponent's line.

Many books are available on the subjects of kites and kiting. Two recommended books that include instructions for building Chinese kites are:

The Penguin Book of Kites, by David Pelham.
Penguin Books, Ltd.   1979
$4.95   228 pp.

Chinese Kites How to Make and Fly Them, by David F. Jue
Charles E. Tuttle Co.   1980
$6.50   51 pp.

The American Kiteflyers Association, 7106 Campfield Road, Baltimore, MD 21207, publishes the best kiting journal in the U.S. It's called "Kite Lines" and appears quarterly with all sorts of information about buying, making, and flying kites.

Chinese kites made in the People's Republic of China are now widely available in the U.S. But if you can't find a good selection in your neighborhood, you might try contacting one of these outstanding kite dealers.

The Kite Site
3101 M Street, N.W.
Georgetown, DC 20007

Kiteworld Inc.
540 De Haro
San Francisco, CA 94107

Go Fly a Kite Store, Inc.
1434 Third Avenue
New York, NY 10028

Let's Fly a Kite
13763 Fiji Way
Fisherman's Village
Marina Del Ray, CA 90291

International Kite Co.
P.O. Box 3248
San Diego, CA 92103

Mah-Jongg

In the early 1920's an American resident of Shanghai named Joseph P. Babcock decided to introduce a Chinese gambling game to the U.S. All kinds of "newfangled" things were being imported to America in the '20's; but Babcock's game, which he called "Mah-Jongg" or "the sparrows," was exotic and exciting enough to make a fairly big hit on the American scene. It is still popular today, perhaps more on the east coast than elsewhere, but the fascination and gambling opportunities still make Mah-Jongg an engaging table game.

Mah-Jongg is an ancient game, believed to have been played in some form as early as the time of Confucius. At one time it was a sort of mock war game, something like chess, played only by men and with the pieces named after military items. It remained a game of the nobility until the nineteenth century. Today in China Mah-Jongg is most often associated with celebration of the New Year, when the game is played continuously for three days and three nights. The gambling possibilities have made Mah-Jongg big business in some of the racier establishments in American Chinatowns. But, most Mah-Jongg in America and elsewhere is played in the home for modest stakes.

When Babcock prepared to introduce the game in America, he modified it considerably to suit U.S. players. Since that time, other alterations have been made as well. The result is a game that resembles the original Chinese game about as much as Chop Suey resembles Chinese cuisine. Its most distinguishing characteristic, however, is still very much the same. It is a game played with small tiles shaped a bit like dominoes. At one time the tiles were made only of ivory. Today they're made of bamboo, wood, bone, and, most frequently, plastic. The tiles are used much like playing cards are used in Western card games. The tiles are even divided into suits. But in Mah-Jongg the suits are a good deal more varied. The suits in Mah-Jongg are called Dots, Craks, and Bams (short for bamboos), plus the Four Winds, Dragons, Flowers, and Jokers. These names refer to the decoration motif on the different tiles much as heart, spade, diamond, club decorate the four suits in Western playing cards.

Although the basic idea in Mah-Jongg is to draw tiles, pass tiles, discard tiles, and try to form "hands" as one would in a game of rummy, it is quite unlike most card games. For one thing, the multiplicity of suits makes forming the hands a much greater challenge. And, the game is usually played with about 150 tiles. The hand that is made must be fourteen tiles in length, but can be combinations of suits, numbers, colors, and so forth. Forming the hands becomes a kind of creative process for the player. Also, there are two ways of building hands; the player may choose to build an exposed or concealed hand. Exposed hands are built from discarded tiles and everyone at the table can see the hand as it develops. Concealed hands are built on the player's own tile rack (something like the rack used in Scrabble) and are hidden from the other players. The rules, the betting, and the procedures are unique in Mah-Jongg. That is part of what makes it interesting to Western players.

Because the formation of hands is crucial to the game, and because the possibilities are almost endless, an organization was formed in the U.S. to standardize play. The group is called the National Mah-Jongg League and is located at 250 West 57th Street, New York, NY 10019. The League publishes an instruction booklet and a yearly up-dated hand chart that lists all the hand formations legally recognized in the U.S.

In order to play Mah-Jongg, you need a Mah-Jongg set. The set includes tiles, racks, dice, etc., and is usually packed in a little carrying case. The sets range widely in price from about $15 to $1,500, depending on materials used and craftsmanship employed. If sets are difficult to find in your area, write to the National Mah-Jongg League for information.

Recommended books on playing Mah-Jongg are:

Learn to Play Mah-Jongg, by Marcia Hammer.
David McKay Company, Inc.
1979   143 pp.

Mah-Jongg, Anyone?/ A Manual of Modern Play by Kitty Strauser and Lucille Evans. This is a classic rule book that has been around for years. Charles E. Tuttle Co., Inc. Tokyo.   1969

Chinese Gardens

When Marco Polo visited the court of Kublai Khan in the late thirteenth century, one of the things he was most impressed with and wrote most glowingly of were the royal gardens he saw. During his visit he saw the fabulous gardens and parks at Xanadu, the summer residence. He also visited Green Hill, an artificial hill planted with trees from all over China and landscaped naturalistically with man-made ponds, groves, streams, and valleys.

Gardens were laid out in China long before the reign of the Great Khan, though. The Han dynasty (206 B.C.—220 A.D.) had such large "pleasure gardens" that they actually began to infringe upon valuable agricultural land. The Han emperor Wu Ti is said to have had palaces with parks and gardens that spread over an area of more than 30,000 acres. But, as with many other artistic endeavors, the highpoint of Chinese gardening came during the era of the Ming (1368–1644).

The basic theory behind Chinese garden design came about as a result of the combination of the Buddhist concept of the picturesque landscape and the Taoist cult of nature mysticism. Chinese gardens can be roughly compared to Chinese landscape painting in that the attempt to capture realism is not by exact reproduction, but by imitation of nature.

Chinese gardens attempt to imitate natural landscapes, and in doing so create a sublime realism of their own. They are reminiscent of the real/surreal nature of classic Chinese scroll landscape paintings.

Taoism, with its emphasis on harmony with nature, gave special impetus to the tradition of flower gardening in China. The Taoists believed that flowers had certain mystical significance and certain flowers were given specific meanings. The four seasons are symbolized by four different blossoms: the peach blossom represents spring; the lotus blossom, summer; autumn is symbolized by the chrysanthemum; and the narcissus

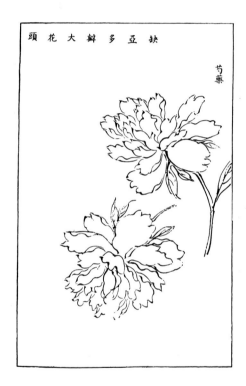

stands for winter. Other plants have other meanings, but the lotus, peony, orchid, cherry and plum blossoms, magnolia, gardenia, chrysanthemum, narcissus, and poppy have always been favorites in the Chinese garden mostly because of their mystical significance.

The Chinese garden recreates a natural landscape in miniature. Earth is piled up to form small hills and rocks are stacked on top of one another to simulate mountains. Miniature waterfalls and ponds are added and flowers, trees, and shrubs are planted informally all around in order to appear as natural as possible. Since the scale of real mountains, lakes, and waterfalls had to be scaled down for the garden, the Chinese horticulturists needed

to dwarf the sizes of trees and shrubs used in the landscapes. Thus began a tradition that was eventually exported to Japan, where it was taken to the extreme in the art of bonsai.

In America, it is easy to find the right plants for a Chinese garden, but somewhat harder to capture the true spirit of Chinese garden design. Still it's fun to try. The main thing to remember is that the Chinese created or tried to create miniature replicas of actual landscapes. So it might be a good idea to look at some photos of Chinese landscapes as well as Chinese gardens. Then try to imagine a space in your own yard that might be made fairly secluded. Choose some rocks—all of the same type—and build a mountain by stacking the rocks and filling in around them with good garden soil. The earth parts of your mountain will have to be planted well with low growing plants such as moss phlox, sand strawberry, or dwarf juniper in order to hold the soil and prevent erosion. You can build in a waterfall, too, if your budget allows. Electric water pumps and plastic pool liners are available at many garden centers and make this an easier task than might be imagined. If you can't afford any special water effects, be content to decorate your mountain with favorite Chinese flowers and shrubs and dwarf trees. Make sure that you include a place to sit in your Chinese garden. One of the most important aspects of this kind of garden is that it provide a quiet place for reflection and meditation.

There are not a great many truly Chinese gardens in America. Most oriental gardens in the U.S. are Japanese. The relationship is very close, however, as Japan imported its gardening style from China. The Japanese refined and codified the style and made it the standard for what we think of as oriental gardens today. Two of the largest oriental gardens in America are located in the Brooklyn Botanic Gardens, Prospect Park, Brooklyn, New York, and in Golden Gate Park in San Francisco, California. The Garden Club of America publishes a handbook called *Guide to Public Gardens.* In it you will find all types of oriental gardens listed by state. These gardens are not only a joy to visit, but provide lots of ideas for your own adventure in oriental gardening.

Write to The Garden Club of America, 598 Madison Avenue, New York, NY 10022 for further information.

Religion and the Occult

Of all the mysteries in the "mysterious east," Chinese religion and occultism must surely be considered one of the most mysterious. Western civilization, a product of the Judeo-Christian religions, has never proven very hospitable to the religions of the east. As a result, Buddhism, Taoism (not to mention Confucianism) are not only not often practiced in the U.S., they are not even very well known. Nor are western occultists very familiar with the practices of their eastern brethren. But, like so many other things, this, too, is changing. Improvements in communication and education have advanced interest in other religious studies. In addition, there seems to be a growing feeling that there are often more things alike than different with regard to the search for theological truths.

One thing is certain, a little knowledge of Chinese religion, philosophy, and folk lore will help illuminate all other aspects of the Chinese culture. The following is a brief examination of the most widespread religious and occult practices in China.

Confucius and Confucianism

In China, Confucianism is called the *Ju* philosophy, *ju* meaning "literatus" or "scholar" in Chinese. Being a scholar in ancient China meant being well versed in the six ancient arts: ceremonials, music (poetry), history (writing), numbers, archery, and charioteering. Confucius is so closely associated with the *Ju* philosophy and with teaching the ancient arts that, in the West, we call the study itself Confucianism. There is little doubt that Confucianism has had the strongest and most lasting effect of any religion or ethical system ever known in the long history of Chinese civilization. It has affected politics, government, education, art, music, literature, justice, and in fact almost every aspect of Chinese thought. Despite devastating political crises and social upheavals, Confucianism has always survived and provided a thread of continuity in Chinese life.

Confucius himself is perhaps the best known philosopher in all the world. His name in English is a romanization of his actual name, K'ung Fu-tzu. It's just as well that we call him "Confucius." The other sounds a bit too much like a modern martial arts film. Anyway, Confucius was born about 551 B.C. in the state of Lu (now known as Ch'u Fu) in Shantung Province. His family could trace its ancestry to royal blood, but Confucius' great-grandfather had lost the family title in a political debacle. His father became a well respected soldier, but died when Confucius was only three years old. This left the K'ung family in a rather precarious financial situation. Confucius could not afford to be a full-time student and was probably self-taught for the most part. He was also forced to take a public service job at an early age in order to help support the family.

When Confucius' mother died, he left his job and began a three year period of study. It was after this that he began to teach, and his reputation grew quickly throughout China. Although Confucius' teachings exerted a great deal of influence on government in China, he was a member of the government for only about three years. This must have been disappointing to Confucius because serving the government was his primary ambition. Confucius died in 479 B.C. He was buried near Ch'u Fu and his tomb and temple are still visited there regularly.

The most common misconception among Westerners is that Confucianism is a religion of some kind. It is a bit like a religion in that it provides a moral system for man to follow, but it does not exact eternal or temporal punishment for not obeying its provisions. And there is no special deity or prophet to worship in Confucianism. There are vague references in Confucius' teachings to god, heaven, and afterlife, but they are general rather than specific to any particular form of worship. Confucius constantly avoided strictly religious questions. His teaching dealt primarily with ethics and the morality necessary for living a "right" life.

Confucianism is really a system of

study developed to produce cultural wisdom and thereby facilitate making the individual and society better. Confucius concentrated on teaching the duties which he considered proper to civilized man. He based these duties on a kind of humanism and something the Chinese call *jen*, which means "fellow-feeling" or humanitarian behavior. Cultivating among men a spirit of moral obligation to one another is primary to the entire Confucian philosophy. Confucius believed that all men deserved love and that expressing this love unselfishly in the family and among all men was an ultimate good here on earth. He also taught two other primary concepts. Confucius believed that conscientiousness, or being faithful to oneself, was a moral obligation as was altruism—developing a genuine understanding of other people. Of course, being true to oneself and understanding others enhances the development of *jen*—humanitarianism. And goodness, Confucius taught, is natural to the human heart. Therefore, the practice of Confucianism can be taken as simply an attempt to preserve the natural instincts of man.

Preservation of what might be called the universal will to civilize oneself is one reason that Confucius believed in teaching from the books of the ancients. Confucius himself worked with the ancient books a great deal in order to make them more accessible to the people of his time. But today we generally look at the *Lun Yu* or *Analects* of Confucius as his major contribution. The *Analects* is a collection of sayings by Confucius and his disciples recorded by the disciples of the Confucian school of thought. In a way, the *Analects* provide a view of Confucius and his philosophy much as the *New Testament* provides a view of Christ.

Confucian philosophy was so practical and so obviously beneficial to man, that it easily became the ideal in government, education, and art in China. Confucianism and the doctrine of *jen* can be regarded as one of the truly great contributions the Chinese have made to philosophical and ethical thought.

Some interesting works on Confucianism are:

Confucianism by Ch'u Chai. Barron's Educational Series, Inc. Woodbury, New York.

Confucian Analects translated by Ezra Pound. London.

The Wisdom of Confucius, edited and translated by Lin Yutang. Modern Library, New York.

The Chinese Classics, James Legge's translation. In 7 volumes. Recently reprinted by Oxford University Press and University Books, Inc.

A Short History of Confucian Philosophy by Wu-chi Liu. Penguin Books.

Taoism

Besides Confucianism, Taoism is the only other major system of ethics in China. It is also the only true and widely practiced religion native to China. No one knows just when it began, but it is generally believed to have run parallel to the development of Confucianism. Taoism, though, has several very distinctive characteristics that set it apart from Confucianism.

One apparent problem with Confucianism is that it is designed for scholars and intellectuals. The practice of Confucianism, after all, began the state examination system that led to the development of the mandarin class in China. Obviously, Confucianism wasn't really meant for everyone. Yet Confucianism *applied* to everyone and the *Tao* or "Way," of Taoism is essentially the accepted *Tao* of Confucianism in that both direct the individual to improved goodness of soul, improvement through introspection, and reliance on the "natural" order of things. Taoism includes along with these ethical guidelines a cult of mysticism that tied together many religious and occult practices from the earliest of China's religious practices. Naturally Taoism was more popular among ordinary people than was the rather elite and esoteric Confucianism.

Later, Taoist philosophy was applied to Buddhism in China and eventually affected the development of what we now know as Zen Buddhism. Before that, however, it developed largely in apposition to Confucianism, sometimes countering it and sometimes supplementing it. But unlike Confucianism, Taoism always grew in the direction of the religious and mystical and away from the purely philosophical.

Lao-tzu is traditionally considered to be the founder of Taoism and is often said to have been contemporary with Confucius. The *Tao* or state of oneness with the universe is common to both Taoism and Confucianism. But in Taoism the oneness becomes the divine All-One godhead. This metaphysical notion of the *Tao* makes it the mother or ancestor of all things according to Taoism. It is the invisible but unchangeable thing that all beings depend upon for life. It is, in other words, God.

Practicing Taoism was in almost direct opposition to the "right life" that Confucius encouraged. Whereas Confucianism promoted the idea of taking action to make things better, Taoism supports the concept of *wu-wei* or "non-action." Actually it is related to the Confucian idea of reliance on the natural state of things. But

Taoism carries the idea to its ultimate conclusion. The Taoist is to be completely spontaneous and non-interfering, taking no direct action but always supporting the natural way of things. These ideas bring Lao-tzu into direct conflict with the Confucians primarily because he felt that laws and government institutions were artificial and thus inhibited the "natural" development of society. Inactivity and "perfect weakness" are primary doctrines of Taoism. Water is often used as the perfect symbol of Taoism. The perfect weakness of water is deceptive, however, as water can destroy the strongest materials. The concept of inactivity and "perfect weakness" often lead to basic inconsistencies in Taoism.

For most Westerners it is the emphasis on nature that distinguishes religious Taoism from other religions. Taoism teaches a oneness with nature, a harmony that deeply influenced Chinese art. In addition, the Taoist provides a deity for just about every animate and inanimate thing in the natural world. The goal of religious Taoism is harmony with nature which will bring good fortune to true believers. And most importantly, true believers will possess the blessing of longevity. Taoism is perhaps the only religion that so emphasizes longevity. It is easy to see why Taoism influenced diet and medicine in China for so many years.

Today Taoism is a fast-fading religion. Many of the old rituals and superstitions remain, but the formal practice of the religion seems oddly out of step with the modern face of China.

A recommended book that compares and traces the development of religions in China is:

The Religion of China/Confucianism and Taoism by Max Weber. The MacMillan Company, New York.

The eight trigrams represent the basic elements of the universe. When the trigrams are combined to make the sixty-four hexagrams, the meanings diversify and represent the multitude of possibilities in the creation. For instance, the fifty-ninth hexagram ☴ combines which stands for (among other things) wood and wind, over ☵ which, as we've seen, stands for water and moon. According to the *I Ching* this explains how the ancients invented boats and sailing—the hexagram stands for wood over water, a boat! Some are even more far-fetched than that. But they are interesting just the same.

During the Han dynasty (206 B.C.– A.D. 220), the *I Ching* was transformed into a workable cosmology that, it was hoped, all Chinese people could understand. It tried to explain the origin of the universe and the elements of change and growth necessary for continued existence. The lines of the trigrams came to represent the Yang (straight line), the masculine, positive, active force; and Yin (broken line), the feminine, negative, passive force in the universe. The combination or balance of Yin and Yang was, of course, the result of an ordered existence and became the basic goal of Confucian and Taoist teachings.

This only scratches the surface of the true meaning and significance of the *I Ching*. Some readers first note that the language of the *I Ching* is rather simple. The words used are few, but the meanings are manifold. No English translation can quite capture the multiplicity of meaning that is inherent in the Chinese language. Several English translations have been done, however. Perhaps the most famous is the one done by James Legge first published in 1882. That version has been amended, improved, and up-dated so as to make it more accessible to Western readers.

A useful version of the Legge translation of the *I Ching* is published by Bantam Books with an Introduction and Study Guide by Ch'u Chai with Winberg Chai.

The *I Ching* is mainly interesting from an historical and philosophical point of view, but it is still used to foretell the future. Yarrow sticks have been replaced by coins, and an individual's fortune and fate may be predicted by making a hexagram based on the toss of three coins. Begin by assigning a value of 2 to heads and 3 to tails, then add the results of six successive throws of the three coins. Each odd number total (7 or 9) represents a straight, Yang line. Each even number total (6 or 8) represents a broken, Yin line. The hexagram is built from the bottom line up. In other words, the first toss of the coins will dictate what the bottom line of the hexagram will be; the second toss, the second from the bottom, etc. Finding out what meaning there is to the resulting hexagram is what the *I Ching* is all about.

I Ching: The Book of Changes

In the late 1960's and early 1970's, many young Americans, discontent with a number of situations in the U.S., turned to the wisdom of other civilizations in hope of finding new answers to age-old problems. Some found inspiration in the simplicity of Zen Buddhism, some in Islam, and some in eccentric cults like the one that developed around the writings of Hermann Hesse. A few rediscovered an ancient Chinese book called the *I Ching* or *Book of Changes.* Here they found an unusual combination of mysticism and philosophy—it was almost made-to-order for the era.

Although the popularity of the *I Ching* in the 60's did not last, it is still an interesting book to study. In many ways it can be a key to Chinese thought, especially in terms of Confucian and Taoist philosophy. Indeed the *I Ching* can be a kind of touchstone to understanding Chinese civilization much as the Bible or Plato's *Republic* might be for our society.

It is important to note at the outset that the basic idea behind the *I Ching* is very old, probably appearing in some form as early as the Shang dynasty (1523–1028 B.C.). The Chou dynasty which followed probably codified and perhaps even printed some early version of the *I Ching*. It was first meant to be a sort of manual of divination. In other words, it was meant to set down a procedure for telling the future. Would crops be good? Would rain come soon? When would a great leader die? The ancient way of forecasting the future depended on a complicated system of reading the cracks that developed on a tortoise shell when it was heated by fire. The cracks were quite intricate and their meanings multitudinous. A simpler way was badly needed. During the Chou dynasty, a method of throwing milfoil (yarrow) stalks on the ground produced certain alignments that could be related to the symbols that form the basis of the *I Ching*. This simplified form of divination became a central part of the Chinese cultural and religious life.

In later years the basic *I Ching* received a great deal of modification by the addition of explanatory or illuminating appendices. The most important addition to the *I Ching* are the appendices known as the Ten Wings or *Shih I.* These are basically Confucian additions that extend the meaning of the *I Ching* beyond simple "fortune telling" to a philosophical foundation for living. Scholars disagree as to exactly how many of the Ten Wings (if any) were actually written by Confucius himself. The point is, the Ten Wings made the *I Ching* the basic sacred text for Confucianism for all time.

The *I Ching* itself is simply an explanation of sixty-four hexagrams (groups of six lines) made by combining two of eight trigrams (groups of three lines) in every possible combination. The eight trigrams are made up of straight lines and straight lines broken in half. Each trigram represents several things. Three straight lines ☰ is the first trigram. It stands for strength, horse, head, father, and heaven. Three broken lines ☷ is the second trigram. It stands for docility, ox, belly, mother, and earth. Combinations of these lines make up the other six. The fifth trigram ☵ , for instance, represents danger, pig, ear, second son, and water and moon.

The Chinese Horoscope

According to an ancient legend, Lord Buddha called on all of the animals of the world to come bid him farewell before he departed from the earth. Of all the animals, only twelve showed up. To honor these twelve, Buddha assigned each of them a year. Thus the twelve years of the Chinese lunar calendar cycle were named Rat, Ox, Tiger, Rabbit, Dragon, Snake, Horse, Sheep, Monkey, Rooster, Dog, and Bear.

The Chinese lunar calendar is the oldest time-keeping system in the world. It dates from 2637 B.C. when the emperor Huang Ti introduced the first sixty-year cycle. Each cycle of the Chinese lunar calendar is made up of five twelve-year periods. The twelve animal signs are combined with five symbolic elements—Earth, Fire, Water, Wood, and Metal. With all of the possible combinations, each year of the sixty-year cycle is different. For instance, 1916 and 1976 were Fire Dragon years; 1908 and 1968 were Earth Monkey years; and 2034 and 2094 will be Wood Tiger years. One particular combination is considered to be unlucky. It comes, like all of the combinations, only once every sixty years. It's the Fire Horse year which occurred in 1906 and 1966 and will occur again in 2026. A child born in the year of the Fire Horse, particularly a female child, is supposedly destined to bring destruction and calamity on her family and spouse. In the Fire Horse year of 1966, the rate of voluntary abortions rose and the birth rate dropped dramatically throughout Asia. Obviously, the Chinese horoscope is still taken seriously by many people.

The years of the sixty-year cycle were further divided by Yin (negative or pas-

sive force) and Yang (positive or active force) probably during the rise of Confucianism in China. The Rat, Tiger, Dragon, Horse, Monkey, and Dog are active Yang signs. The Ox, Rabbit, Snake, Sheep, Rooster, and Boar are the Yin or passive signs. All of these things are taken into account when the Chinese astrologer predicts the future or reads an individual's personality and destiny.

One of the most distinctive aspects of the Chinese lunar calendar is its accuracy in terms of predicting seasonal changes and favorable conditions for growth of plant and animal life on the earth. For this reason, one of the main occupations of

the Chinese astrologer has been to forecast and document the most suitable periods for agricultural activity. The Chinese relied heavily on the horoscope to predict rain. If the natural element of a certain year was Water it would supposedly bring either an abundance of water or destructive flooding depending on the positive (ample) or negative (destructive) aspect of the animal sign. The year 1983 was a Water Boar (negative) year. The destructive flooding in California, New Orleans, Mississippi, and the Northeast seems to give credence to the Chinese lunar formula for predicting rain!

The Chinese horoscope is not as popular in China as it once was. The PRC does not encourage belief or adherence to the reading of the lunar signs. And Chinese astrology has never been as popular in America as the Sun signs of the Western Zodiac—Aries, Taurus, Capricorn, etc. Still, it is interesting to look into the Chinese horoscope if only for the sake of comparing it with Western astrological ideas. One of the things that draws Westerners to the Chinese zodiac is its ability to forecast the future by predicting how the different sign personalities will fare during different astrological years. The Chinese horoscope predicts, for instance, how a Water Rabbit personality gets along in a Metal Snake year.

The following chart shows the years of the Chinese lunar signs from 1900 to 1995.

RAT	1900	1912	1924	1936	1948	1960	1972	1984
OX	1901	1913	1925	1937	1949	1961	1973	1985
TIGER	1902	1914	1926	1938	1950	1962	1974	1986
RABBIT	1903	1915	1927	1939	1951	1963	1975	1987
DRAGON	1904	1916	1928	1940	1952	1964	1976	1988
SNAKE	1905	1917	1929	1941	1953	1965	1977	1989
HORSE	1906	1918	1930	1942	1954	1966	1978	1990
SHEEP	1907	1919	1931	1943	1955	1967	1979	1991
MONKEY	1908	1920	1932	1944	1956	1968	1980	1992
ROOSTER	1909	1921	1933	1945	1957	1969	1981	1993
DOG	1910	1922	1934	1946	1958	1970	1982	1994
BOAR	1911	1923	1935	1947	1959	1971	1983	1995

Note: Since Chinese New Year varies between January and mid-February, people born during that period will need to check with another source (local newspaper or library) to find out what Chinese astrological year it was when they were born.

The Signs of the Chinese Zodiac

The following are short sketches of the personality traits most often associated with the various signs of the Chinese zodiac. The signs appear in the order their animal symbols appeared to bid farewell to Buddha and therefore represent the chronological order they assume in the twelve-year lunar cycle.

RAT

The Rat personality is characterized by being industrious and forthright. Occasionally supercritical, the Rat is usually easy to get along with and is often quite sociable—especially at gatherings of friends and relatives. He has an innate love of money and success, but also exhibits strong feelings for cherished family members. The Rat person is easily irritated by lazy and wasteful people. He has a weakness, however, for "sucker deals" and is often separated from his money by them. He will be successful if he can control his native avarice and learn to stay and face up to problems rather than pulling the "quick exit" routine.

OX (Buffalo)

Responsibility and steadiness are sure signs of the Ox personality. He is an organized and methodical person, astute but rather shy and inward. His integrity is usually unimpeachable. Somewhat unsophisticated in affairs of the heart, he is an old-fashioned traditionalist about most relationships. His mind is clear and uncluttered. His approach to life is a no-nonsense practical approach. On the negative side, an Ox can hold a grudge. He is also victim to falling into ruts that he has trouble breaking out of. Honest, patient, and hard-working, the Ox may not be rich, but what he earns will be rightfully his.

TIGER

A dynamic and passionate individual, the Tiger is an exciting and surprising personality. He exhibits an infectious *joie de vivre* and an adventurous approach to living. Somewhat quick-tempered, he can also be very happy-go-lucky if the mood strikes him. The eternal optimist, a Tiger often adopts a fadish or trendy lifestyle in order to show disdain for the staid, traditional, or conservative. His intensity can sometimes lead to a very selfish or hedonistic lifestyle, too. The Tiger is most glorious in his youth when his volatile and expressive personality is admired by

all. He will need to find a stabilizing influence (perhaps work or a spouse) to knit the wildly loose ends of his life together.

RABBIT (Hare)

In Chinese mythology, the Hare is closely associated with the moon. He is associated with love of beauty and luxury and is a sensitive, graceful being. The Rabbit personality is very rarely flustered or out-of-sorts. Everything in a Rabbit's life is tempered by good taste, tranquility, and cultivated behavior. Although he may appear to be a snob, the Rabbit is destroyed by harsh criticism. But hurt or insulted, the Rabbit very rarely resorts to violence. In fact, the Rabbit always seeks the easy way out. His greatest weaknesses are love of luxury, and love of self. He is often distant and aloof from his family. And though he may appear weak, he is usually bolstered by a great strength of will. A Rabbit is generally happy and satisfied during his entire lifetime.

DRAGON

Just as the mythical character of the dragon is perceived, so the Dragon personality is grand, powerful, and ablaze with energy. In the Dragon's mind there is nothing he cannot accomplish. He is the original mover-and-shaker. Usually blessed with intelligence and persuasiveness, the Dragon commands love and respect. His boundless energy suits him well for the Herculean tasks he sets up for himself. Not particularly wise or sensitive, the Dragon is often criticized for being egocentric. Most of all the Dragon despises all things petty. His is a big world with most of its problems his own responsibility. Seldom thwarted and never defeated, his resilience and self-confidence make him an almost sure winner in life.

SNAKE

Beautiful, elegant, powerful, and mysterious are usually the most common adjectives used to describe a Snake personality. He is not a communicative person and does not allow himself to depend on others. He's a bit of a skeptic and is often cynical about ideas or lifestyles that do not match his own. Frequently victim to ulcers and nervous breakdowns, the Snake is sometimes suspicious to the point of being neurotic. There is often a mystical or deeply religious aura about

Snake people. Unfortunately, their deep-set single-mindedness can lead to fanaticism and intolerance. A superior tactician, he is an excellent diplomat. And if paranoia does not destroy him, his charismatic personality and cunning intelligence can lead him to enormous success.

HORSE

The Horse personality is one that is rife with inconsistencies. This individual can be stubborn but also accommodating, rashly independent and yet hopelessly victimized by love. There is very little middle ground for the Horse. He has flair and style and a love for the fun things in life—especially sports. The Horse is agile of both mind and body. He loves variety in his life, and sometimes this leads him into abrupt changes that can be either constructive or destructive depending on the circumstances. The Horse is a changeable personality not easily reined into docile conformity. His sense of time is usually at odds with the rest of the world. When most people are asleep, the Horse is at work; and in the midst of great activity, the Horse may take time out for a nap. There is great unbridled passion in the Horse person. In the case of the Fire Horse, this passion can result in destructiveness. This brash and sometimes unprincipled personality must fight boredom his entire life. His interests must be kept alive if happiness is to be found.

SHEEP

The Chinese associate the Sheep with gentleness and understanding. This sign is the most feminine of all the signs. Women born under this sign will be delicate and coquettish; men sheep will be kind, well-groomed, and sensitive. The Rabbit is the Sheep's soul mate, and they make very close friends. Sheep appreciate the finer things in life and very often get them through no real effort of their own. Most people love them and many admire them so much that they assume responsibility for them. Sheep are often the recipients of expensive gifts and surprise inheritances. Basically creative people, the Sheep must fight against a morose and often pessimistic nature. The Sheep will indulge in self-pity sometimes and frequently overspend on personal luxuries. Approval makes the Sheep person bloom. He likes nothing better than an appreciative audience. Good fortune usually smiles on the Sheep because he is basically very good at heart.

MONKEY

A person born in the year of the Monkey is a clever but often duplicitous individual. The most intelligent sign in the Chinese zodiac, the Monkey is an inventor and a strategist. Nothing the Monkey does is unplanned. His life, his work, even his relationships with others are controlled by a constantly maneuvering intellect. There is almost nothing a Monkey can't learn or do. But he is an extremely jealous type, too. Anything that someone else has that he wants will spark a deeply envious desire in him. The Monkey is extraordinarily competitive, and often suffers from an acute superiority complex. He is an elitist and practically nothing can convince him that he might have an equal in the world. He is saved from himself by charm, a sense of humor, and a light-hearted approach to life. Things are fun with a Monkey if you can forget that there is probably a motive beneath the merriment.

ROOSTER

An accountant, efficiency expert, or loan shark is very likely to be born under the sign of the Rooster. These people are meticulous, exacting, and extraordinarily adept at handling money. The Rooster's personal money matters are always in complete order. Roosters are often talkative and extroverted, but they sometimes put others off by being overly candid and critical. The Rooster has lofty, splendid goals, but usually succeeds by doing something simple with matchless precision. A bit of a miser, the Rooster is almost never down-and-out. Prudent to a fault in money matters, the Rooster never sidesteps controversy. In fact, he often tries to pick a fight. He is the kind of heroic personality often undone by an impossible dream. Yet there is a nobility about Rooster people that is universally admired.

DOG

No one could wish for a better friend than the kind of friend the Dog sign produces. Not easily fooled, the Dog selects the right companions carefully. Once you prove your worthiness to a Dog person, you have a valuable friend for life—valuable because the dog is a model of stability and insight. The Dog can survive an incredible amount of stress and pain. The Dog person is a warm and affectionate human being, often a crusader for what is right and good. A Dog is rarely a money monger; he prefers simple dress and a comfortable, practical lifestyle. The Dog person has an incisive wit and an amazing gift for logical thinking. A born worrier, the Dog gives vent to many shortlived bursts of annoyance. Most people enjoy having Dogs around because they are generally attractive, friendly, and honest.

BOAR (pig)

The Boar is the very image of magnanimity. What wealth he accumulates (and it is often considerable) he is likely to share with the world and most especially lavish on his family. Capable of achieving unbelievable tasks, the Boar is never afraid of work. He often takes on another's responsibilities because he knows that he will have no trouble handling them. He is guileless and even naive, and can easily be taken in by tricksters. He is magnanimous of character, too, slow to criticize, and accepting of almost every kind of human being. The Boar will avoid open conflict and quarrelsome hostility at almost any cost. He is a great peacemaker and a forgiving friend. The Boar is the original "party animal." His love of food, wine, and the opposite sex can, in fact, be his undoing. No one, though, is blessed with more friends or has more heart or strength of character than the trusting, generous Boar.

This diagram is called the "Affinity Triangles." Each triangle connects those astrological signs that make the best partnerships in business and marriage. Recommended for further reading:

The Handbook of Chinese Horoscopes by Theodora Lau. Harper & Row, 1979 314 pp. $11.95

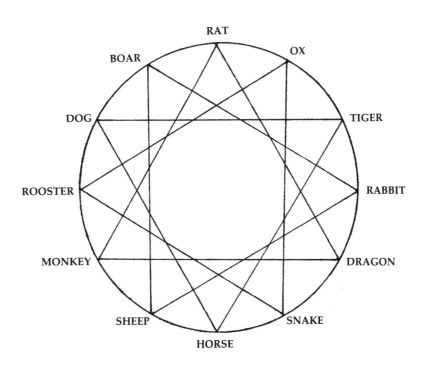

Literature, Language, and the Performing Arts

All three of these areas of interest are fairly new to Americans. Certainly there has never been any widespread desire in the U.S. to learn to speak or write Chinese. And, partly as a result, very little Chinese literature has ever been translated into English. The performing arts in China were never meant for export and so are rare and practically unknown in this country. Almost all of this is attributable to the profound differences between the two languages. Yet interest in these areas is growing. The Chinese, of course, are most anxious to learn English—the language that predominates in our modern age. But Americans are also expressing interest in learning the Chinese language. Travel enhances this interest, but the discovery of a wealth of heretofore unknown treasures in literature and the performing arts is even more alluring. Slowly, more sophisticated methods of teaching Chinese are being developed. One by one, the great works of Chinese literature are being translated into English, and the Chinese are even beginning to share with us some of the classics from their performing arts.

Chinese Poetry

Verse writing in China had a long but rather restricted history. It is generally agreed that poetry has been written in China for more than 2,500 years. Few Chinese, however, have had much to do with it. For many centuries, poetry was the exclusive province of the mandarin and noble classes. It was not written in common, everyday Chinese, but in a stilted literary language. Most Chinese in Imperial China could not read anyway, but even if the general public heard a recitation or song made from this poetry, it would not have been very well understood. Poetry was to the Chinese the ultimate literary endeavor. It was the most refined and specialized form of literature, suitable only for the scholar-official.

The social revolutions in China over the last seventy years changed literary directions in China completely. A change was badly needed. The poetry of the Chinese elite had become as pointless and ineffectual as the dynastic form of government itself. There had been literally no contact with the outside world in terms of modern literary traditions. Change and growth in Chinese literature were literally nonexistent as a result of the in-grown and self-serving nature of mandarin poetry. First under the Nationalist's republic and then under the People's Republic of China, the structure of traditional Chinese literature was torn

down. Almost all forms of literature written in the mandarin literary style were judged imitative and disreputable. Naturally, the early revolutionists went too far. Slowly, a reevaluation of the poetic tradition in China is producing a number of "accepted" ancient poets who, although writing in an artificial language, wrote about ordinary people and very real human experiences.

The very personal nature of Chinese poetry is perhaps its most interesting characteristic for the Western reader. Very often the Chinese poet reveals himself in his verse, and the reader feels an identification with the author that is both personal and spiritual. This personal tradition in Chinese poetry developed gradually from its earliest forms.

The oldest recorded poetry in China is contained in an anthology called *Shih-ching* or *Book of Songs*. This collection existed during the time of Confucius (551–479 B.C.) and, in fact, became one of the primary Confucian scriptures. The *Book of Songs* addressed such varied subjects as marriage, war, hunting, agriculture, and courtship. Its importance in terms of social, political, and educational impact cannot be overemphasized.

Following the collapse of Confucian China the Han dynasty introduced a new poetic form called *fu. Fu* is not considered by the Chinese to be true poetry. It is not like the song poetry of earlier periods, and although it is often rhymed, it is not meant to be set to music. Nevertheless, it is poetic by Western standards and certainly served to broaden the vocabulary and form of Chinese verse. Under the Han, the mandarin class was first established, and it was to them that the responsibility for the poetic tradition fell. This gentry class of Chinese wrote poetry based very much on the events of their own lives. The Confucian idea that poetry should address itself to social criticism did not die; it simply took a somewhat secondary place to personal contemplation and the joys of word play.

Form in Chinese poetry is based mostly on the number of words per line. This is perhaps because Chinese words are usually only one syllable long. The most

common forms are the five-word and seven-word lines. Chinese poetry, until the twentieth century, almost always rhymed—usually the even lines (2, 4, 6, 8, etc.). As the Han dynasty disintegrated and the T'ang established itself, the five-word *shih* form became firmly established. Another form called *tz'u* was developed under the T'ang during what is now called the "golden age" of Chinese poetry (seventh and eighth centuries A.D.) This *tz'u* form would become more fully realized during the poetic flowering of the Sung dynasty. But by the end of the Sung era, poetry would be fixed and static and remain unchanged to modern times.

Established forms are extremely limiting and the five-line form was often made to work by employing antiquated literary expressions from as far back as the *Book of Songs*. In addition, the Chinese poetic convention of addressing poems to other poets living and dead, and of filling verse with complex and subtle allusions to other poems became a troublesome influence. It was not long before Chinese poetry was based on a kind of insider's information, and slowly it lost relevance to all but those who were writing it.

English translations of Chinese poetry have never been terribly popular with Western readers. The People's Republic of China, however, has done the West a great service in going back and reviewing all of the writings of the ancient poets and choosing those most relevant to modern times. As those are translated, it will doubtless provide us with a much better view of traditional Chinese poetry. Of course, today Western forms are being used in China along with the old mandarin forms. Because the writing of Chinese poetry was limited to so very few, it would seem that the future of Chinese verse will be one of great growth and fascinating experimentation.

Some anthologies in English translation that can be recommended are:

The Penguin Book of Chinese Verse, Translated by Robert Kotewall and Norman L. Smith. Edited with an Introduction by A.R. Davis. Penguin Books, Baltimore, MD. 84pp.

Translations from the Chinese by Arthur Waley. Vintage Books, Random House, New York. 1971. 325 pp.

The Book of Songs, translated by Arthur Waley. Grove Press, first Evergreen Edition 1960. New York. 358 pp.

Sunflower Splendor/Three Thousand Years of Chinese Poetry. Co-edited by Wu-chi Liu and Irving Y. Lo. Anchor Press/Doubleday, Garden City, New York. 1975. 630 pp.

Reading Chinese Fiction

The basic traditions in Chinese literature grew out of the teachings of Confucius. The single most important aim of literature, according to Confucius, was to teach men to be good. Moral scrupulousness was always judged to be more important than artistic brilliance by Chinese literary critics. Nothing had so profound an influence on Chinese literature as this imposition of Confucian morality.

Chinese fiction is very much a product of the Confucian literary tradition. True fiction did not exist during the life of Confucius. But tales, fables, and legends sometimes showed up in historical and philosophical works. These tales and legends were commonly repeated, embellished, and imitated among common people. When minor court officials began writing down and collecting the stories, they became known as the work of *hsiao-shuo chia* or "minor-talk writers." Chinese fiction has from that time on been known as *hsiao-shuo*. And, for the most part, Chinese fiction has adhered to the Confucian goal of being written primarily to teach mankind how to be better.

Ancient Chinese fiction is similar in many ways to early Western fiction. The stories, based on the lives of heroes and gods. the creation of the universe, miraculous jouneys, and magical transformations, are fairly artless in style. In the T'ang dynasty (618–906 A.D.), however, the first accomplished fiction with an artistic narrative style began to appear. A good example of the first true fiction in China is a story called "The White Monkey." The author is unknown, but it dates from the very early days of the T'ang dynasty. Other stories of interest from T'ang times are "The Man with the Curly Beard" probably by Tu Kuan-t'ing, "A visit to the Fairy Lodge" by Chang Tsu, "Jen, the Fox Fairy" by Shen Chi-chih, and "the Tale of the Peerless" by Hsieh T'iao. One of the best and most sophisticated pieces of T'ang fiction is a story by the writer Po Hsing-chien called "The Story of Li-Wa." It is a love story about a well-bred student and the beautiful prostitute who nearly does him in. It is rich with detail and remarkable in terms of characterization.

Full-length Chinese novels appeared much later, during the Yuan and Ming

dynasties (thirteenth through seventeenth centuries). The two earliest novels, *Romance of the Three Kingdoms* and *Tale of the Marshes* are both historical tales that probably spring from popular theatrical dramas about the same subjects.

Romance of the Three Kingdoms was published in the first half of the sixteenth century. Its characters interact against the background of a turbulent period in Chinese history when the Han dynasty fell and China broke into three separate kingdoms. Unlike Western historical fiction, the *Romance of the Three Kingdoms* does not focus on one particular hero or one family's struggle through political and cultural upheaval. Instead, it is a broad panoramic view of many heroes, many families, and many historical events. The reputed author was Lo Kuan-chung, but the *Romance of the Three Kingdoms* has been changed and modified over the years as new editions were printed. *Tale of the Marshes* is probably by Shih Nai-an and tells the story of a band of Robin Hood characters who were active during the mid-Sung dynasty (twelfth century). They supposedly revolted against the high taxation leveled on the common people during the lavish reign of the Sung. This fictional piece is loosely put together and is really more a collection of tales with a set group of characters than it is a true novel.

During the last century of the Ming dynasty, fiction established itself as one of the recognized literary genres. Fiction was printed more regularly and purchased more readily by the educated classes. Groups of stories such as those in Ling Meng-ch'u's *Striking the Table in Amazement at the Wonders* were incredibly popular. It is surprising to most Western readers to discover how strikingly explicit with regard to sexual relationships these early stories are. Certainly many must have been written as purely erotic and pornographic literature. Many of them survive today only because they were sent to Japan for safekeeping during the various censorship crusades of the Ch'ing dynasty.

From Ming times to the twentieth century much fiction has been written in

China. Three classic novels from Chinese literature stand out, however. *Journey to the West, Gold Vase Plum*, and *Dream of the Red Chamber* are perhaps the most famous and possibly the greatest Chinese novels ever written.

Journey to the West (also known as *Monkey* in the West) is a supernatural adventure novel. It is the story of a somewhat less than brilliant saint named Tripitaka and his journey to the Western Heaven to find sacred sutras and so redeem himself in the eyes of Buddha. Monkey (one of the animal spirits that accompanies him on his journey) becomes the main character. The adventures of Monkey and his quest for power make up the major part of the novel. Based on a number of stories and legends, it has evolved as a novel from its first edition written by Wu Ch'eng-en and published in 1593.

The *Gold Vase Plum* first appeared in the early seventeenth century and is known in English as *The Golden Lotus* and *The Adventurous History of Hsi-men and His Six Wives*. Its author remains anonymous but used the pen name Hsiao-hsiao sheng (Laughing, laughing scholar). It is the first realistic social novel written anywhere in the world. English and French novels of this type did not appear until more than a hundred years later. It tells the story of the self-destructive Hsi-men family adrift in the corrupt society of the late Sung dynasty. The novel was probably meant to be social criticism aimed at mandarin society of the late Mings. The *Gold Vase Plum* is without doubt one of the best Chinese novels ever written.

Dream of the Red Chamber was written by Ts'ao Chan during the 1700's. It is another sprawling novel of family life. This time the house of Chia represents Chinese society. At the center of the novel is a triangle love affair, but hundreds of characters make up this expansive story. It is especially interesting in terms of social history. One gets a very insightful look at the complex extended family system in Imperial China. It is also meant to be social criticism, casting serious doubts upon the integrity and nobility of the Chinese intellectual.

Fiction and the novel form did not fare

especially well during the last dynastic period—the Ch'ing or Manchu. Censorship and criticism discouraged many authors. Western influence began to rekindle an interest in fiction in the late nineteenth century, but social upheaval in China has not been conducive to a flourishing literati. Still, experiments in Chinese fiction are taking place and will undoubtedly produce some significant works in the future.

To experience Chinese fiction for yourself, these English translations can be recommended.

The Chinese Classics, translated by James Legge. In 5 volumes by Oxford University Press. New York. (Bilingual text)

Anthology of Chinese Literature edited by Cyril Birch, various translators. In two volumes by Grove Press, Inc. New York. 1972.

A Treasury of Chinese Literature, translated and edited by Ch'u Chai and Winberg Chai. Appleton-Century. New York. 1965.

Monkey by Wu Ch'eng-en, translated by Arthur Waley. Allen & Unwin, London. Classic translation first printed in 1942. Waley's translation is considerably abridged from the original.

The Journey to the West by Wu Ch'eng-en, translated and edited by Anthony C. Yu. In four volumes by The University of Chicago Press. Chicago. 1983.

The Golden Lotus, translated by Clement Egerton. In 4 volumes by Grove Press, Inc. New York. 1954.

Dream of the Red Chamber by T'sao Chan, translated by Chi-chen Wang. Doubleday. New York. 1958.

Dream of the Red Chamber by T'sao Chan, translated from the classic German version of Franz Kuhn by Florence and Isabel McHugh. Pantheon. New York. 1958.

For examples of contemporary writings from China, **The New Realism,** edited by Lee Yee, brings together a volume of selections from the years 1979–1980. Hippocrene Books. New York. 1983.

For an overview of Chinese literary history:

An Introduction to Chinese Literature by Liu Wu-chi. Indiana University Press. Bloomington. 1966.

Shadow Puppetry

Early Chinese historians, eager to prove that China was truly the "mother of all civilization," made up an interesting story about the discovery of shadow puppetry. According to the legend, the Han emperor Wu-ti fell into a deep depression after the death of his wife, Wang. He did not recover until the God of Compassion convinced him that he could bring the spirit of the emperor's wife back to him in the form of a shadow. Every night behind a thin silk screen Wang would appear to talk with the emperor. Of course, this Wang was simply a puppet's shadow moved by the God of Compassion himself. The trick was discovered eventually by the emperor, but he was so impressed by the artistry involved in his deception that he ordered shadow puppetry to be taught and performed in China from that day forward.

That makes a nice story, but there is actually no record of puppetry in China until around the eleventh century. What's more, some evidence seems to suggest that the tradition began in India and was introduced to China as a means of teaching Buddhism to the people. But this is only another theory; no one really knows how or why shadow puppetry first came into existence. What is known is that the Chinese brought the art of shadow puppetry to a very high degree of development.

Shadow puppetry is essentially a puppet show based on the manipulation of moveable silhouette puppets behind a lighted screen. The effect is produced by holding the puppets directly against a back-lighted screen of paper or cloth. The flat puppet silhouettes are jointed usually at the neck, shoulders, elbows, hips, and knees. They are operated with three rods attached at right angles to the silhouette. The main rod, called "the rod of life," is attached either to the puppet's torso or just below the neck. With this rod the puppeteer moves the character's body, legs and head. The other two rods are attached to the arms and control all of the puppet's arm and hand gestures. Although the experienced puppeteer can easily maneuver the puppet into walking, kneeling, and sitting positions, it is the animation of the hands and arms that truly brings the puppet to life.

There are four major elements involved in a shadow puppet show. The screen is a major element because it acts as the medium for the illusion. The Chinese first used paper, but later turned to cloth for their screens. Paper and cloth both need to be stretched taut within a wooden frame because the puppets must be

moved smoothly over the back surface of the material. Then a source of illumination is needed. Originally this was done with either a torch for night performances or with sunlight coming into a dark room through a cloth-covered window. Modern performances have the advantage of sophisticated electrical lighting. The puppets and the scenery are the two other elements that contribute to the shadow performance. These two are the most complex and artistic elements, and the Chinese proved both their skill and imagination in their creation.

Both the stage scenery (which is attached directly to the back side of the screen) and the puppets themselves are perfectly flat. But in the Chinese puppet theatre these elements are known for being executed with a remarkable amount of incised and cut-out designing. In shadow, of course, this adds a great deal of interest to the figures. The average Chinese shadow puppet is about twelve inches high. Traditionally animal skins were used to make the puppets. The skins were oiled and pressed to make a light, translucent, durable, and non-warping material much like plastic. Today, plastic is normally used to make shadow puppets. One of the interesting elements of early Chinese puppets is their coloring. Since the skins were worked until nearly transparent, the idea of coloring the skins to elaborate costuming and so forth must have come naturally. But to the audience, seeing the first shadow shows done in color must have seemed almost as wonderful as seeing the first color TV programs. The Chinese also attacked the problem of overlapping pieces that created darker shadows at every moveable joint on the puppet. Chinese puppet masters created a kind of wheel-shaped joint that almost completely eliminated the bothersome black spots caused by overlapping. The joints themselves were then connected with a nearly transparent thread. The faces of both animals and humans are always highly stylized in Chinese puppets, and the whole head is usually detachable so that several characters with distinguishable faces can be used on the same puppet body.

Chinese puppet plays themselves have changed over the centuries. Probably the first widely seen Chinese productions were based on the adventurous tales of the Three Kingdoms. Other legends and probably some religious instruction were done on early puppet stages as well. Later, as the puppeteer's art began to be refined, operas and more serious dramas were staged to entertain in the homes of the mandarins. It is believed that puppetry gained such prominence in dynastic China because women were not allowed to attend the sometimes ribald live stage performances of the time. The puppeteers provided cleaned up versions for the ladies and children at home.

Shadow puppetry has never been as popular in the U.S. as either marionette or hand puppetry has been. Excellent collections of Chinese shadow puppets can be seen in many U.S. museums and there seems to be a growing interest in presenting shadow puppet shows in these museums. The Field Museum of Natural History in Chicago and the Museum of Natural History in New York City have extensive collections of Chinese shadow puppets. With renewed cultural exchange, Chinese puppet touring companies may be making more appearances in the U.S. as well.

For more information about Chinese shadow puppetry, these books can be recommended.

Dictionary of Puppetry by A. R. Philpott. Plays, Inc. Boston. 1969.

The World of Puppets by Rene Simmen. Thomas Y. Crowell Co. New York. 1975.

Puppet Theatre in Performance by Nancy H. Cole. William Morrow & Co., Inc. New York. 1978.

The Shadow Puppet Book by Janet Lynch-Watson. Sterling Publishing Company, Inc. New York. 1980.

The Peking Opera

The Peking Opera, which made a triumphant tour of the U.S. in 1980, is enormously popular in China. And as cultural exchanges stabilize between the U.S. and the People's Republic, there are sure to be more tours of the Opera in America.

What is known today as the Peking Opera has a long history. It began in ancient times as an adjunct to religious ceremony where certain spiritual/historical stories were mimed or sung about as a way of teaching the people. Soon little dramas became standardized, and certain playlets became favorites and were repeated and embellished as time passed. Jugglers, dancers, and acrobats often performed with the actors and singers, and all of these elements combined to make the unique stage presentation that is the Peking Opera.

There is really no equivalent to Peking Opera anywhere in the world. It is both opera and drama, with dancing, comedy, and acrobatics integrated to suit the characters and plots. Masks and painted faces combine with lavish costuming, stylized movements, and lots of jumping and tumbling all over the stage to make up the traditional opera event. Some newer operas with revolutionary soldiers

in battle fatigues and characters like "Chiang Shui-ying, Party Branch Secretary of the Dragon River Brigade," are costumed in contemporary clothes and wear regular stage makeup (a little heavy). But they also move with stylized gestures and dance and jump and tumble in production numbers that are truly spectacular. Peking Opera is like a musical tragi-comedy circus!

Traditional or classical Chinese opera deals mainly with the legends and history of imperial China. The costumes are elaborate, and their colors signify the rank of the characters wearing them. Yellow robes are for the emperor and his family. Red and purple robes are for persons of high rank, blue for people of slightly lower rank. Brown and olive green are colors associated with older characters, and black is reserved for the lowest ranking characters in the cast. Makeup and masks also have symbolic meaning. The painted faces are said to have come about because a famous actor's face was too effeminate to play warrior roles. The style and color of the painted face may signify the character as ugly, good, short-tempered, or elderly; or it may represent the character as being a warrior, god, or even an animal.

Actors of classical Chinese opera are trained in one of four role categories. Each role category has distinct costuming, gesture pattern, voice quality, and stage movement. The four are: *Sheng*, the male role, which includes military characters plus young and old man roles; *Tan*, the female role, includes virtuous, flirtatious, young, married, and old woman roles; *Ching* (painted face) incorporates the roles of all extroverted characters, often generals, bullies, or expert fighters; and *Ch'ou*, the comedian, has a number of comedic roles from the eccentric scholar to the rascally prince. Classical Chinese opera combines these roles in all sorts of variations to come up with the characters needed for various story lines.

It wasn't until about 1930 that the female roles actually began to be played by women. Imperial China considered the opera and all theater for that matter to be of and for men only. When Chinese actors, writers, and directors began coming to the West for schooling in the early '30's, "new" ideas were incorporated into the opera. The Peking Opera did, as a matter of fact, even tour the U.S. in the 1930's. It did not reappear in the U.S. until 1978 when a small troupe toured briefly, followed by the 1980 tour when a full company arrived and played in ten cities throughout America.

The Peking Opera has had a rather difficult time of it since the end of World War II. The Japanese occupation didn't do much for it, and just as it feebly got back on its feet, Mao's wife and the infamous "cultural revolution" stopped it dead. That is to say she stopped "classical" productions. The Peking Opera still gave performances but they were new propaganda plays called things like "Taking Tiger Mountain by Strategy." And many of the most famous and gifted classical opera stars were sent out to plant rice and make tractor tires. Luckily this period of insanity lasted only a few years. In 1977 the classical operas returned to the stage, stars were brought back, and most of the highly-charged, political garbage was dumped.

During the American tour in 1980 most of the operas were adjusted to make them more appealing to Western eyes and ears—mainly ears. Naturally there is a lot of music and singing in the Peking Opera, but it is not "melodic" in the Western sense, and to many untrained ears it seems terribly off-key. So, for the U.S. productions a lot of the singing was cut. Also, in Peking Opera almost every movement is accompanied by a musical sound effect. To Americans, however, the accompaniment sometimes sounds like an amateur saw player backed up by a very loud four-piece kitchen band and someone on gongs. So the music was cut a bit, too, for American audiences.

The choreography and the plots of the operas remained pretty much the same, although the productions were shortened

considerably. This was probably for the best because most of the plots require a familiarity with Chinese mythology and cultural and historical detail. And, like Wagner and other Western opera classics, some scenes just seem too long anyway.

While in America in 1980, the big hit of the repertoire was an opera called "The Monkey King Fights the 18 Lo Hans." Anything about the Monkey King, the famous character from the classic novel *The Journey to the West*, is a big hit in China, too. The mischievous but lovable and brave Monkey is a dazzling role for the male acrobatic dancer. In this opera, Monkey fights off eighteen sword and spear carrying meanies with comic and skillful alacrity. The plot is fairytale-like and easy to follow. In addition, there is a great deal of action and sensational costuming. Monkey stars in other operas, too, since he is such a favorite. "The Magic Palm Fan" is a popular vehicle for Monkey and his friends and probably will be seen here on a future tour.

Another popular opera on the American tour was a classic called "The Crossroads." English-speaking audiences also know this opera as "Fight in the Dark" because of its most famous scene. An innkeeper, trying to protect an old general who has stopped at the inn for the night, arms himself and sneaks into the general's "darkened" room. The stage lights are on, of course, but the illusion of the two men in a pitch black room confusing each other for would-be assassins is

brilliantly executed and makes this opera a great favorite.

"White Snake" is another opera that is often played. It is a romantic, mythological tale of two "heavenly" snakes, a white one and a blue one, who change themselves into beautiful maidens and descend to earth. A young man falls in love with White Snake but the ruse eventually brings tragedy to the two lovers. This opera is a bit less accessible to Western audiences because the mythological source is somewhat obscure.

"The Drunken Concubine" is probably the most famous opera performed in China. The plot is simple. A concubine is angered when the emperor stands her up. She orders the palace eunuchs to bring her wine. She slowly gets drunk as more and more wine is ordered. Her drunken behavior and the frantic efforts of her maids and the eunuchs to get her out of sight before the emperor returns, make up the entire opera. It is a favorite because it is a *tour de force* for the female lead.

Not much Western critical interest has ever been generated by the Peking Opera. However, one book about this remarkable art form is very informative. It's called *Peking Opera*. It was written by Elizabeth Halson and published by Oxford University Press in Hong Kong in 1966. It's worth looking into if you get the chance to see the Peking Opera on tour in America.

Speaking and Writing Chinese

The spoken language that Westerners think of as "Chinese" is really just one part of a complex family of languages referred to by linguists as the Sino-Tibetan group. Chinese itself has many dialects, some of which are mutually unintelligible. The official Chinese language of the People's Republic of China and the one taught in the U.S. and elsewhere is called "Mandarin" or *Kuo yü* as the PRC renamed it. Mandarin was the official dialect of the court at Peking during the dynastic era in China, and represented the cultivated language of the Northern Chinese. Even Mandarin, however, is broken down into several dialects, and there is really no "Standard Chinese" by which all other dialects are judged. It is rather informally agreed that the educated speakers in Peking set the standards for language in China. This situation, however, is bound to change as China struggles toward modernity.

A spoken language never did unite China. It was the written language that all educated people in China understood. But the written language has very little to do with a phonetic reproduction of speech. Chinese writing, the calligraphy that is so famous and that spread so far throughout the Orient, is basically a pictographic or ideographic language. This is, words are formed with characters that represent pictures or ideas related to actual objects. Thus the character for "man" is a torso with two legs, and a circle with a dot in the middle is the character for "sun." Of course, over the years the calligraphy has become quite stylized and characters have been combined in order to make new words. For instance, when the character for "lightning" is combined with the character for "language," the result equals "telephone"!

Chinese writing originated over 4,000 years ago, and there are currently over 50,000 characters in use. They are organized under 214 radicals that hint at a part of the meaning of each word. Characters that represent words that relate to wood, for example, like "tree," "table," etc., include the "wood" radical as part of the character. Chinese dictionaries organize words by their radicals. Needless to say, not many Chinese, and far fewer foreigners, have complete command of this complex written language. Memorization of more than 5,000 characters is necessary for a working literacy in written Chinese. Efforts to simplify and even phoneticize it have been going on for many years but those who can read the written language find it of great value in China.

Spoken Chinese differs a great deal from English in one remarkable respect. Every word in Chinese is a single sylla-ble. Since the number of possible spoken syllables is limited, a number of words with different meanings are pronounced the same way. The Chinese word *shi*, for instance, can mean "house," "ten," "poetry," "cadaver," "excrement," and a few other things. Context helps to clarify meanings; in addition many words are made by combining two words. Chinese place names are good examples of this. "Shanghai," for instance, means "mountain sea." But Chinese is also a tonal language. In Mandarin Chinese there are four tones: high, rising, slight fall followed by rise, and abrupt fall. These four inflections added to a single syllable give that syllable four different meanings, sometimes more.

Obviously, learning written Chinese and learning spoken Chinese require two entirely different courses of study. Written Chinese can be learned by memorizing the meanings of the symbols and by practicing the writing of the calligraphic characters. Parts of speech, as such, do not exist in Chinese. Grammatical meaning is derived by word order. Learning to speak Chinese cannot be a result of learning the written language. Spoken Chinese must be learned by sound and by utilizing romanized transcriptions of the language.

Some recommended books and study materials are:

How to Study and Write Chinese Characters, by W. Simon. This is a classic text first printed in 1944 by Lund Humphries & Co., London.

Beginning Chinese, by John DeFrancis. Yale University Press, New Haven, CN & London.

Chinese Language/30 an Educational Services Teaching Cassette by Dun Donnelley Publishing Corp., 666 Fifth Ave., New York, NY 10019.

PICTOGRAMS

| Sun | Moon | Hills | Eye | Child | Horse |

INDICATORS

| Morning | Evening | Above | Below | Union | Centre |

IDEOGRAMS

| Bright | Obstructed | Forest | To see | To sit | Emperor |

DEFLECTIVES

| Right hand | Left hand | Sundered (threads) | Continuous | Body | Turned (body) |

PHONOGRAMS

Ngo, a goose

Ho, a river

Chinese Cookery

Beyond Rice and Egg Rolls

When Americans think of Chinese food, they invariably think of rice. So do the Chinese. In ancient China, famines were so common that growing and storing rice became a national preoccupation. So much so, that the Chinese phrase that means literally "to eat rice" became "to eat dinner." But rice is only a small part of a traditional cuisine that reaches back over the millennia for its beginnings.

Almost everyone enjoys eating Chinese food. And despite the fact that it contains some of the oldest recipes and involves the most ancient methods of food preparation, it is remarkably well suited to modern life. Because so much of the Chinese tradition in cookery was based on a sparse economy, the recipes are usually high in vegetables, chicken, and fish, and low in red meats and expensive dairy products. The method of cooking is quick and uses very little energy. And traditional Chinese flavorings substitute quite nicely for salt and sugar—two things we moderns are constantly being warned against.

Many Americans know Chinese foods only as they appear in Chinese restaurants—egg rolls are available just about everywhere nowadays. But Chinese restaurant food includes much more than egg rolls. There are, in fact, a staggering number of different dishes in Chinese cuisine. One of the reasons for so much variety is that regional cooking in China is so strikingly diverse. Most of us are fairly familiar with the Cantonese variety of Chinese cookery, but there are other interesting styles that are only now becoming well known and widely available in America.

This section of *The Chinese Catalog* presents a number of aspects of Chinese cookery. For the cooks we've gathered information about Chinese foods, groceries, vegetable gardening, cooking schools, cookbooks, and utensils. For the eaters (which, of course, does not exclude the cooks) we've put together some valuable information about eating in Chinese restaurants. We've listed some of our favorite restaurants in the U.S. and also tried to provide some tips on ordering a Chinese meal. Whether you're a cooker or an eater, or both, this section is going to help you make some discoveries about Chinese food that will take you far beyond rice and egg rolls. Enjoy!

Yes We Have No Cloud Ears

Admittedly you can't walk into your neighborhood 7-Eleven and expect to find bok choy and shark fin, but Chinese foods are becoming more available every day. With a little investigation, you'll be surprised what you can find. Of course, one of the peculiar delights of Chinese cookery is that substitutions (broccoli for bamboo shoots, leeks for bok choy) lead to some wonderful culinary discoveries. Still, it's fun to use real Chinese foods if only because the new flavors and textures are so exciting. Here's a list of some of the most common and most often called for ingredients in Chinese cookery.

ABALONE

Abalone is the meat from a mollusk with an iridescent shell. It's available fresh on the west coast, but usually comes from Japan or Mexico in one-pound cans. It is very tender and can be eaten directly from the can as a cold appetizer. Don't cook it much because it quickly becomes tough. Use the juice from the can in the recipe or freeze it for use later. Experts differ on the length of time it can be stored—either one week or two. In either case, keep it in the refrigerator in water and change the water daily. It's not cheap—prices start at about $6 per pound—so you're hardly likely to forget where you put it.

AGAR-AGAR

This is a dried seaweed, grayish-white, with almost no flavor. It looks like a cross between bean thread noodles and rice sticks. Soak it in cold water and it becomes more resilient. After soaking, cut the long strips up and use in salads. Or dissolve the strips in hot water and use as a thickening agent. Agar-agar needs no refrigeration and keeps indefinitely. A four-ounce bag should cost from $2.50 to $4.00.

ANISE, STAR

This Chinese spice is about half an inch in diameter and looks like a little eight-pointed star. It is reddish-brown in color and smells a lot like licorice when dried. It is sold by weight or in four-ounce packs. Best to transfer it to a tightly sealed jar where it will keep indefinitely. Another reason for keeping it sealed is that its distinctive flavor transfers easily to other foods. It is one of the spices used

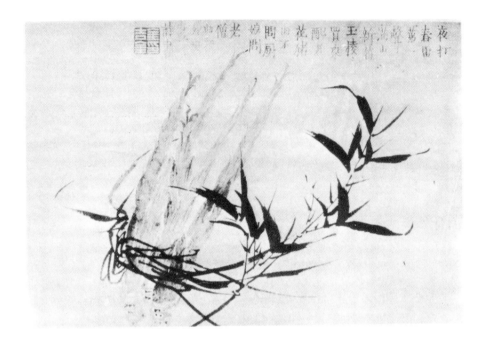

in Five Spice Powder described below. Used alone, don't overdo it—a little goes a long way.

BAMBOO SHOOTS

Most bamboo shoots in this country are available only in cans. Rarely will you find fresh shoots. These ivory-colored, cone-shaped vegetables have a distinctive texture—tender and crisp but slightly chewy. Once you open a can, store the shoots in slightly salted water. Change the water regularly and they should keep for about a month. Be sure to rinse them thoroughly before using. This will eliminate a slightly sour and musty taste. And don't use the water in which they have been packed since it contains preservatives that give it a very odd taste. Winter shoots are the more tasty and are smaller. But they're anywhere from two to three times as expensive as the spring shoots. A 19-oz. can of spring shoots should cost you about a dollar. You'll pay around three dollars for the same amount of winter shoots.

BEAN CURD (Tofu)

Although we have evidence of consumption of bean curd 2,000 years ago, it could very well be one of the foods of the future. And it is distinctively Chinese. Soybeans are soaked, boiled, and drained until curds form. Then the curds are pressed and formed into soft, whitish cakes with the consistency of custard. In China, where almost nothing is wasted, the residue is fed to animals. What remains is extremely high in protein and has the potential to become a very popular meat substitute in this country because it is inexpensive. It is also almost tasteless, stimulating your palate about the way unflavored gelatin would. But the texture is unique, so tofu contributes to the range of textures in a dish as well as to its food value. And because it doesn't intrude a distinctive taste, it combines well with many ingredients. It can be used in dishes that employ most cooking methods because it is fairly resilient.

In this country there are two types of fresh tofu, Chinese and Japanese. The Chinese type comes in smaller squares and is more solid, having less water content. The Japanese type comes in larger squares and tends to fall apart a bit more easily.

Bean curd is sold in many grocery stores throughout the U.S., usually in the produce department in sealed plastic containers. It will keep in the refrigerator for about a month if the container is unopened. If you open the pack or if you have bought fresh tofu from the large vat at your Chinese grocers, store it in fresh water in the refrigerator, change the water daily and keep covered. It should keep for at least a week.

BEAN CURD, PRESSED

This is simply bean curd cake from which much of the water has been extracted. The result is a fairly chewy substance with the consistency, roughly, of American cheeses, but less likely to crumble. Cut it small and it goes well with almost any dish. Left in chunks, it tastes good after being simmered awhile. Some types of pressed bean curd are darker in color because soy sauce has been added. It will keep for several days if refrigerated. Eight ounces should cost about $2.50.

BEAN CURD CHEESE OF RED BEAN CURD

This is bean curd that's been fermented with beans, red rice, salt, water and rice wine. It is pungent and salty in taste and is used mostly as a seasoning. Usually sold in cans, it will keep for months if put in a jar and refrigerated. You should be able to buy a pound for about $1.50, but different brands may be $2 and up.

BEAN PASTE

This thick brown paste is made from fermented soybeans, flour and salt. It comes in two styles, one of which includes whole beans and is preferred by some experts. It is also harder to find than the second type in which the beans have been thoroughly mixed with the other ingredients. Type two is also a little more salty. Bean paste is a major seasoning ingredient in two important styles of Chinese food, northern and Sichuanese. It adds its own flavor and thickens sauces. If you don't plan to use it for some time, transfer it from the can to a jar, and store in the refrigerator because it will keep much longer there. You should be able to buy eight ounces for less than a dollar. It's a good thing to have on hand on a regular basis because it can be used in so many different dishes.

BEAN PASTE, HOT

This is the standard bean paste to which crushed chili peppers have been added. We have the Sichuanese to thank. It's usually a lighter brown in color and more expensive than the regular paste.

BEAN PASTE, RED
(And Usually Sweet)

Made from red beans that are pureed together with sugar and shortening. Red bean paste is often used as a filling in pastries and as part of the sauce in sweet dishes. Most of the time it is sold in cans,

Additional crops and beans (A, taro; B, yam; C, soybean; D, red bean) from Wu Ch'i-chün, *Chih Wu Ming Shih T'u K'ao*, 1848

but the rare Chinese pastry shop in this country may stock quantities of it from which small amounts are sold by weight. It will keep for months if kept refrigerated in a covered jar.

BEAN SPROUTS

These are the sprouts of mung beans with a white body, yellow head, green hoods and small tails. They are available either canned or fresh and are sold by weight in grocery stores all over the U.S. The canned variety will remain fresh for at least three days if transferred to a glass jar. One week is usually the limit. If sprouts, fresh or canned, begin to look slightly brownish with a faint smell, they're over the hill. A number of experts say that the canned sprouts cannot compare with the fresh because they've lost some of their very delicate flavor and their crispness—which is important because the crisp quality adds to the texture mix of a given dish. The other attractive quality of sprouts is that they are very low in calories and fairly high in protein.

BIRD'S NEST

Bird's nest may not be the first thing that springs to mind next time you're really hungry. It may not even be the second or third. But the nests of small Asian swifts are highly prized in Chinese cooking. Much of this bird's nest is made up of actually digested seaweed that the bird is recycling. This gelatin-like material hardens, and the nest is like a small translucent cup. Nest collectors along the coast of the South China Sea risk life and limb to climb the steep walls of limestone caves in search of the finest nests. The greater the percentage content of digested seaweed, the better the price.

Nests come in three forms, the whole, the whole broken up, and ground. The first two forms are very expensive, and you must clean them well. The ground-up variety works just as well because it's the texture that is important.

Bird's nest will cost you at least $3.50 per ounce, with higher grades costing much more. The nests are almost pure protein and are regarded by traditionally minded segments of the Chinese population as an elixir of youth.

Green Cabbage and Radishes. Yun Shao-ping.

Taro and Green Cabbage. Chin Nung, Ching Dynasty.

CELLOPHANE NOODLES

Also known as bean-thread noodles, these thin, hard, clear noodles are made from mung beans. They are very absorbent and become soft, translucent and gelatinous after soaking. They are almost tasteless and easily absorb the flavor of other ingredients in a dish. They should be soaked for about 20 minutes until soft. As with the rice noodles, no need to soak them if you're going to deep-fry. They become jelly-like if overcooked.

CHESTNUTS, SWEET

Rarely available fresh, these chestnuts are usually found canned or dried. The fresh ones must be put in the oven at about 325 degrees for 20–30 minutes or until they begin to pop. Let them cool, then peel away the outer shells and inner skins with a paring knife. The canned variety must be rinsed thoroughly before using. Sprinkle dried chestnuts with baking soda, pour boiling water over them, and allow to soak for an hour. Then rinse off the baking soda in warm water. Make sure all the inner red skin is removed, using a toothpick to get it out of the creases if necessary. Then simmer them for another hour over very low heat. Chestnuts should be added to a dish just long enough to allow the sauce to permeate them. Four ounces of dried chestnuts will cost between $.80 and $1.

CHILI PEPPERS, DRIED

The type recommended by most Chinese chefs is about two inches long and scarlet in color. They pack a wallop, so don't use too many. Most often they are used to season the oil before the ingredients are added to a stir-fry dish. Make sure to use the seeds because they contribute to the hotness. Generally, the smaller the chili pepper, the hotter. It's best to remove them once the oil is seasoned—when chopped up, they're often too small to detect, and eating even a small piece can bring tears to the eyes of all but the most hard-core afficionados of hot food. Best to go easy until you have a clear idea of the consequences.

BITTER MELON

This has the shape of an oversized sweet potato with a green and lumpy body. The meat is, indeed, quite bitter.

BLACK BEANS, FERMENTED

Black beans, black soybeans preserved in garlic, ginger and other spices, are used as a seasoning agent. They usually are covered with salt and should be rinsed in hot water before use. And they should be chopped up or mashed because they are strongly flavored and need to be mixed well throughout the dish. They will keep indefinitely if put in a tightly sealed jar. If they begin to dry out, add a few drops of peanut or vegetable oil. Black beans do not require refrigeration. They are packed in jars, often with chilies. Eight ounces should cost about $1.30 to $1.50.

BOK CHOY
(Chinese Cabbage)

The words literally mean "white vegetable." It has foot-long white stalks that look a little like celery, but it also has large, dark green leaves. It is sold by the bunch or by weight in Chinese grocery stores. Sometimes it is available in the produce section of supermarkets. Boy choy tastes a little like Swiss chard, but is a bit sweeter. Wrap it tightly in a plastic bag and it should keep in the refrigerator for up to a week.

CELERY CABBAGE

This is a variety of Chinese cabbage that grows like celery, but has wide, yellow-white stalks 14–16 inches long. The leaves are yellow-green and wrinkled. It is sold only in Chinese groceries, so you may need to use a substitute ingredient. Celery is the best bet, especially in dishes where crunchiness is important. Store it the same way you would bok choy.

CLOUD EARS

Also known as wood ears, this is a tree fungus with a strange look—small, black, and crinkled. They should be soaked in hot water for thirty minutes and in the process will expand to two or three times their original size. They become soft and resilient, but don't have much taste. But their texture is unique and adds to a dish.

Cloud Ears.

A large cluster of cloud ears may have a hard "eye" in the center which should be removed. You pay about a dollar for half an ounce.

CORIANDER (Chinese Parsley)

Early records indicate that the herb was brought back to China from central Asia over 2,000 years ago. It has a long stem and flat leaves. The taste and aroma are very strong, having a somewhat metallic quality. It is used as a seasoning and a garnish—sparingly. It is also sold in Spanish and Italian groceries by its western name, cilantro. It will keep for about four days if you simply wrap it and put it in the refrigerator. But it will keep twice that long if you keep the roots in water and cover the leaves with a plastic bag.

CUCUMBERS, ORIENTAL

Another of the important imports into China of over 2,000 years ago. The oriental variety is seedless, sweet and firm—ideal for cooking. The pickled type is made from the Chinese "flower cucumber," having been soaked in a soy sauce brine. Four ounces will cost you about a dollar, but they make a good relish, or they can be used as a seasoning agent in cold dishes.

EGG ROLL SKINS

Usually eight inch squares, often sold in two-pound packages.

What we call egg rolls in this country are called "spring rolls" in China. There are two different types of skins, one from the Canton area in south China and one from Shanghai. The latter are very thin and fragile, and almost transparent, resembling rice paper. After deep-frying they become brittle and hard because they have absorbed relatively more oil. The Shanghai wrappers are usually circular in shape and often sold in packages of twelve. The Cantonese kind are a little thicker and softer and don't absorb as much oil. They are usually seven-inch squares and are often sold by the pound, about 14 of them comprising one pound. Best to wrap them in plastic, tightly, and then wrap that in aluminum foil. They will keep for a week in the refrigerator and indefinitely in the freezer. Just make sure they don't dry out. The drier they become, the more difficult they will be to pull apart.

FIVE SPICE POWDER

This is a combination of five finely ground spices: anise, cinnamon, fennel, clove and Sichuan pepper. It is very strong and the dominant flavor is that of the anise. Five spice is most often used to season meats. It keeps well at room temperature if tightly sealed. Allspice is a suitable substitute, but there are some variations in the composition of the ingredients, the most notable being the substitution of ginger for the Sichuan pepper. Five spice is very useful in Chinese cooking. Because it's cheap and keeps indefinitely, it's wise to buy some even if you don't think you're going to use it right away.

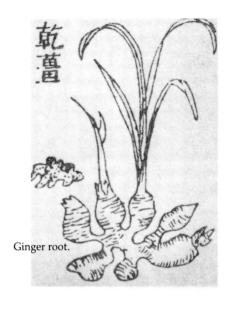

Ginger root.

GINGER ROOT, FRESH

Not really a root but an underground stem with an intense, aromatic taste, it's one of the most common seasonings used in Chinese cooking. Fresh ginger is brown, irregularly shaped and gnarled, about three inches long. In recent years it has become more widely available in supermarkets throughout the U.S. Ginger is useful in mitigating fish and gamy odors and, used sparingly, does not add too much of its own distinctive taste.

There are several ways of storing fresh ginger. One is to wrap it in plastic and put it in the refrigerator, where it will last for months. Another way is to wash the ginger, put it in a jar and cover it with any

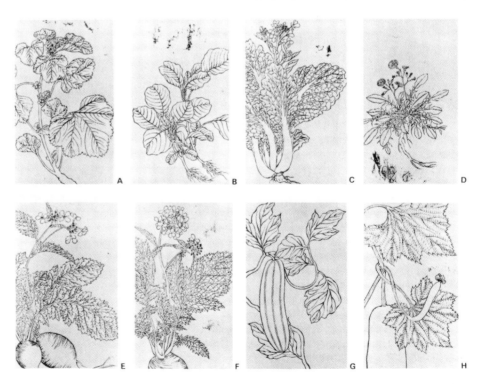

Some Chinese vegetables (A, malva; B, amaranth; C, Chinese cabbage; D, sonchus; E, radish; F, turnip; G, melon; H, gourd)
from Wu Ch'i-chün, *Chih Wu Ming Shih T'u K'ao*, 1848

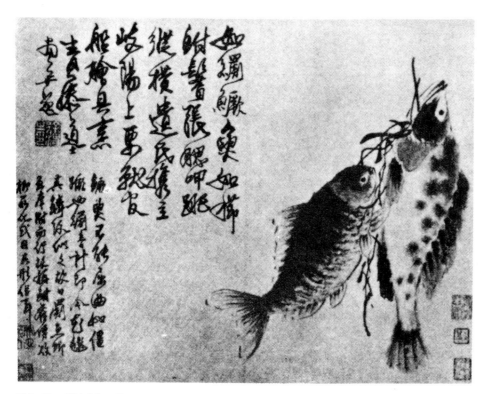

Fish. Hsu Wei, Ming Dynasty.

white wine or dry sherry. Finally, you can keep it in the freezer, bringing it out just long enough to slice off what you need for the meal and then returning it before it thaws. When a recipe calls for a slice of ginger, it usually means a piece about one inch in diameter and one-eighth inch thick. Experts usually caution against substituting ginger powder or dried ginger for fresh.

GINGER ROOT, PICKLED AND PRESERVED IN SYRUP

This consists of chunks of ginger dyed a red color and preserved in syrup. It is sweet, hot and crunchy. It's often used in sweet and sour dishes for color. The Chinese sometimes eat it straight as a kind of candy. It comes in small bottles and should be refrigerated after opening.

GINGER ROOT, PRESERVED IN BRINE

It's red and sometimes referred to by its Japanese name, *benishoga*. It comes in bottles and should be refrigerated after opening.

GINKGO NUTS

Available either fresh or canned. Like water chestnuts, though, the canned variety lose much of their taste in the canning process. But you can be sure of getting really fresh ones only in early spring. Ginkgo nuts are the beige-colored

pits of the ginkgo fruit and are used in soups and vegetarian dishes. You're going to have to take a whack at the fresh ones to crack the shell. A hammer will do nicely, but don't hit it so hard as to mash the meat inside.

GOLDEN NEEDLES (Lily Buds or Tiger Lily Buds)

The thought of eating flowers may not appeal to you, but that's what you're doing when you eat lily buds. The buds are a pale gold color, two to three inches in length, with a slightly pungent taste and a chewy texture. The better kinds are flexible, not brittle. They are sold dried and should be soaked in warm water for half an hour before use, then rinsed and the water squeezed out. Some of the buds will have a hard little knot at one end which must be cut off. They will keep indefinitely without refrigeration if stored in a tightly sealed jar. A four-ounce package should cost about a dollar.

HOISIN SAUCE

This sauce is made from soybeans, flour, sugar, salt, garlic and chili peppers. It is reddish brown and has a creamy texture. Though its name means "seafood sauce" in Chinese, it is used primarily as a dip or in marinades. It is also used in some stir-fry dishes and barbecue sauces. It is packaged in jars or cans and is fairly cheap—one pound for about $1.50 and up. Once you've opened the can, keep it refrigerated in a tightly covered jar. It will keep for months.

LYCHEE NUTS

This, of course, is actually a fruit, grown in the south of China. The meat is white, almost translucent, surrounding a large pit. In this country it's pretty hard to find the fresh ones, but if ever you're so lucky, and if they look ripe, throw caution to the wind and indulge yourself—lychee are great. They have a very limited season, so keep your eyes open starting about the middle of June.

The canned ones are, well, canned. They have been pitted and the tough, reddish-brown skin has been removed. Sometimes sugar has been added to the juice they're packed in, masking much of the very delicate flavor.

MSG

Originally this wasn't monosodium glutamate, but rather a home-made seasoning agent made from dried, fermented wheat gluten or soybean protein, often with a little powdered dry shrimp or seaweed added. Its name in Chinese literally means "taste essence," and it was used to enhance weak flavors in soups and meat. Today it is strictly a chemical compound, probably best known to Americans under the brand name Accent. Most authors of cookbooks will tell you to use it sparingly or not at all because it doesn't really contribute to the taste of food, can upset the stomach in sufficient doses, and adds to our already high intake of sodium.

MUSHROOMS, DRIED BLACK

There are several varieties of dried mushrooms, ranging in size from a half inch to three inches in diameter. They can be a speckled brown or gray a well as black. They should be rinsed in cold water because there's usually a little sand left on them. Then soak them in warm water for from 30 minutes to an hour. Make sure to remove the stems. Save the water they are soaked in for the next time you make soup. The dried mushrooms will keep indefinitely in a tightly sealed jar. The reconstituted ones are good for about two days if refrigerated. You won't want to waste them—they're anywhere from $1.25 to $2 per ounce depending on the size and on whether or not they still have the stems.

NOODLES

The Chinese have been making and eating noodles since 100 B.C. when techniques for large-scale grinding of wheat into flour were imported into China. Noodles are the staple food in north China. You can't go more than a block in most Chinese cities without seeing a noodle stand or a noodle vendor pushing his cart. The very best kind are freshly made egg noodles, which usually can be found in Chinese groceries. Packaged noodles that are found in any supermarket are definitely second best.

OILS

Sesame oil should be thick and light brown in color. If it's yellow and runny, it's the American kind and not nearly as aromatic as the Chinese variety. Sesame oil is made from roasted sesame seeds. It is used more as a flavoring agent than for cooking because it burns too easily. When buying sesame oil be sure to check the label to see what percentage of the contents actually is sesame oil and not vegetable oil. It can turn rancid in a months, so don't buy too much at one time. Sesame oil can help cut the taste of "fishy" fish and so is often used in marinades.

Soy oil is the most widely used oil in China because it is the cheapest. Peanut oil is the oil preferred by most Chinese cooks. Corn oil is gaining in popularity among people who cook Chinese food in this country. And, like safflower oil, it is fairly low in saturated fats.

Oils can be reused many times. They should be refrigerated so that they don't become rancid. They should be taken out and left at room temperature at least 15 minutes before using. Although oils can be reused, they do tend to absorb odors.

In order to get rid of the odor, heat the oil to a deep-fry temperature and put in two quarter-sized pieces of fresh ginger root or raw peeled potato. Fry them until they turn golden. Remove them from the oil. Now you're set. Oil doesn't have to be discarded until it becomes dark and heavy with residues.

OYSTER SAUCE

This is one of the most commonly used sauces in Chinese cooking. It is made from oyster extract, soy sauce and brine. It is pungent and salty and is used to add flavor to meat and poultry. There are many grades, the best kind being thinner and more runny. It will keep indefinitely if tightly covered. It comes in bottles or cans. You should be able to buy six ounces for about $1.75.

PLUM SAUCE (Duck Sauce)

Made from plums, ginger, apricots, vinegar, sugar and water, this sauce is thick and spicy, sweet and sour, something like chutney. It is often used as a condiment for duck. It comes in a can and once the can is opened, the sauce should be put in a jar in the refrigerator. Plum sauce is also one of the ingredients in dips for such wonders as spring rolls and fried wontons.

RICE, GLUTINOUS

This is a round-grained rice which becomes soft and sticky when cooked. In Chinatowns it is also called sweet rice or sticky rice. It is most often used in making dumplings, pastries and puddings. It is usually sold by weight in bags.

RICE NOODLES

Also called rice sticks, these thin, whitish noodles are made from finely ground rice. They are often used in soups. Rice noodles tend to disintegrate more readily than noodles made from flour, so don't soak or cook them too long. They are often deep-fried and used as a garnish. But don't soak them if you're going to deep-fry and don't deep-fry for more than two seconds. Rice noodles keep for a year without refrigeration, but keep them in a jar or canister.

RICE POWDER, GLUTINOUS

This is basically rice flour and is used in the dough wrappers for specialty desserts and snacks. It becomes very soft and chewy when cooked.

SAUSAGES, CHINESE

Usually made with minced pork and seasonings, they sometimes include pork liver or duck liver. They come in hard little links about six inches long and half an inch in diameter. They are red and white in color and very rich-tasting, but they're also loaded with fat. Steam them until soft and slightly bloated or slice them up for a quick stir-fry with other ingredients.

SESAME PASTE

This comes in a jar covered with a little oil. The paste is fairly hard, resembling clay in both color and consistency. It is used as a seasoning or as a dressing for cold vegetables and meats. Since it's so thick, you may have to dilute a glob scooped from the jar with hot oil or water and stir until the consistency is creamy. A word of caution: some people feel that the sesame paste in this country has lost its flavor due to the long trip across the Pacific. Therefore they suggest using peanut butter creamed with a little sesame oil. A six-ounce jar of sesame paste is about $2.

SHARK'S FIN

A distinctively Chinese food, shark's fin is long, threadlike pieces of dried cartilage from a shark's fin. After being cooked they look like translucent needles. They are esteemed as highly nutritious because they're high in protein and trace minerals. Shark's fin is very expensive and is a prestige food, so you will usually see it only at better restaurants or at Chinese banquets. After cooking they are relatively tasteless and tend to take on the flavor of other ingredients in a broth. You can pay over $20 for an eight-ounce box of dried shark's fin.

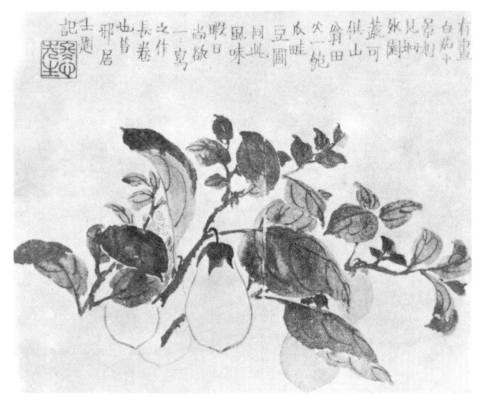

White Eggplant. Chin Nung, Ching Dynasty.

STRAW MUSHROOMS

Also called grass mushrooms, these are small and yellowish with a pointed black cap. They are sold dried or in cans. The dried variety will keep for months in a sealed jar in the refrigerator. The canned type will keep for only two or three days in water in the refrigerator, but you're better off to use them right away because the water tends to absorb the delicate flavor. The canned ones tend to be sweeter and crisper, while the dried ones have a stronger flavor. The canned are much cheaper than the dried.

TEA

Ever hear the expression, "I'd give all the tea in China to . . ."? The idea was that the speaker would give anything to do whatever—all the tea in China was perceived as a fantastic amount at one time because China supplied virtually all the world's tea. This began to change many years ago as tea, often at the instigation of the colonizing British, began to be cultivated in other areas that offered the hot, wet climate required. India and Ceylon are two examples, along with Indonesia and some areas along the east coast of Africa. In 1981 the United States imported about 13 million pounds of Chinese tea, only about five percent of total imports. And we don't know how much you'd be giving if you gave all the tea in China because the Chinese don't release figures for their exports or internal consumption.

We know that the Chinese drank tea during the Han Dynasty about two thousand years ago, and it might have been much earlier—Chinese legend says, after all, that the mythical emperor Shen Nung (Divine Farmer) discovered tea after the leaves of a nearby bush dropped into his boiling drinking water around 2737 B.C. Tea did not become really popular—and then mostly among the literate, upper class—until the eighth century A.D. Late in that century, about 780, a man by the name of Lu Yu wrote *The Classic of Tea*, the definitive handbook on the subject. (The Japanese were greatly influenced by this book and a cult of tea, far more elaborate than anything in China, later grew up in that country.) The first tax on tea was apparently imposed around 793, providing circumstantial evidence of its increasing popularity. It wasn't until roughly the eleventh century that tea drinking existed at all levels of Chinese society. By about 1300 it was

SHRIMP, DRIED

These shrimp are shelled and dried in the sun. They have a very strong flavor, so go easy. They range in size, but the important thing is the color—make sure they're orange-pink and about one inch long. They should be soaked in hot water for at least 30 minutes before being mixed with other ingredients. If the "fishy" taste is just too intense, soak them overnight in sherry. They should keep well so long as they're stored in a tightly sealed jar. Again, prices vary widely depending on the size, but you should be able to get half a pound for about $3.50.

SICHUAN PEPPERCORNS

This is a very small, reddish-brown peppercorn with a strong and pungent smell, but is not as hot as black peppercorns. They are used extensively in Sichuan-style cooking, which is rapidly becoming more popular in this country. There are two kinds on the market, the seeded and the whole. Buy the seeded ones because much of the flavor and aroma come from the husks. Sichuan peppercorns are sold by weight, usually about 40 cents per ounce. Keep them in a tightly covered bottle and they'll retain their oomph for a long time.

A lot of Sichuanese dishes call for dry-roasting these peppercorns. A good way to get the maximum flavor out of them is to heat them over a very low fire for about five minutes, shaking the skillet occasionally to avoid burning them. Wait until they're cool before you crush them up.

SOY SAUCES

No one would dispute that soy sauce is the most important seasoning in Chinese cooking. Soy sauces are made from fermented soybeans, wheat, yeast, salt and sugar. There are all sorts of different kinds, ranging from good to bad, so you'll be doing yourself a favor by learning about soy sauces and buying only the better brands.

Basically there are two categories of soy sauce, thin or light and dark or black. Thin soy sauce is the liquid extract from the combination of soybeans, flour, salt and water after slow fermentation. The first extraction is the best. A good thin soy sauce should have a clear brown color, not murky, and should smell, not surprisingly, of beans. It has a more delicate flavor than the dark soy sauce. The dark should be slightly thicker, should taste sweeter and less of beans. The major difference in components is that the dark has caramel or molasses. A good one is very dark with a kind of sheen to it.

Both types of soy sauce come in bottles or large cans. Once the can is opened the contents should be transferred to tightly covered bottles or jars. It should keep just fine for months on the shelf, but some experts think it's a good idea to keep it refrigerated during the hot months. The best brands are imported from Hong Kong, Taiwan and China. And even the very best brands are fairly cheap, so don't scrimp.

reported to be "one of the things that people cannot do without every day"—along with firewood, rice, oil, salt, soy sauce, and vinegar. Tea had come a long way. It was the most prestigious drink of the day and has remained popular throughout Chinese society ever since.

Tea is the dried leaf of an evergreen plant related to the camellia family. It is a hardy jungle plant which can withstand nature's punishment. Hence it is able to grow in elevations up to about 6,000 feet as long as there is plenty of heat and moisture. Without attention a tea plant will grow to twenty feet and more in height, but early on the plants are severely pruned to induce them to grow more side branches. The bushes are kept to about four feet in height so that the harvesters can reach all the leaves. It takes between three and five years for a plant to produce suitable leaves.

So-called "black" tea leaves go through, with some variation, a five-stage process. WITHERING, by spreading the leaves in the sun or by artificial drying, rids the leaf of much of its water content so that it becomes soft and pliable. ROLLING twists and rolls the leaves to break up the leaf cells and free the juices which give the tea its flavor. The beginning of an important chemical change happens here because the juices adhering to the leaf begin to turn into a kind of oil. ROLL BREAKING breaks up the lumps which emerge from rolling, allowing the finer pieces to fall through a sieve. These are taken to the fermenting room. The remaining bigger pieces go back for another round of rolling. FERMENTATION basically means oxidation. The leaves are spread out in a cool, damp atmosphere, finishing the oxidation process. The leaves turn into the bright copper color of a new penny. FIRING them arrests any further oxidation, drying the leaf evenly without scorching it.

Again, the preceding process refers only to black tea. Over 95% of the tea consumed in the United States is of this type. Green tea, which most Chinese prefer, is simply dried and rolled and dried again until crisp. There is no oxidation and the leaves remain green. Finally, oolong tea is a compromise between the two. The leaves are partially oxidized and they turn a greenish brown. These are the three kinds of tea. They all come from the same tea bush. It's what happens after they're picked that makes the difference.

Grades of tea as we know them are determined by the size of the leaf fragments in the box or the tin or the tea bag. It's that simple. What are known as leaf grades comprise about 20% of the total crop. Because the pieces are bigger, flavor and color come out more slowly. Leaf grades generally produce more subtle and delicate flavors and are therefore

Brewing Tea.

Tea Vendors.

Preparing Tea. Ch'i Pai-shih.

THOUSAND-YEAR EGGS
(Hundred-Year, Ancient)

These uncooked duck eggs are coated with clay mixed with lime, ashes and rice husks, then buried in an earthen pot for about three months. The whites become a dark amber color and the yolks turn green and somewhat elastic. Slice them up for a great appetizer. Chinese people regard them as a delicacy. You should be able to buy them individually at many Chinese groceries for about 40 to 50 cents apiece. They'll keep for about a month if refrigerated. It may take a little getting used to the color, but they taste good.

VINEGARS

Chinese red vinegar made from rice usually has a clear color in the bottle but turns reddish-brown after the bottle is opened. It is used in cooking and in dips. Black vinegar, sometimes known as Chenkong rice vinegar, is milder and has a very distinctive, mellow flavor. Chinese sweet vinegar is made from a combination of black vinegar and sugar. It is black and very pungent and combines well with dishes that use some ginger. It is thought to be very nutritious. Chinese white vinegar has a sharp taste and is much like American vinegars. It is recommended that you use the very best vinegar available as it is an ingredient that can make a big difference in the results of your cooking efforts.

WATER CHESTNUTS

Water chestnuts are available fresh and canned. Each has its advantages, the major one for the fresh variety being that they are very, very good to eat. And the consistency (about like that of your average uncooked potato) adds another dimension to any dish, the water chestnut being nice and crunchy even when cooked. The fresh ones have a deep purple skin and you may find some mud on them—don't bother to wash it off until just before you're ready to peel the water chestnuts because it will help keep them from drying out.

The canned variety are peeled and packed in water. This type has almost no sweetness, flavor or food value. But they are much more widely available and cost about a fourth as much. As with bamboo shoots, do not use the water they're packed in . . . preservatives, you know.

sought by connoisseurs. The three leaf grades are orange pekoe (pron. peck-o), pekoe and souchang, from best down. Then there are the broken grades, smaller and broken leaves all the way down to the leaf particles, "dust." These are about 80% of the tea crop. From the top down they are broken orange pekoe, broken pekoe, broken pekoe souchang, fannings and fines. These broken grades make stronger and darker tea and usually go into tea bags.

Once again, it should be emphasized that the Chinese prefer the green and oolong teas. Black tea, which the Chinese refer to as red tea, is produced primarily for export. So if you want to really "go native," you should try some green tea, and drink it as the Chinese do. Put about a teaspoon of tea in a cup or 1 tablespoon per three people in a teapot and pour just a little boiling water over it. Cover it and let it sit for a minute, then fill the cup or pot the rest of the way with water that is at a full boil. The tea may float around on the surface, but no matter. Let steep three to five minutes. The cup should always be refilled at least once—many people think the second go-around is better than the first. By the way, the color of the tea is just as important to a Chinese connoisseur as the aroma and the taste. Perhaps this is why most Chinese drink their tea from glasses. The glasses usually have little lids to keep the contents hot while steeping.

WATER CHESTNUT POWDER

As a thickening agent, most Chinese cooks prefer to use water chestnut powder. Although cornstarch or tapioca starch may be used in its place, water chestnut powder has a couple of advantages: it lends deep-fried dishes a crunchier, lighter consistency than does cornstarch; and it gives to sauces the kind of sheen so characteristic of genuine Chinese cuisine. On the other hand, it is a bit expensive—from $1.75 to $2.00 for a half-pound box.

WONTON SKINS

Wonton skins, also known as *shao-mai* skins, are usually 3½ inches square. They're made from the same ingredients as egg roll skins—eggs, flour and water, but are slightly thinner. That's okay because they don't have to hold as much. They usually come in one-pound packages and can often be found in American supermarkets. You can keep them in the refrigerator for about five days, but after that they will dry out, at which point it will be much more difficult to keep them from breaking after the ingredients are put inside.

WINTER MELON

This is a large, light green, squash-like melon with white flesh and a center core of seeds. It can weigh over 20 pounds, so often the Chinese grocer is willing to slice off a chunk. A whole winter melon will keep for several months if stored in a cool place. Wedges will last a week if wrapped in aluminum foil.

Fish and Vegetables. Ch'i Pai-shih.

A Shopper's Guide To Chinese Groceries

Listed below, in alphabetical order by state, are some selected Chinese grocery stores in the U.S., and at the end of the list are some in Canada. These stores were selected because they stock a good variety of Chinese foodstuffs, and, in most cases, other useful culinary equipment. Every Chinese grocery store in the United States is not included here, but if you find that you favorite is not among those we enumerate, please let us hear about it so that it may be included in the next edition of *The Chinese Catalog*.

The stores that are listed may be expected to carry all of the major ingredients called for in most Chinese recipes—bamboo shoots, oyster sauce, lily buds, sesame oil, and the like. They all carry tea and some have fresh vegetables and fish. Specialty items such as fresh vegetables, wine or beer, utensils (usually including dinnerware), cookbooks, and gifts, and special services such as mail order, are noted below each store entry. Along with these entries you'll also find some interesting information about various Chinese foods, including explanations of some of the more exotic items (like thousand-year eggs).

Inevitably, there will be some readers who will not be able to find a store in their locality. Those of you who find yourselves in this situation may have to rely on mail order shopping, but if your home is in or near a fairly large city or town, there is probably a Chinese grocer somewhere near. The best advice for seeking out the elusive Chinese grocer is to locate another kind of business (gift shop, florist, dry cleaner, etc.) that either employs or is owned by people of Chinese descent. Patronize this establishment and ask either an employee or proprietor if there is a Chinese grocer that he might recommend. If one exists, he will be more than happy to direct you to it.

ALABAMA

Asian Supermarket
1407-A Montgomery Hwy.
Birmingham, AL 35216
Tel. (205) 822-0140
(utensils, gifts, mail order)

Chai's Oriental Food Store
2133 7th Ave. South
Birmingham, AL 35233
Tel. (205) 324-4873
(cookbooks, utensils, gifts, mail order)

ALASKA

Sagaya Oriental Groceries
3309 Spenard Rd.
Anchorage, AK 99509
Tel. (907) 279-2811
(utensils)

Kobe-Ya
401 Idaho St.
Anchorage, AK 99510
Tel. (907) 333-8896

ARIZONA

House of Rice
3221 N. Hayden Rd.
Scottsdale, AZ 85251
Tel. (602) 947-6698
(utensils, cookbooks, gifts)

ARKANSAS

Kim's Oriental Grocery Store & Gifts
1714 S. University Ave.
Little Rock, AR 72204
Tel. (501) 661-1660

CALIFORNIA

China Native Products, Inc.
2005 San Fernando Rd.
Los Angeles, CA 90065
Tel. (213) 227-1945
(arts & crafts)

Kwong On Lung Co.
680 North Spring St.
Los Angeles, CA 90012
Tel. (213) 628-1069
(utensils, cookbooks)

Easy Foods Company
299 Castro
Mountain View, CA 94041
Tel. (415) 969-5595
(utensils, cookbooks, mail order)

Sacramento Tofu Co.
1915 6th
Sacramento, CA 95814
Tel. (916) 447-2682

Quang Fat Co., Inc.
1142 Grant Ave.
San Francisco, CA 94133
Tel. (415) 982-0514

Shing Chong & Co.
800 Grant Ave.
San Francisco, CA 94108
Tel. (415) 982-0949

Sin Ma Imports Co.
1551 Minnesota
San Francisco, CA 94108
Tel. (415) 282-1949

Wing Sing Chong Co., Inc.
685 7th Street
San Francisco, CA 94103
Tel. (415) 982-4171

Oriental Trading Co.
131 West Harris Ave.
South San Francisco, CA
Tel. (415) 761-0266
(liquor)

COLORADO

Dynasty Chinese Kitchen
2743 W. Bellview Ave.
Littleton, CO 80123
Tel. (303) 797-3685
(utensils, gifts)

CONNECTICUT

Young's Oriental Grocery
243 Farmington Ave.
Hartford, CT 06105
Tel. (203) 246-2998

Kinm's Gift Shop
202 Park Road
West Hartford, CT 06119
Tel. (203) 232-5046
(utensils, cookbooks)

Lee's Oriental Grocery Store
455 Williams St.
New London, CT 06320
Tel. (203) 443-9665

International Food, Inc.
1565 South Main St.
Waterbury, CT
(314) 574-5356

FLORIDA

Aloha Food, Inc.
226 SW 21st Terr.
Ft. Lauderdale, FL
Tel. (305) 587-9333

Fashion Imports, Inc.
3270 E. 11th Ave.
Hialeah, FL 33013
Tel. (305) 836-0571
(utensils)

W-East Trading Corp.
4559 Shirley Ave.
Jacksonville, FL 32210
Tel. (904) 384-7233
(gifts)

Siam Exotica Corp.
Oriental Food & Gift Shop
6453 Beach Blvd.
Jacksonville, FL 32216
Tel. (904) 721-1644

Asia Market
1241 E. Colonial Drive
Orlando, FL 32803
Tel. (305) 894-8065
(utensils, gifts)

Oriental Food & Gift
1531 S. Dale Mabry Hwy.
Tampa, FL 33609
Tel. (813) 251-0262
(utensils)

GEORGIA

Asia Imports Co.
Oriental Food Mart
1665-B La Vista Rd. NE
Atlanta, GA 30329
Tel. (404) 329-9234
(utensils, gifts)

Asian Supermarket
2581 Piedmont Rd. NE
Atlanta, GA 30324
Tel. (404) 266-0362
(beer, utensils, cookbooks)

ILLINOIS

Golden Country Market
2422 S. Wentworth Ave.
Chicago, IL 60616
Tel. (312) 842-4111

Oriental Food Market
2801 W. Howard St.
Chicago, IL 60645
Tel. (312) 274-2826
(utensils, cookbooks)

Star Market
3349 No. Clark St.
Chicago, IL 60657
Tel. (312) 472-0599

IOWA

Oriental Food Store
112 E. 4th St.
Davenport, IA 52801
Tel. (319) 323-3141

A&A Supermarket
924 Locust
Des Moines, IA 50309
Tel. (515) 288-4734
(utensils, cookbooks)

Jang's Oriental Food Store
913 E. University
Des Moines, IA 60316
Tel. (515) 266-3891
(utensils, cookbooks, gifts, mail order)

INDIANA

A-B Oriental Grocery & Gift Shop
3709 N. Shadeland Ave.
Indianapolis, IN 46229
Tel. (317) 545-3438
(utensils, gifts, mail order)

Indy Oriental Grocery
6430 E. Washington
Indianapolis, IN 46229
Tel. (317) 359-2137
(utensils, gifts)

KENTUCKY

Oriental Foods & Gifts
357 Southland Drive
Lexington, KY 40503
Tel. (606) 276-2013
(fr. veg., utensils, cookbooks, mail order)

Oriental Grocery
2350 Woodhill Drive
Lexington, KY 40509
Tel. (606) 269-7722

Dixie Oriental Supermarket
4030 Dixie Hwy.
Louisville, KY 40216
Tel. (502) 447-1287
(utensils, cookbooks, gifts)

Ting Hou Oriental Food & Gift Shop
4742 Bardstown Rd.
Louisville, KY 40218
Tel. (502) 499-1087

MARYLAND

The Chinese Cookery, Inc.
1049-R Rockville Pike
P.O. Box 2042
Rockville, MD 20852
Tel. (301) 340-0995
(utensils, cookbooks)

MASSACHUSETTS

Mirim Trading Co., Inc.
152 Harvard Ave.
Allston, MA 02134
Tel. (617) 783-2626
(utensils, cookbooks, gifts)

Joyce Chen Unlimited
The Oriental Market
172 Massachusetts Ave.
Arlington, MA 02174
Tel. (617) 643-1930
(utensils, gifts)

New England Food Supply Co.
225 Harrison Ave.
Boston, MA 02111
Tel. (617) 426-8592
(mail order)

MICHIGAN

Manna Oriental Foods & Gifts
1162 Broadway
Ann Arbor, MI 48105
Tel. (313) 663-6868
(beer, utensils, cookbooks)

Oriental Food Groceries
18919 W. 7 Mile
Detroit, MI 48219
Tel. (313) 534-7773
(fr. veg., utensils, cookbooks)

MINNESOTA

Asia-Mart
908 Marquette Ave.
Minneapolis, MN 55402
Tel. (612) 338-1058
(utensils, cookbooks, gifts)

First Oriental Foods, Inc.
3225 E. Hennepin Ave.
Minneapolis, MN 55413
Tel. (612) 331-3343
(utensils, cookbooks, gifts, mail order)

International House of Foods
75 West Island Ave.
Minneapolis, MN
Tel. (612) 739-2335

Kwong Tung Foods, Inc.
326 Cedar Ave.
Minneapolis, MN 55455
Tel. (612) 338-1533
(utensils, cookbooks, mail order)

Oriental Plaza, Inc.
24 Glenwood Ave.
Minneapolis, MN 55402
Tel. (612) 338-2677
(fr. veg., utensils, cookbooks, gifts, mail order)

United Noodles, Inc.
2001 E. 24th St.
Minneapolis, MN 55406
Tel. (612) 721-6677

International Grocery and Health Foods
476 N. Lexington Parkway
St. Paul, MN 55104
Tel. (612) 647-9795

Kims Oriental Grocery
689 Snelling Ave.
St. Paul, MN 55104
Tel. (612) 646-0428
(utensils, cookbooks, mail order)

MISSOURI

Oriental Trading Co.
925 DeMun Ave.
Clayton, MO 63105
Tel. (314) 727-5994
(fr. veg., utensils, cookbooks)

China Food Company
1714 W. 39th St.
Kansas City, MO 64111
Tel. (816) 756-0001

Eastern Foods
449 N. New Ballas Rd.
St. Louis, MO 63141
Tel. (314) 872-7077
(utensils, gifts)

NEBRASKA

Omaha Oriental Food
7051 Maple
Omaha, NE 68104
Tel. (402) 551-2187
(utensils, gifts, cookbooks, mail order)

Midwest Oriental Foods
8243 Hascall
Omaha, NE 68124
Tel. (402) 391-7730
(utensils, mail order)

Aki's Oriental Food
4425 S. 84th St.
Omaha, NE 68127
Tel. (402) 339-2671
(fr. veg., utensils, mail order)

NEW YORK

Ching Chow Grocery
887 Nostrand Ave.
Brooklyn, NY 10525
Tel. (212) 778-6628

Lily Oriental Foods
2837 Church Ave.
Brooklyn, NY 11226
Tel. (212) 287-3435

Oriental Foods
3409 Church Ave.
Brooklyn, NY 11203
Tel. (212) 282-5264

East Wind
2801 Broadway
New York, NY 10025
Tel. (212) 666-6644
(utensils, cookbooks, gifts)

Kam Kuo Food Corp.
7 Mott St.
New York, NY 10013
Tel. (212) 349-3097
(beer, utensils, mail order)

Katagiri & Co, Inc.
224 E. 59th St.
New York, NY 10022
Tel. (212) 755-3566
(utensils, mail order)

Kam Man Food Products
200 Canal St.
New York, NY 10013
Tel. (212) 571-0330
(beer, utensils, cookbooks, mail order)

MFW
36 Pell St.
New York, NY 10013
Tel. (212) 962-9980

New Frontier Trading Corp.
2394 Broadway
New York, NY 10024
Tel. (212) 799-9338
(cookbooks, gifts)

Summit Import Corp.
415 Greenwich St.
New York, NY 10013
Tel. (212) 226-1662

Wing Woh Lung
50 Mott St.
New York, NY 10013
Tel. (212) 962-3459
(utensils)

J & S Oriental Food Co.
1706 Erie Blvd. E.
Syracuse, NY 13210
Tel. (315) 479-8812

NORTH CAROLINA

Oriental Imports
4808 E. Central Ave.
Charlotte, NC 28205
Tel. (704) 537-4281
(utensils, cookbooks, mail order)

Oriental Food Store
3008 Spring Garden St.
Greensboro, NC 27403
Tel. (919) 292-2613
(fr. veg., cookbooks)

Oriental Store of Raleigh, Inc.
3310 North Blvd.
Starmount Shopping Center
Raleigh, NC 27604
Tel. (919) 876-6911

OHIO

Far East Co.
889 W. Galbraith
Cincinnati, OH 45231
Tel. (513) 521-6611
(utensils, cookbooks, gifts, mail order)

Soya Food Products Co.
2356 Wyoming Ave.
Cincinnati, OH 45208
Tel. (513) 661-2250

Friendship Chinese Foodland
3415 Payne
Cleveland, OH 44114
Tel. (216) 431-8334
(utensils, cookbooks)

Hall One Chinese Imports
3126 St. Clair Ave.
Cleveland, OH 44114
Tel. (216) 566-7430

Sam Wah Yick Kee Co.
2146 Rockwell Ave.
Cleveland, OH 44114
Tel. (216) 771-0054
(gifts)

Columbus Oriental Food Shop
2659 N. High
Columbus OH 43202
Tel. (614) 267-2837
(Utensils, cookbooks, gifts)

OKLAHOMA

Ha's Asian Market
1140 NW 24th
Oklahoma City, OK 73106
Tel. (405) 524-7333
(utensils, gifts, mail order)

Far East Foods
6929 S. Sheridan Rd.
Tulsa, OK 74133
Tel. (918) 492-5500
(utensils)

Su's Oriental Market
3313 E. 32nd Pl.
Tulsa, OK 74103
Tel. (918) 743-0007
(utensils, gifts)

PENNSYLVANIA

Joy Dragon Food Market
1022 Race
Philadelphia, PA 15218
Tel. (215) 925-2329

Hsin Kuo Oriental Shop
2022 Murray Ave.
Pittsburgh, PA 15217
Tel. (412) 421-1201
(utensils, gifts)

RHODE ISLAND

East Sea Oriental Market
90–92 Warren Ave.
East Providence, RI 02914
Tel. (401) 434-3251

TENNESSEE

Conjean Imports
1470 Wells Station Rd.
Memphis, TN 38108
Tel. (901) 767-5843
(utensils, cookbooks, gifts, mail order)

Orient Blessing Grocery
1513 Church
Nashville, TN 37202
Tel. (615) 327-3682

TEXAS

Oriental Market
502 Pampa
Austin, TX 78752
Tel. (512) 453-9058
(liquor, utensils, cookbooks, mail order,
fr. veg.)

Pacific Orient Market
6617 Airport Blvd.
Austin, TX 78752
Tel. (512) 458-8333

Say Hi
5249 Burnet Rd.
Austin, TX 78756
Tel. (512) 453-1411

Sangroksu Oriental Groceries & Gifts
5501 N. Lamar
Austin, TX
Tel. (512) 453-8607

E's Oriental Food Market
5107 W. Davis St.
Dallas, TX 75211
Tel. (214) 339-8412

Edo-Ya Oriental Food Store
232 Farmers Branch Shopping Center
Dallas, TX 75234
Tel. (214) 247-0393
(utensils, cookbooks, gifts)

Young Ho Pak Food, Inc.
3201 Ross Ave.
Dallas, TX
Tel. (214) 821-0542

Oriental Import-Export Co.
2009 Plok St.
Houston, TX 77003
Tel. (713) 233-5621

Alice's Food Products and Gifts
From the Orient
343 N.E. Parkway
San Antonio, TX 78218
(liquor, utensils, cookbooks, mail order)

Kim Long Market
2003 Austin Highway
San Antonio, TX 78218
Tel. (512) 653-0820
(utensils, gifts, mail order)

Sachiko's
2504 SW Loop 410
San Antonio, TX 78227
Tel. (512) 674-7791
(fr. veg., gifts)

UTAH

Oriental Food Market
667 S 700E
Salt Lake City, UT
Tel. (801) 363-2122
(fr. veg., utensils, gifts, cookbooks, mail
order)

Sage Farm Market
1515 S. Main
Salt Lake City, UT 84115
Tel. (801) 484-4122
(utensils, mail order)

Yu's Chinese Market
944 E. 200 S.
Salt Lake City, UT 84111
Tel. (801) 355-3294
(gifts, cookbooks)

VIRGINIA

Mekong Center
3107 Wilson Blvd.
Arlington, VA 22201
Tel. (703) 527-2779
(liquor, utensils, mail order)

WASHINGTON

TC USA Corp.
15325 6th SW
Seattle, WA 98114
Tel. (206) 246-2840

Tsue Chong Co. Inc.
801 S. King
Seattle, WA 98112
Tel. (206) 623-0801

WISCONSIN

Asian Food Store
910 Regent St.
Madison, WI 53703
Tel. (608) 255-9046
(utensils, cookbooks)

International House of Foods
440 W. Gorham St.
Madison, WI 53703
Tel. (608) 255-2554
(utensils, cookbooks, gifts, mail order)

Oriental Shop
618 South Park
Madison, WI 53715
Tel. (608) 251-7991
(fr. veg., utensils, cookbooks)

The Asian Mart
1107 N. 3rd St
Milwaukee, WI 53203
Tel. (414) 765-9211

Hong Fat Co.
1112 N. 3rd St.
Milwaukee, WI 53203
Tel. (414) 273-1727
(gifts)

Oriental KP Grocery & Gift
821 N. 27th St.
Milwaukee, WI
Tel. (414) 344-4467

Peace Oriental Foods & Gifts
4250 W. Fond du Lac Ave.
Milwaukee, WI 53216
Tel. (414) 871-1818

CANADA

Ching Products Co.
492 Dundas St. W.
Toronto, Ontario
Tel. (416) 977-2449

Min Sheng Chinese Grocery
121 Percy
Ottawa, Ontario
Tel. (613) 235-3134

Leong Jung Company Ltd.
999 Clark
Montreal, Quebec
Tel. (514) 861-9747

A Note on Phone and Mail Orders

Even though we have almost 150 stores listed here, inevitably many readers do not have handy access to a store. About half of the stores listed do accept either mail or phone orders, sometimes with conditions—only over $20, prepaid, C.O.D., and the like. Others say that they will provide this service only if they know the customer. Our advice is that if you foresee the prospect of periodic shopping at a Chinese grocery and your access to one is limited, try to get yourself there at least once. Almost none of these stores has a mail order list, so one benefit of going there in person will be to find out just what is available. Secondly, many Chinese groceries are "mom and pop" stores, and an in-person visit may help you to establish a personal relationship with the proprietor. Several proprietors have told us that their rules against mail or phone orders are waived for known customers.

Mail Order Grocers

EAST

Asia House Grocery
2433 St. Paul St.
Baltimore, MD 21218

Lee's Oriental Gifts & Food
3053 Main St.
Buffalo, NY 14214

Bloomingdale's Food Dept.
1000 Third Ave.
New York, NY 10022

Yuit Hing Market Corp.
23 Pell St.
New York, NY 10013

Crestview Foodtown
200 E. Crestview Rd.
Columbus, OH 43202

Harmony Oriental
247 Atwood St.
Pittsburgh, PA 15213

Hon Kee Company
935 Race St.
Philadelphia, PA 19107

Da Hue Foods
615 I Street N.W.
Washington, D.C. 20001

MIDWEST

Kan Shing Co.
2246 S. Wentworth St.
Chicago, IL 60616

Shiroma
1058 W. Argyle St.
Chicago, IL 60640

Kings Trading
3736 Broadway
Kansas City, MO 64111

WEST

Wing Chong Lung Co.
922 S. San Pedro St.
Los Angeles, CA 90015

Manley Produce
1101 Grant Ave.
San Francisco, CA 94133

SOUTH

South Eastern Food Supply
6732 N.E. 4th Ave.
Miami, FL 33138

Mail Order Bazaar

Suppose you live in the wilds of deepest Nebraska. There are no Chinese markets for miles around, but you want to cook Chinese food. Well, you should write or call the folks at The Chinese Grocer and ask them to send you their most recent shopping list. They have whatever you need when it comes to Chinese cooking—food, utensils, cookbooks, decorative items—even personalized fortune cookies. It's all available on a mail order basis, so all you need is a post office. They promise to get the items to you in four weeks, even if shipped from their Hong Kong office.

As you will see from their list, they can supply you with all of the standard Chinese culinary supplies that you could ever need. But they can also supply a number of not-so-standard things you may never have dreamed you needed. Take, for instance, a stainless steel vegetable cutter in the shape of a dragon or a phoenix, or garnet-colored clay pots from southwest China. For personalized fortune cookies, you write your own message and the cooks at The Chinese Grocer will print it and put it in the cookies as they bake. You can also order an authentic Chinese "chop" with your name carved in English, Chinese or both.

Get a shopping list by writing or calling The Chinese Grocer, 209 Post St., San Francisco, CA 94108. Tel. (415) 982-0125.

Section #1 — VEGETABLES

Item		Size (oz.)	Cost
Dried Lotus Roots in Slices	Boxed	8	2.89
Lotus Root Slices (sweetened)	Canned	19	1.09
Lotus Root in Water	Canned	19	1.09
Water Chestnut	Canned	6	.55
Water Chestnut	Canned	19	1.29
Bamboo Shoots	Canned	6	.49
Bamboo Shoots	Canned	19	.89
Bamboo Shoots	Canned	11	1.19
Szechuan Pickles (char choy - chopped fine)	Canned	6	.59
Szechuan Pickles (char choy - large pcs.)	Canned	12	1.29
Szechuan Pickles (char choy - large pcs.)	Canned	16	1.59
Preserved Snow Cabbages	Canned	6	.59
Braised Bamboo Shoots Tips	Canned	13	1.59
Braised Bamboo Shoots Tips w/chili	Canned	10	.95
Black Mushrooms (sm. w/o stems)	Bagged	1	1.29
Black Mushrooms (med. w/o stems)	Bagged	4	4.95
Black Mushrooms (shredded)	Bagged	1	1.49
Black Mushrooms (lg. w/o stems)	Cello	1	1.89
Cloud Ears (tree ears)	Bagged	½	1.00
Cloud Ears (tree ears)	Cello	1½	2.59
Wood Ear	Cello	4	2.99
Lily Flowers (golden needles)	Cello	4	.95
Button Mushrooms (sliced)	Canned	4	.89
Button Mushrooms (whole)	Canned	4	1.69
Oyster Mushrooms	Canned	10	.98
Straw Mushrooms (dried)	Bagged	1	2.59
Straw Mushrooms	Canned	10	1.29
Golden Mushrooms	Canned	10	1.29
Baby Corns	Canned	15	1.29
Bamboo Shoot Tips	Canned	19	1.19
Pa Pao Chai	Canned	13½	1.49
Pickled Mustard Green	Canned	19	1.09
Mandarin Jah Jan	Canned	10	.89
Sliced Sour Bamboo Shoot	Canned	19	1.00
Bitter Melon	Canned	19	1.09
Preserved Turnips	Bagged	8	.69
Red in Snow	Canned	6½	.59
Dried Bok Choy	Cello	5	1.99
Hot Pa Pao La Jan	Canned	10	.89
Braised Snow Cabbage with Beans	Canned	10	.95

Section #2 — SAUCES, CONDIMENTS & SEASONINGS

Item		Size (oz.)	Cost
Black (dark) Soy Sauce	Bottled	12	1.19
Black (dark) Soy Sauce	Bottled	21	1.79
Black (dark) Soy Sauce	Canned	5#	3.99
Thin (light) Soy Sauce	Bottled	12	1.19
Thin (light) Soy Sauce	Bottled	21	1.79
Thin (light) Soy Sauce	Canned	5#	3.99
Hoisin Sauce (paste)	Jar	4	.89
Hoisin Sauce (paste)	Jar	16	1.99
Hoisin Sauce (paste)	Canned	16	1.59
Hoisin Sauce (paste)	Canned	5#	5.99
Plum Sauce	Jar	5	.95
Plum Sauce	Jar	16	2.09
Plum Sauce	Canned	5#	6.99
Oyster Sauce	Bottled	6	1.59
Oyster Sauce	Bottled	16	2.89
Oyster Sauce	Canned	5#	8.99
Sesame Oil	Plastic Bottled	8	1.49
Sesame Oil	Plastic Bottled	16	2.59
Sesame Oil	Plastic Bottled	½ gal.	8.49
Cooking Wine (aji-marin)	Bottled	10	1.69
Chili Oil	Bottled	8	1.99
Chili Oil	Bottled	5	1.69
Chili Sauce	Bottled	6	.79
Black Vinegar	Bottled	19	1.69
Sesame Paste	Jar	6	1.99
Monosodium Glutamate	Bagged	3	.55
Monosodium Glutamate	Bagged	16	2.59
Hot Bean Sauce (paste) (Szechuan)	Canned	6	.69
Hot Bean Paste (sauce) (Szechuan)	Jar	8	1.69
Bean Sauce (brown)	Jar	8	.89
Bean Sauce (brown)	Jar	16	1.69
Chili Paste with Garlic	Jar	8	1.29
Chili Paste with Soy Beans	Jar	8	1.29
Black Bean Sauce with Chili	Jar	8	1.29
Black Bean Paste with Chili	Jar	16	1.99
Chee Hou Sauce (different blend of hoisin sauce)	Canned	16	1.55
Salted Chili Sauce with Sesame Oil	Canned	6	.69
Barbecue Sauce	Jar	4½	1.09
Barbecue Sauce	Jar	7	1.79
Barbecue Sauce	Jar	8	1.75
Barbecue Sauce (Chinese style)	Jar	16	1.99
Red Vinegar	Bottled	12	1.19
Red Vinegar	Bottled	21	1.79
Lemon Sauce	Jar	16	1.89
Maggi Sauce	Bottled	1½	.69
Fish Sauce	Plastic Bottled	6	.69
Fish Sauce	Plastic Bottled	21	1.39
Fish Sauce	Bottled	21	1.39

Sec. #2 — SAUCES, etc. (Continued)

Item		Size (oz.)	Cost
Shrimp Paste	Plastic Container	2	.89
Shrimp Sauce	Jar	8	1.49
Sweet & Sour Sauce, for cooking	Jar	13	1.59
Sweet & Sour Sauce, for egg roll	Jar	8	.79
Hot Mustard Sauce, for egg roll	Bottled	5	.59
Hot Mustard Powder	Cello	2	.29
Preserved Radish with Chili	Jar	8	1.29
Fermented Black Beans	Cello	8	.75
Fermented Black Beans	Canned	16	1.69
Rock Sugar (bing tong)	Cello	16	1.29
Slab Brown Sugar (wong tong)	Cello	16	.95
Preserved Plum in Brine	Jar	16	1.99
Fermented Red Bean Curd (nam yee)	Jar	12	1.99
Fermented Bean Curd (foo yee)	Jar	16	1.99
Dried Red Chili Pepper	Cello	4	1.09
Lotus Root Powder (thickener, etc.)	Cello	3½	1.00
Arrow Root Powder (thickener, etc.)	Boxed	8	1.00
Water Chestnut Powder (thickener, etc.)	Boxed	8	1.69
Tapioca Starch (thickener, etc.)	Cello	15	.69
Red Pickled Sweet Ginger	Bottled	16	2.99
Mixed Pickled Ginger (fruits)	Canned	16	1.89
Pickled Scallions	Bottled	16	1.59
Pickled Garlic	Bottled	9	1.09
Pickled Cucumbers (tea melon)	Canned	6	.89
Mixed Vegetables (preserved - garnish	Canned	16	1.99
Seasoned Cucumber with Soy Sauce	Bottled	4	1.09
Pickled Plum (akaume zuke)	Bottled	8	1.49
Pickled Ginger (beni shoga)	Bottled	9	2.09
Satay (barbecue sauce)	Bottled	6	.75
Mushroom Soy Sauce	Bottled	22	1.89
Steam Powder (for steaming meat & seafood)	Boxed	4	.69

Section #3 — OTHER SPECIALTY FOODS

Item		Size (oz.)	Cost
Bird's Nest (dried)	Cello	1	3.50
Shark Fins (dried)	Boxed	8	19.95
Chinese Macaroni	Cello	8	.79
White Fungus (snow fungus)	Cello	½	1.29
Sweet Rice Flour (JFC)	Boxed	16	.79
Sweet Rice Flour	Plastic Bagged	18	1.19
Regular Rice Flour	Plastic Bagged	16	1.09
Wheat Starch	Bagged	16	.99
Tapioca Pearl	Bagged	16	.59
Red Beans	Cello	14	.89
Mung Beans	Cello	16	.75
Bean Thread	Cello	3.5	.69
Bean Thread	Cello	16	2.10
Rice Sticks	Cello	7	.89
Rice Sticks	Cello	14	1.29
Rice Sticks	Cello	16	1.19
Dried Bean Curd Sticks	Bagged	8	2.49
Dried Bean Curd Sheets	Bagged	8	2.49
Shai Ho Fun (dried wide rice noodles)	Boxed	16	1.09
Rice Pudding (eight precious pudding)	Canned	8	.59
Tempura Batter Mix	Boxed	12	1.29
Chinese Style Gelatin (grass jelly)	Canned	19	.69
1000 Year Old Egg	Single	ea.	.40
Quail Egg	Canned	15	1.69
Hot and Sour Soup	Canned	19	1.29
Agar-Agar	Bagged	½	1.89
Agar-Agar	Bagged	3½	2.59
Jelly Fish (preserved in salt)	Bagged	½	1.89
Bamboo Leaves (dried)	Bagged	16	1.89
Lotus Leaves (dried)	Bagged	16	3.50
Rice Paper Wrappers	Bagged	100shts	5.99
Shrimp Chips (puff-up when deep fried in oil)	Cello	8	1.00
Prawn Chips (puff-up when deep fried in oil)	Cello	8	1.00
X-rated Fortune Cookies	Cello	1 doz.	.79
Regular Fortune Cookies	Cello	1 doz.	.49
Almond Cookies	Cello	25 pcs.	1.20

Section #4 — SPICES & HERBS

Item		Size (oz.)	Cost
Star Anise	Cello	1	.39
Fennel Seeds	Cello	1	.39
Szechuan Peppercorns or Flower Pepper	Cello	1	.39
Dried Spiced Ginger	Cello	1	.39
Dried Tangerine Peel	Cello	½	.39
White Pepper Powder	Cello	1	.39
Ground Szechuan Pepper Powder	Cello	4	1.00
Dried Red Hot Peppers	Cello	4	1.00
Red Hot Pepper Flakes	Cello	1	.39
Five-Spice Powder	Cello	1	.39
Licorice Root (kam cho)	Cello	1	.39
White Peppercorns (whole)	Cello	1	.35
Black Peppercorns (whole)	Cello	1	.35
Red Berries (for soup)	Cello	1	1.50
Red Dates (for seasoning or soup)	Cello	1	.59
White Poppy Seeds	Cello	1	.49
Holy Basil	Cello	¼	.49
Laos (dried galanga)	Cello	1	.75
Dried Sweet Basil	Cello	.05	.69

Growing Your Own

If all else fails, and you still can't find the Chinese groceries you need, or if you just prefer the taste of garden-fresh vegetables and herbs, you might like to try your hand at a little Chinese vegetable gardening. Here are some tips on Chinese gardening, plus seed sources and a valuable Chinese gardening guide.

BETTER VEGETABLE GARDENS THE CHINESE WAY
Peter Chan with Spencer Gill
Graphic Arts Center Publishing Co.
96 pp. $4.95

In China there is an old saying: If you wish to be happy for a few hours, drink wine until your head spins pleasantly; if you wish to be happy for a few days, get married and hide away; if you wish to be happy for a week, roast a tender pig and have a feast; if you wish to be happy all your life, become a gardener.

Peter and Sylvia Chan, both from southern China, have long experience in working the soil. Both graduated from South China Agricultural College in Canton. Peter later worked at an agricultural extension center and then taught plant pathology for seven years. After Peter worked four years on an experimental farm near Hong Kong, the Chans came to the United States. Since 1969 Peter has been associated with Portland State University, where he is now a research technician in the biology department. The Chans began gardening while in Portland, employing the same techniques used by farmers in south China. Their garden was selected as the best of 1,400 gardens in the *Sunset* magazine contest of 1976.

Raised-bed gardening is many centuries old and has withstood the test of time because, simply, it is more efficient than the flat-planting method. A raised-

THE CHAN FAMILY GARDEN

THIS YEAR

Matrimony Vine (perennial)		
Tomato, Pepper & Eggplant	Blue Lake Bean	Zucchini Squash
Nursery bed for Bonsai plants & etc.	Blue Lake Bean	Chinese Leek (Perennial)
Pea Pod (Before June) Lettuce, Spinach, Swiss Chard (After June)	Chinese Broccoli, Head Cabbage & Garlic	
Pea Pod (Before June) Lettuce, Spinach, Chinese Cabbage (After June)	Chinese Cabbage, Celery, Green Onion & Garland Chrysanthemum	Rhubarb (Perennial)
Scallion (Before July) Chinese Cabbage, Mustard Green (After July)	Cucumber, Lettuce & Leek, Kohlrabi	

NEXT YEAR

Matrimony Vine		
Scallion & Lettuce	Chinese Broccoli, Head Lettuce & Garlic	Zucchini Squash
Pea Pod (Before June) Lettuce, Spinach, Swiss Chard (After June)	Chinese Cabbage, Green Onion Carrot & Garland Chrysanthemum	Chinese Leek
Chinese Broccoli, Chinese Cabbage Cucumbers & Leek	Blue Lake Bean	
Pepper, Egg Plant & Onion	Blue Lake Bean	Rhubarb
Pea Pod (Before June) Lettuce, Kohlrabi, Mustard Green (After June)	Tomato & Scallion	

bed system requires less space, allows for a longer season, requires less fertilzer and water, and produces more vegetables than a conventional garden. The raised beds in the Chan garden are 25 feet long, four feet wide, and one foot serves as a pathway between the beds. The 100-square-foot area makes it easier to figure out applications for fertilizer, instructions for which are usually based on this size area. An important benefit of raised-bed gardening is that the plants can be tended without stepping on the beds. Thus the soil stays loose, aerated, year after year. Drainage is better and harvesting in one bed doesn't disturb the plants in another.

Farmers in China, according to Peter Chan, stress eight aspects of working the

land to produce a successful crop: water, fertilizer, the earth, seeds, spacing of plants, management, tools and protection of plants from bugs and weather. The book is organized on this basis, with some extra chapters on making the mounds and planting various crops. In the back is a diagram for the planting and harvesting of certain crops along with a schematic of the Chan's own garden for two different years. The apparent competence of the author and the obvious delight he takes in his garden makes this an attractive book. "Giving pleasure to yourself and others is one very important reason for making a home garden." He even admits on p. 13 that some of his best friends still use the flat-planting method.

GROW YOUR OWN BEAN SPROUTS!

It's easy to grow bean sprouts. Most health food stores sell kits with instructions for growing sprouts, but you can do it on your own.

To start, wash half a cup of dried mung beans. Be sure to get rid of any bad ones. Soak them overnight at room temperature. Next morning, put the beans between double thicknesses of damp cheesecloth in a colander. Sprinkle the cloth covering the beans with half a cup of warm water, then put the colander in a dark place that you're sure is above 68°F. (The ideal temperature for sprouts is 75°F.) It's a good idea to put a pan under the colander in order to catch any dripping from the warm water you'll need to spray on the sprouts at four to five hour intervals. (Spray about half a cup each time.) In about four or five days you should have sprouts to eat. Be sure to rinse them well and get rid of the little green hoods that may still be attached. The half cup of beans should yield about three cups of sprouts. And, don't think sprouts are only for Chinese dishes. They're great in salads and lots of other standard western fare.

CHINESE LETTUCE?

Chinese cabbage or *bok choy* should probably have been called Chinese lettuce. It's a cool weather plant, best when planted for fall harvest—about three months before the first frost comes to your neighborhood. It has a flavor reminiscent of very good lettuce and is leafy rather than bowling-ball-like when mature. As with lettuce, you can use it raw in salads or cooked in a variety of dishes. One thing to remember, *bok choy* needs a deep (8" to 10") soil enrichment of compost or manure. Check your seed packet or gardening guide carefully before planting.

DOUBLE YOUR FLAVORS!

Coriander and Chinese parsley are the same plant but are not the same flavors. Confusing? Well, not really. The plant, *coriandrum sativum*, produces lemony-flavored coriander seeds often used in baking and in spice mixtures such as curry powder. It also produces leaves (the Chinese parsley part) with a strong and rather exotic flavor used in many Chinese dishes. So, by adding coriander to your herb garden you'll really be doubling your flavors. Who knows, maybe you'll be doubling your fun, too!

SEED SOURCES

TSANG AND MA INTERNATIONAL
1306 Old County Road
Belmont, CA 94002

This organization tries to take the mystique out of Chinese cooking and make it understandable for westerners. This is the case in each of their three product lines: cookware, seasonings, and Chinese vegetable seeds. That's why each package containing one of the sixteen varieties of seeds tells you what the vegetable tastes like, its consistency, how to plant it, and how to cook it for best results. (Otherwise, how would you know that *bok choy* goes to flower immediately in long daylight periods.)

In addition to *bok choy* and other Chinese favorites, Tsang and Ma feature unusual vegetable seeds, such as Chinese Bitter Melon and Chinese Fuzzy Gourd! You can get the Tsang and Ma catalog by writing to the above address.

AMERICAN SEED CORPORATION
New Haven, MI 48048

This company packs a vegetable seed line called the Medallion Series. This group of seeds is designed to acquaint the American gardener with the best of flower and vegetable varieties from around the world. The "Oriental Cuisine Garden" is a part of this series. It features a number of hybrid seeds such as Hybrid Chinese Cabbage (*Siew Choy*) and Hybrid Eggplant (*Ichiban*).

W. ATLEE BURPEE COMPANY
Fordhook Farms
Doylestown, PA 18901

What could be more American than a Burpee seed catalog? Well, you might be surprised by the number of Chinese vegetable seeds you can order from this venerable old American institution. For instance, Burpee offers Mung Beans for sprouting, Bush Soybeans for making your own tofu, several varieties of edible podded peas (Snowbird, Dwarf Gray Sugar, etc.) and many other interesting herb and vegetable seeds perfect for Chinese cookery. Besides that, the Burpee catalog itself, with its beautiful color photos and easy-to-use order form, is a delight to any gardener. You can get the catalog by writing to the above address.

ORIENTAL FOOD MARKET
2801 W. Howard St.
Chicago, IL 60645

This Chicago food market offers some vegetable seeds on its mail order form. They feature such vegetables as Chinese broccoli, Chinese celery, and swamp cabbage. Also available are a number of indoor/outdoor herb seeds. Write to the above address for a mail order list.

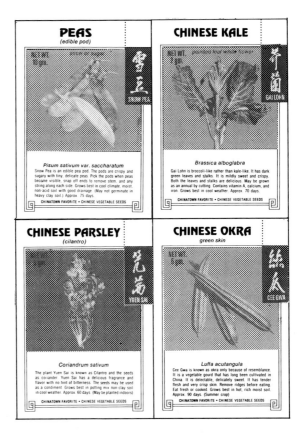

Chinese Cooking Schools

For a Post-Chow Mein Education

Probably the most effective way to learn about genuine Chinese cuisine is to attend a cooking school. Listed below are 12 cooking schools that truly specialize in Chinese food preparation. To be sure, they teach with different methods and viewpoints, but all approach Chinese cookery with enthusiasm and devotion. Most offer a variety of classes, and all include some eating of the subject at hand. If you are lucky enough to live near one of these schools, and you really want to master the art of Chinese cooking, enroll and enjoy!

CLASS MENUS

"BASIC CHINESE" course includes:
* LONG GRAIN RICE
* CHICKEN CHOW MEIN
* FRIED PORK WONTONS
* SWEET + SOUR SAUCE
* WON TON SOUP
* SWEET + SOUR CHINESE CABBAGE
* OYSTER SAUCE RICE
* BOK CHOY + BEEF
* EGG FU YUNG
* FRIED RICE
* SZECHUAN CUCUMBERS
* CABBAGE + MUSHROOMS
* EGG FLOWER SOUP
* CHINESE SPONGE CAKE
* SHRIMP CHIPS
* EGG ROLLS

"CHINESE + VEGETARIAN" course includes:
* STIR FRIED RICE STICKS WITH SHRIMP
* STEAMED SPICED BEEF * EVERY DAY RICE DISH
* TOFU WITH BBQ PORK
* PICKLED TURNIP * ORANGE FLAVORED BEEF
* PRAWNS WITH SOUR SAUCE
* TAIWAN STYLE NOODLES
* FRIED BANANA ROLLS
* VEGETARIAN SWEET + SOUR MEATBALLS
* VEGETARIAN ROAST DUCK
* VEGETARIAN STIR FRIED FISH
* HOT + SPICY BEAN SPROUT SALAD

"BASIC JAPANESE" course includes:
* SHORT GRAIN RICE * TERIYAKI CHICKEN
* TERIYAKI BEEF SKEWERS * OSUIMONO (SOUP)
* CHICKEN OVER RICE * TEMPURA * SUKIYAKI
* NORIMAKI * BARASUSHI * MISO SOUP
* MANJU (STEAMED DESSERT) * PORK KORROKKE
* NOODLES W/DIP * JAPANESE CUCUMBER SALAD

"CHAU'S HOT + SPICY" course includes:
* CHICKEN + CASHEWS IN CHILI SAUCE
* MOON CAKES * STIR FRIED BEEF + NOODLES
* PEPPERED PORK MEATBALL SOUP * SHRIMP TOAST
* PUN PUN CHICKEN SALAD * ZUCCHINI FRI
* RICE BUNDLES IN BAMBOO LEAVES
* HUNAN STIR FRIED VEGETABLES
* SPICED BEEF * SPICY CHICKEN LEGS

"CHINESE II" course includes:
* ALMOND CHICKEN * STIR FRIED MIXED VEGETABLES
* LITTLE DRUMSTICKS
* PORK SAIFUN * BARBECUED PORK
* CHINESE CHICKEN SALAD * BEEF and PEPPERS
* STEAMED MEAT BUNS
* SWEET + SOUR PORK * CHICKEN and SUGAR PEA SOUP
* ORIENTAL FRUIT and GELITIN DESSERT

"CHINESE III" course includes: * ROAST DUCK
* SIZZLING RICE SOUP * CANDIED BANANAS
* PAPER WRAPPED CHICKEN * SWEET + SOUR FISH
* MOO SHOO PORK WITH MANDARIN PANCAKES
* STIR FRIED CHICKEN * STEAMED RICE PUDDING
* PORK SHUMAI * ALMOND COOKIES

"GOURMET CHINESE" includes:
* STIR FRIED PORK + BEAN CURD (HOT)
* HOT + SOUR SOUP * MONGOLIAN HOT POT
* CHINESE NOODLE + MEAT PLATTER
* EGGPLANT WITH MEAT SAUCE
* ALMOND JELLO * SZECHUAN SHRIMP
* POT STICKERS * DEEP FRIED TOFU W/ BLACK BEAN SAUCE
* RICE SOUP

"APPETIZERS and DESSERT" course includes:
* CHINESE SAUSAGE CANAPE * KIM CHEE
* PORK PEARLS * SWEET, SOUR + HOT BALLS
* RICE + MEAT RECTANGULAR OMLETTE
* DEEP FRIED EGGPLANT SANDWICH
* PORCUPINE SHRIMP * ROSETTES
* STUFFED MUSHROOMS * CURRY PUFFS
* SESAME SEED TORTILLA CHIPS
* HOUSE OF RICE BEEF BOMBS

"NEW ORIENTAL" course includes:
* KOREAN BARBECUE * RICE WITH BEAN SPROUTS
* LEMON CRISPS
* BEAN THREADS AND VEGETABLES
* SAMOSA * INDONESIAN CABBAGE SALAD
* INDONESIAN CHICKEN CURRY
* PORK SATE * TONKATSU (PORK CUTLETS)
* FRESH GREEN BEANS W/ SESAME DRESSING
* JAPANESE EGG CUSTARD
* SUMMERTIME NOODLES
* DEEP FRIED EGGPLANT WITH MEAT SAUCE

STORE HOURS – Monday 12 to 6:30
Tues. thru Fri. 10:30 to 6:30
Saturday 10:00 to 5:30

Class menus at the House of Rice.

THE HOUSE OF RICE
3221 N. Hayden Rd.
Scottsdale, Arizona 85251
Tel. (602) 947-6698

Kiyoko Johnson, the owner of The House of Rice, has organized a number of Chinese cooking classes. There are three courses from basic to advanced that concentrate on standard Chinese cuisine. In addition, there are four specialized courses in such areas as Sichuanese and Hunanese (hot and spicy dishes), Chinese gourmet cookery and appetizer and dessert preparation.

Courses are offered in series—three two-hour classes, one class a week. Maximum class size is ten students. They are participation classes, and the needed food, recipes, and equipment are supplied by the school. The cost is around $29.50 per student for a series. Write to the store for a schedule of classes. This school encourages participation by men as well as women.

WEI-CHUAN'S COOKING
1434 S. Atlantic Blvd.
Alhambra, California 91803
Tel. (213) 289-8288

Classes at Wei-Chuan's meet daily with series classes meeting twice a month in the morning, afternoon or evening. They are two hours long and are taught in English, Japanese and Chinese. In addition to learning standard Chinese food preparation, Wei-Chuan offers classes in Chinese Seafood and Chinese Snacks. Mrs. Su-Huie Huang-Chang is the head of the Wei-Chuan operation in Alhambra. She was a teacher for twenty years in Taiwan and is the Director of Wei-Chuan's home economics department in Taiwan. (Wei-Chuan is a giant food processor and distributor, mostly of dairy products and canned goods, in Taiwan.)

The fee at Wei-Chuan is $16 per class, $60 for four classes, and $360 for twenty-four classes. Students learn to prepare three dishes per class. There is at least one class in session at all times.

DYNASTY CHINESE KITCHEN
2743 W. Bellview Ave.
Littleton, Colorado 80123
Tel. (303) 797-3685

One of the teachers at Dynasty Chinese Kitchen, Madam Chui, has thirty years of professional cooking experience in Hong Kong and the U.S. Emily Ko, from north China by way of Hong Kong and Hawaii, has a degree in hotel management and has been trained in all four major regional styles of Chinese cooking. That gives you some idea of the expertise around the woks and steamers at Dynasty. They offer three levels of cooking classes plus a *dim sum* class. The classes meet once a week for six weeks and range in price from $65 for the introductory course to $90 for the advanced. That's pretty reasonable, considering that all ingredients are included and you take home what you cook. Emily says that usually seven classes are going on at any one time, so there's no problem in terms of availability.

CONSTANCE QUAN COOKING SCHOOL
P.O. Box 387
Old Greenwich, Connecticut 06870
Tel. (203) 637-9302

Constance Quan is an authority on food. Besides teaching both Chinese and French cooking classes, she writes a weekly column on food for the local newspaper. She has won national and international honors in the culinary arts, including a bronze medal from the 1980 International Culinary Olympics in Frankfort and a silver medal from the American Culinary Federation.

Standard classes are four sessions of two and one-half hours each, noon or evening, for $160. At each class, preparation of several dishes is demonstrated and students hear discussions of ingredients, recipes and techniques. The classes are small and tastings, of course, are a part of each class. Occasionally Ms. Quan offers short courses in *dim sum* and Chinese fire pot. Classes or guest-chef lecture demonstrations for groups can be arranged by request.

JOANNE HUSH'S KITCHEN
The Green Farms Store
1254 Post Road East
Westport, Connecticut 06880
Tel. (203) 227-4152

Joanne Hush, co-author of *The Chinese Menu Cookbook*, teaches a three-part series of full participation classes four times a year. She also gives one-day workshops throughout the year. Her classes are lim-

Constance Quan

ited to fifteen people so everyone can join in and really learn by doing. That means you get to chop vegetables and dice chicken with four partners at one of the round work tables. Later, you will learn to handle the wok and steamer. At the end of each class you grade yourself by eating the results of your labors. This course is set up for beginners, as is the *Menu Cookbook*. Classes are on Saturdays so as not to conflict with work schedules.

The Green Farms Store, where the classes meet, has a large selection of Chinese cooking utensils as well as ingredients for Chinese cooking. And feature this: you can arrange for a Chinese cooking class/party/banquet at the Kitchen. Now *that* sounds like fun, especially with the expert there to supervise if it turns into more party than class.

THE CHINESE COOKING SCHOOL OF ATLANTA
1725 Merton Road N.E.
Atlanta, Georgia 30306
Tel. (404) 876-1177

Mrs. Deen Terry runs this cooking school in Atlanta and she has some pretty definite ideas about how to teach Chinese cooking. She states emphatically that she teaches *methods*, not recipes. She concentrates on the five major methods—stir-fry, steaming, deep-frying, red cooking and white cooking. And the students do their share of concentrating, too, inasmuch as classes are 99% participation and four hours long. Because classes are limited to six students, everyone has extended contact with the teacher.

As of this writing, Mrs. Terry only has time for introductory-level classes, either over the lunch or supper hours. (She says that the supper-hour classes don't take as long as the noontime ones because everyone is hungry in the evening.) For each class, students prepare, cook and eat a Chinese home-style meal under Mrs. Terry's supervision. Classes run in series of five and there may be two or even three

On right, Huang Su-Huie on television series.

Deen Terry

per week. Students will not see much in the line of red meat, sugar or animal fat because Mrs. Terry thinks our intake of these ingredients is much too high.

And there are some sidelights to Mrs. Terry's classes, too. Each class usually includes a smattering of the artistic and cultural background of China as it relates to food. Another interesting feature is that every other Saturday Mrs. Terry leads a tour of the Asian Supermarket, probably the largest store of its kind in the southeast.

Chu-Yen and Pansy Luke

ORIENTAL FOOD MARKET AND COOKING SCHOOL
2801 W. Howard St.
Chicago, Illinois 60645
Tel. (312) 274-2826

Chu-Yen and Pansy Luke preside over this Chicago food emporium. They offer a variety of interesting cooking classes. The courses run for six weeks, one two-hour class per week, for a fee of around $65. Each session includes instructions, three printed recipes and a wonderful meal. The Lukes ask only that you bring a pencil and an empty stomach to each class. There are also one-shot classes given on Saturdays. These classes last for two and one-half hours and cost about $16 each. These "Saturday Specials" concentrate on one specific subject such as "Chinese Style of Cooking Tofu with No Meat or Seafood," or "Chinese Cooking with the Food Processor and Cleaver."

Incidentally, at the Oriental Food Market and Cooking School you can purchase the nifty "Lady or Man at Wok" chef's aprons.

INTERNATIONAL GOURMET CENTER ORIENTAL COOKING SCHOOL
323 Park Ave.
Baltimore, Maryland 21201
Tel. (301) 752-5501

This is the only Chinese cooking school we've run across which puts its major emphasis on principles of nutrition. This is attributable to the influence of Katherine M. Chin, the Chinese cooking instructor and a registered dietician. She has a B.A. in food and nutrition, did an internship at Johns Hopkins Hospital, and later taught normal nutrition and dietetics at the JHH School of Nursing. Ms. Chin has been teaching Chinese cooking with the focus on nutrition for thirteen years. She is recognized as an authority on Chinese cooking in the Baltimore area and has made numerous media appearances.

Classes are on Mondays, Tuesdays, and Wednesdays, one two-hour session a week for either three or six weeks. The fee is $40 and $80 respectively. It's lecture and student participation in preparing a complete Chinese meal. All ingredients are included in the fee. Lecture topics include geographical areas of China as related to regional cooking, nutritive values of the foods used, cutting and preparing of vegetables, explanation of ingredients and cooking techniques, menu planning, serving and eating.

THE CHINESE COOKERY, INC.
1049-R Rockville Pike
P. O. Box 2042
Rockville, Maryland 20852
Tel. (301) 340-0995

Ever notice that sometimes you have no idea what a particular entry on a Chinese menu really is? "Eight jewels chicken, Yu-xiang chicken, Assorted three shreds," are some of the dishes you can learn how to cook—and find out what's in them—at Joan Shih Carducci's The Chinese Cookery in Rockville, a northwest suburb of Washington, D.C. Actually Ms. Shih offers cooking classes at six levels: basic and advanced, gourmet I and II, special demo (at this stage you're in a position to show off for guests), and Sichuan. She hands out printed recipes and you do some sampling before you leave each two-hour session. One class per week, five weeks, $53. Morning or evening. Not bad, though classes may have up to 15 students—which could tend to leave a reticent rookie cook holding a spare steamer rather than participating.

Ms. Shih also offers a complete line of Oriental cooking utensils, cookbooks and groceries.

A teacher is known by his or her students, sometimes, and in this regard Ms. Shih has registered an impressive achievement. She directed her students' catering for the Peking Opera Company—74 people—who were performing at the Kennedy Center in Washington. She and her students prepared three meals a day for two weeks, apparently with great success, according to a long article in the *Washington Post*. If it's good enough for Chinese actors and singers, it's probably good enough for us.

Jeanne Tahnk

JEANNE TAHNK'S GOURMET KITCHEN INC.
910 Main St. (Rte. 38)
Winchester, Massachusetts
Tel. (617) 729-8027

The Gourmet Kitchen really sounds great for those aspiring to master Chinese cookery. It offers five-week courses at a number of levels depending on the student's interest and ability. The courses are in series, last five weeks, one two-hour session per week. In Chinese I, the beginner learns how to cook vegetables, how to use and care for cooking utensils and how to make a number of fairly simple dishes. By Chinese V, you'll be wowing your family or guests with shark fin soup and lobster Cantonese style. There are also two courses each in Sichuan cuisine and Chinese appetizers, or *dim sum.* This might be the largest variety of offerings of any school in this catalog.

Classes consist of both demonstration and participation. Recipes are provided to students at class time, and dishes prepared in the class are served to students at the end of each lesson. The five-week classes are $80 and meet on the same day of the week. Finally, there is a comprehensive one-week program for out-of-town students.

The Gourmet Kitchen also offers a catering service and has a range of Chinese cooking utensils for sale.

KAREN LEE
CHINESE COOKING CLASSES
AND CATERING
142 West End Ave.
New York, NY 10023
(212) 787-2227

Karen Lee, author of *Chinese Cooking for the American Kitchen,* tries to leave no stone unturned in teaching Chinese cooking. Her primary concern is that students master the necessary basic techniques: handling the cleaver, chopping, shredding, slicing, mincing, roll-oblique cutting, stir-frying, deep-frying and steaming. The idea is that with this background a graduate of her course will have confidence to open a Chinese cookbook and try a totally unfamiliar recipe.

Another feature of her courses is a tour through Chinatown. She recommends markets which stock all the items necessary for successful Chinese cooking in the home and holds forth on how to substitute fresh American vegetables for their Chinese counterparts.

Classes include basic, intermediate and advanced levels. In both the basic and

Basic Class Menu
First Class
Home Style Egg Drop Soup
Braised Gingered Spareribs
Shrimp with Snow Peas
Broccoli with Oyster Sauce
White Rice

Second Class
Deep-Fried Wontons
Wonton Soup
Chicken with Bean Sauce and Nuts
Shrimp and Roast Pork Fried Rice
Spicy Dipping Sauce

Third Class
Shanghai Spring Rolls with Plum Sauce
  and Mustard
Pon Pon Chicken
Kung Pao Scallops
Fresh Pineapple and Strawberries

Fourth Class
Hot and Sour Soup
Roast Duck Lo Mein
Barbecued Roast Pork
Almond Milk

Fifth Class
Sichuan Steamed Whole Fish
Orange Spiced Duck
Barbecued Shrimp
Spicy Charcoal peppers

Sixth Class
Pearl Balls
Butterfly Shrimp
Orange Beef
Dry Sauteed String Beans

intermediate classes students learn at least 25 dishes. Reprinted at the right is a recent menu from a basic class. It looks pretty ambitious, but there's time—classes convene, day or evening, for four hours, one session a week for six weeks.

That's a total of 24 contact hours. And with a maximum class size of eight, it would be hard to avoid learning something. The price is $230 for the basic and intermediate courses. It includes the complete meals prepared during each class, served with wine. All utensils and ingredients are provided for students.

Ms. Lee has recently started up some week-long, intensive cooking courses for out-of-towners. So, if you're planning to visit New York City and would like to study with Ms. Lee, it might be a good idea to write for her out-of-towner's course schedule. These special classes are also limited to eight students. There are five four-hour sessions and the fee is $300.

MARGARET SPADER'S CHINESE COOKING SCHOOL
235 E. 50th St.
New York, NY 10022
(212) 755-2661

Margaret Spader moonlights as a teacher of Chinese cookery. By day she has a full-time job in the food product information industry. But often she returns home to teach a class limited to five students. What does she teach them? Here's a description of what goes on in the beginning class: "Comparison of Chinese/American meals in uses of food, preparation, presentation and nutrition. Taste tests acquaint students with sauces and a variety of Chinese ingredients. Practice in cutting and preparing meat, poultry, seafood and vegetable combination dishes. Students participate in family style meal at end of each session. One class period is held in Chinatown for shopping and a family style meal."

Classes are two-hour sessions, once a week for five weeks. Tuition is $125.

More Cooking Schools

Most of the cooking schools and cooking teachers listed below are members of an organization called the International Association of Cooking Schools. This list is an attempt to mention cooking schools and teachers on a nationwide basis. They are listed in alphabetical order by state and they all claim to offer some kind of instruction in Chinese cuisine. This list does not pretend to be all-inclusive. There are doubtless many other schools and teachers giving instruction in Chinese cookery, and some listed may no longer be holding classes. Most of the schools on this list offer Chinese cooking classes as part of a much larger instructional program. A good idea might be to contact the International Association of Cooking Schools, 1001 Connecticut Ave. NW, Suite 800, Washington, D.C. 20036, Tel. (202) 293-7716, and ask what kind of Chinese cooking instruction is going on in your area.

ALABAMA

Kitchen Things, Inc.
2916 Linden Ave.
Birmingham, AL 35209
Tel. (205) 871-8785

ARIZONA

The Tasting Spoon
2559 East Ft. Lowell Rd.
Tuscon, AZ 85716
Tel. (602) 327-8174

CALIFORNIA

Martin M. Yan
P.O. Box 833
Davis, CA 96517
Tel. (916) 758-0451

Creative Cuisinieres
Frazier Farms Cooking School
P.O. Box 1247
Escondido, CA 92025
Tel. (714) 747-6877

Eileen Gillespie
2024 Janson Glen
Escondido, CA 92026
Tel. (714) 741-9143

Ruth G. Smith
102 Navarre
Irvine, CA 92715
Tel. (714) 559-1836

Sarah Williamson
Something More
6122 Lake Murray Blvd.
La Mesa, CA 92041
Tel. (714) 462-4440

Josephine A. Gatan Cooking School
2030 Fairburn Ave.
Los Angeles, CA 90025
Tel. (213) 474-3600

Lesands Articles de Cuisine
1139 Chestnut St.
Menlo Park, CA 94025
Tel. (415) 325-1712

Phyllis Ann Marshall Cooking School
5506 La Colline
Orange, CA 92667
Tel. (714) 637-6063

Good Cooks & Co.
321 Stanford Shopping Ctr.
Palo Alto, CA 94304
Tel. (415) 326-4952

Inner Gourmet Cooking School
484 Bellefontaine St.
Pasadena, CA 91105
Tel. (213) 441-2075

Fran Jenkins
Box 318
Rancho Santa Fe, CA 92067
Tel. (714) 756-2785

William Glen Cooking School
2651 El Paseo Lane
Town & Country Village
Sacramento, CA 95821
Tel. (916) 483-2935

The Perfect Pan
4901 Morena Blvd.
Suite 809
San Diego, CA 92117
Tel. (714) 274-7131

Cantonese Gourmet Cooking School
1715 Clement Street
San Francisco, CA 94121
Tel. (415) 221-5804

Tante Marie's Cooking School
271 Francisco Street
San Francisco, CA 94133
Tel. (415) 771-8667

Le Cordon Rouge
1020 C Street
San Rafael, CA 94901
Tel. (415) 459-2026

Rachel Cronin
Montana Mercantile
1324 Montana Ave.
Santa Monica, CA 90403
Tel. (213) 451-0401

Mitzie Cutler
13624 Ventura Blvd.
Sherman Oaks, CA 91423
Tel. (213) 995-0568

Karen J. Berk
19064 Wells Drive
Tarzana, CA 91356
Tel. (213) 344-6496

Marlene Sorosky's Cooking School
18440 Burbank Blvd.
Tarzana, CA 91356
Tel. (213) 345-4003

What's Cooking
24572 Hawthorne Blvd.
Torrance, CA 90505
Tel. (213) 373-1773

CONNECTICUT

Cooks Corner, Inc.
70 E. Putnam Ave.
Greenwich, CT 06830
Tel. (203) 869-2653

The Culinary Arts
Gateway Shopping Center
Wilton, CT 06897
Tel. (203) 637-7575

DELAWARE

Patricia Tabibian
2018 Gravers Lane
Wilmington, DE 19810
Tel. (302) 475-4564

DISTRICT OF COLUMBIA

Chez Wok
1015 Wisconsin Ave. NW
Washington, D.C. 20007
Tel. (202) 333-9220

FLORIDA

Deborah Carrow
2231 Belleair Rd.
Clearwater, FL 33516
Tel. (813) 536-3723

Peggy M. O'Donnell
Rt. 1, Box 208F
Land O'Lakes, FL 33539
(813) 996-4380

Bobbi & Carole's Cooking School
7251 SW 57th Court
Miami, FL 33143
Tel. (305) 667-5957

Pot 'n' Pan Tree
213 Esplanade
150 Worth Avenue
Palm Beach, FL 33480
Tel. (305) 655-0905

Claire A. Moderelli
11502 Carrolwood Drive
Tampa, FL 33618
Tel. (813) 932-2380

Dorothy Sims
6161 N. Memorial Hwy. Apt. 611
Tampa, FL 33615
Tel. (813) 885-5330

GEORGIA

Shirley O. Corriher
3152 Andrew Dr. NW
Atlanta, GA 30305
Tel. (404) 233-0923

Ursula's Cooking School
1764 Cheshire Bridge Rd. NE
Atlanta, GA 30324
Tel. (404) 876-7463

ILLINOIS

The Complete Cook
405 Lake Cook Plaza
Deerfield, IL 60015

Barbara Pisik
539 Susan Lane
Deerfield, IL 60015
Tel. (312) 945-5311

The Persimmon Tree
127 S. Third Street
Geneva, IL 60134
Tel. (312) 232-6446

Patty Godfrey
318 East Prospect Ave.
Ottawa, IL 61350
Tel. (815) 433-1234

The Proper Pan
Metro Centre
4620 N. University
Peoria, IL 61614
Tel. (309) 692-6382

INDIANA

The Clay Kitchen
4213 Grape Rd.
Mishawaka, IN 46544
Tel. (219) 277-2006

KANSAS

The Back Burner
6964 W. 105th St.
Overland Park, KS 66212
Tel. (913) 642-3553

KENTUCKY

Helen L. Lang
4110 Crestview Road
Louisville, KY 40207
Tel. (502) 893-5530

Lillian Marshall's School for Cooks
1431 St. James Court
Louisville, KY 40208
Tel. (502) 637-4111

LOUISIANA

Wok and Whisk, Inc.
2295 Hollydale Avenue
Baton Rouge, LA 70808
Tel. (504) 344-5511

Marilyn Farrow
P.O. Box 4111
Luling, LA 70070
Tel. (504) 785-2275

Lee Barnes Cooking School
7808 Maple St.
New Orleans, LA 70118
Tel. (504) 866-0246

MARYLAND

Sandra M. Naumann
P.O. Box 82
Accident, MD 21520
Tel. (301) 826-8376

L'Acadamie de Cuisine
5021 Wilson Lane
Bethesda, MD 20014
Tel. (301) 986-9490

Lee R. Ehudin
11401 Woodland Drive
Lutherville, MD 21093
Tel. (301) 321-8292

Sheilah Kaufman
10508 Tyler Terrace
Potomac, MD 20854
Tel. (301) 299-5282

Ginger Silvers
8609 Red Coat Lane
Potomac, MD 20854
Tel. (301) 983-1993

What's Cooking! Inc.
1776 E. Jefferson St.
Rockville, MD 20852
Tel. (301) 881-2430

NEW JERSEY

Mai Leung Classic Chinese
Cooking School
29 Fairview Ave.
Madison, NJ 07940
Tel. (201) 822-2293

East/West Cooking School
137 Sibbald Dr.
Park Ridge, NJ 07656
Tel. (201) 391-7068

Sylvia Lehrer's Cooktique
9 Railroad Ave.
Tenafly, NJ 07670
Tel. (201) 568-7990

NEW YORK

Learn-To-Wok
145 Hicks St. Apt. B10
Brooklyn Heights, NY 11201
Tel. (212) 875-7899

Rosa Ross' Wok on Wheels
76 Pierrepont St.
Brooklyn Heights, NY 11201
Tel. (212) 875-5854

China Institute in America
125 East 65th St.
New York, NY 10021
Tel. (212) 744-8181

Lilah Kan's Chinese Cook Classes
884 West End Ave. Apt. 74
New York, NY 10025
Tel. (212) 749-0550

Ana Wong
c/o Society of Ethical Culture
2 West 64th St.
New York, NY 10023
Tel. (212) 874-5210

Liang's Chinese Cooking School
8 Pleasantville Rd.
Pleasantville, NY 10607
Tel. (914) 769-6611

PENNSYLVANIA

The Classic Cook Ltd.
440 S. Main St.
Pittsburgh, PA 15220

TEXAS

The Happy Wok
1614 Preston Ave.
Austin, TX 78703
Tel. (512) 478-4808

Cooks That Teach

Listed below are ten expert Chinese cooks who, though they may teach from time to time in various cooking schools, are best known as teaching cooks rather than as cooking school teachers. These folks are often on the road spreading their culinary knowhow near and far. Most have written cookbooks, but all approach Chinese cuisine with a distinctively individual reverence. It would be a very valuable experience to attend classes or demonstrations given by any of these very special cooks.

FLORA CHANG'S
CREATIVE CHINESE COOKING MADE EASY

ONE MARINADE GOES ON FOREVER AND EVER AND EVER...

	METHOD	* INTERCHANGEABLE INGREDIENTS	DISH

CHICKEN + BASIC MARINADE

STIR-FRIED — cashew → Cashew chicken
STIR-FRIED — special sauce → Kung Pao chicken

STEAMED — green onion → Cantonese style steamed chicken
STEAMED — special sauce → Steamed chicken in black bean sauce

BRAISED — mushrooms → Braised chicken with mushrooms
BRAISED — special sauce → Chicken wings in oyster sauce

DEEP-FRIED — ginger → Paper wrapped chicken
DEEP-FRIED — special sauce → Lemon chicken

*The particular ingredients, marinades and sauces in each recipe should be regarded as suggestions. Use whatever combination that appeals to you, and experiment with the cooking methods to create original dishes of your own.

GOLDEN PACIFIC ENTERPRISES
P.O. Box 510
Reseda, CA 91335

FLORA CHANG
P.O. Box 510
Reseda, California 91406
Tel. (213) 343-2823

Flora Chang's calling cards could easily say, "Have wok, will travel," because she demonstrates Chinese cooking in many places, responding to requests. Time and distance are the two main factors she considers in her fee.

Chang takes a structured approach in teaching Chinese cooking. Sauce and marinade ingredients for each recipe are grouped separately, and the student is encouraged to switch them from dish to dish. Take, for example, chicken. It can be cooked by four methods—stir-frying, steaming, braising or deep-frying. By adding one of four different sauces which are interchangeable, the student can create sixteen different dishes. By the addition of certain groups of vegetables, fruits and nuts, which are also interchangeable, the student already has over one hundred recipes. The combination is up to the student and it is he or she who creates the recipe.

Another area of emphasis in Chang's traveling school is the ease with which Chinese cookery can be adapted to the modern kitchen. Many of her dishes can be made ahead of time and frozen. These ideas and more are detailed in her book, *Creative Chinese Cooking Made Easy.*

KEN HOM
P.O. Box 4303
Berkeley, California 94704
Tel. (415) 842-5579

Ken Hom, according to Craig Claiborne in the New York *Times,* is "one of the best-known Chinese cooking school teachers on the West Coast." Certainly, with his latest book, *Chinese Technique,* his nationwide personal appearances (22 cities in 1981), and his classes in the U.S. and Hong Kong, he might just be on his way to becoming one of the first "superstars" of Chinese cookery.

A sort of missionary zeal pervades Ken's enthusiasm for Chinese cuisine.

"It's the perfect food for our generation. It requires very little energy in its preparation; it's healthy and low calorie, and all of the ingredients are fresh or preserved naturally without chemicals. Chinese cuisine is the original fast food, perfect for busy people who still like to eat well." No doubt Ken's attitude has had something to do with his success in teaching Chinese cooking.

Ken has taught at the California Culinary Academy in San Francisco, a school for professional chefs, and at La Cuisine in San Francisco. And he conducts professional seminars twice a year at home in Berkeley. Quite recently, Ken has begun a culinary tour of Hong Kong. (See Travel section for more info.) It includes seven action-packed days, learning about Chinese food from a real pro, and staying in one of the world's most exciting cities. Check it out.

Watch for Ken in your city, or you might even want to take the initiative and inquire about setting up a personal appearance and/or cooking class yourself. Ken Hom's Chinese cooking classes are a good way to promote a new cooking school opening or other Chinese "event." Contact him at the address above.

HONG SISTERS
6126 N. Pershing Ave.
Stockton, California 95207

These Chinese-American sisters, natives of Stockton, California, are the authors of an innovative idea about Chinese cooking. They have adapted authentic Chinese recipes (their mother's) for preparation in the microwave oven. Their cookbook, *The Hong Sisters Microwave to the Orient,* explains the basic idea. But, the Hong sisters also teach microwave Chinese cooking in Stockton and "on the road." Since both Hong sisters have full-time occupations other than teaching cooking, they usually try to schedule their classes during the summer. Anyone really "into microwave" can learn a lot from the Hongs.

JOYCE JUE
262 Corbet Ave.
San Francisco, California 94114
Tel. (415) 863-7881

Joyce Jue has been teaching in the Bay Area since 1975. She teaches regularly at schools such as Tante Macrie's (San Francisco), Le Cordon Rouge (San Rafael), Peck's (Burlingame) and Good Cooks and Company (Stanford), as well as outside the Bay Area as a guest teacher.

She also teaches at home, and will conduct classes in private kitchens by special arrangement. In addition to teaching, she organizes cooking workshops, leads shopping tours through San Francisco's Chinatown, consults and caters (for small, special occasions).

Ken Hom

Joyce's approach is very technique-oriented. She stresses Stir-frying, steaming, roasting, and the other techniques, and also concentrates on designing meals and dishes to reflect a correct balance of taste, texture, and color. Her range is from true Cantonese home cooking to Mandarin banquet dishes and regional specialties.

Joyce's schooling in Chinese cooking began in the most demanding situation—her mother's kitchen—and continued with classes in Hong Kong and the constant challenge of perfecting her own classes.

RUTH LAW
P.O. Box 323
Hinsdale, Illinois 60521
Tel. (312) 986-1595

Ruth Law owns an outfit called "What's Cooking," which is located just outside of Chicago in the suburban town of Hinsdale, Illinois. Ruth has studied Chinese cuisine with master chefs in Shanghai, Canton, and Sichuan Province, at the Wei-Chuan Cooking School in Taipei, and with internationally famous Lucy Lo in Hong Kong. She holds most of her classes in the Chicago area, but she is

available for wok demo's and conducts a very informative slide show called "Tastes of China," which gives a personal view of many aspects of cuisine in China.

FRANCES NEEL
Route 1, box 84
White, Georgia 30184
Tel. (404) 382-5659

Most people interested in learning the art of Chinese cookery, with emphasis on Mandarin and Sichuan dishes, would probably not look to the little town of White, Georgia, for inspiration. It would be a mistake not to, though, because White, Georgia (forty miles north of Atlanta on I-75) is where Frances Neel makes her home.

Mrs. Neel has studied Chinese cooking extensively with the likes of Grace Chu at the Good Cooks Cooking School and Ging Young Ching, chef at Atlanta's Forbidden City restaurant. Most of her classes are organized by would-be students who are from the local area or who make the forty-five minute drive from Atlanta. Mrs. Neel does, however, teach in Atlanta from time to time and will, in fact, travel up to 150 miles from her home if requested.

NINA SIMONDS
P. O. Box 363
Manchester, Massachusetts 01944
Tel. (617) 526-1358

It was quite a shock to call Nina Simonds and encounter a recording in Chinese that said to leave a message at the "beeb." Later, when we asked how people who don't speak Chinese normally reacted, she laughed and allowed as how most of them figure out what they're supposed to do. She went on to say that the biggest problem is that word gets around and people call for the novelty of it.

Ms. Simonds writes for *Gourmet* magazine and teaches Chinese cooking. Most of her regular teaching is done in conjunction with the continuing education program at Salem State College near her home in Massachusetts. But two or three times a year she packs up and tours around the country, giving demonstrations and teaching short courses in cooking schools.

Certainly the most interesting thing Ms. Simonds has done recently was to lead a tour of "serious students of Chinese cuisine"* to Taipei and Hong Kong. Her group attended classes at Taiwan's foremost cooking school, enjoyed nightly banquets, and saw a good deal of both cities. Having lived in Taipei for some years and taken cooking classes there, Ms. Simonds is uniquely qualified to lead such an expedition and hopes to be able to do it again in subsequent years.

*Not to scare anyone off, but the group attended ten three-hour cooking classes; if you're along just for the sights and eats, the classes could turn into a grind.

Frances Neel

CHINGWAN TCHENG'S CHINESE COOKING
40 Sixth St.
Cresskill, New Jersey 07626
Tel. (201) 567-5310

Mrs. Tcheng grew up in a milieu of gourmets to whom good cooking was an art, a hobby and a source of enjoyment. She learned cooking mostly from experts among relatives and friends from different regions of China. She has also studied at the China Institute of America in New York City with Florence Lin. Mrs. Tcheng has over ten years' experience teaching both in schools and at home. Her teaching emphasizes technique and refinement of the finished product to make it pleasing to the eye. The menus in her classes cover the best dishes from all regions of China.

Currently Mrs. Tcheng only accepts teaching assignments in schools or demonstrations. Her home teaching is limited to private lessons by appointment, four people maximum. Cresskill is just north of Tenafly, about 15 minutes from the George Washington Bridge.

BARABARA TROPP
2142 Filbert
San Francisco, California 94123
Tel. (415) 922-4789

Barbara recently finished a cookbook entitled *The Modern Art of Chinese Cooking*. It emphasizes use of the food processor in Chinese cookery, but also includes a wonderful chapter on desserts and an interesting chapter on serving wine with Chinese food. Barbara has conducted demonstration classes at Le Cordon Rouge in San Rafael, California, but also arranges specially tailored participation, demonstration or even private classes for beginners through professionals.

IRENE WONG
2215 Alta Vista Ave.
Austin, TX 78704
Tel. (512) 441-5986

Irene Wong describes her Great Asia Cooking School as a "traveling" one. She basically works out of Austin, Texas, holding classes in gourmet shops, department stores and at the University of Texas. But, Ms. Wong also travels throughout Texas and the southwest teaching and demonstrating on a contract basis. Her specialty is steam cooking, which is also the subject of her cookbook, *Great Asia Steambook*.

Irene Wong

Now You're Cooking!

If the previous sections have helped you find (or grow) your Chinese groceries, and led you to enroll in a Chinese cooking class, you should be cooking by now. And, sooner or later, you're going to want to invest in one or more Chinese cookbooks. In order to help you choose, the next few pages are devoted to reviews of a cross-section of cookbooks about Chinese cuisine. Of course, many more are available, and you may want to begin your cookbook search at the library. There, you will probably be surprised by the number and diversity of the Chinese cookbooks that have been written. Check out one or two that appeal to you and try at least one recipe from each. if you're happy with the results, if you find the recipes easy to follow and clearly written, and if you find other things in the cookbook that you like (photos, method or ingredient info), it's probably worth purchasing. Unfortunately, not all of the cookbooks you'll find in the library are still in print. The trick is to find one you like that is also currently available at the bookstores.

The group of books presented here are all available. They are either relatively new or are still being reprinted. They represent the variety of books about Chinese cookery that is currently in vogue, and all of them meet with certain standards of quality that should be expected in any good cooking manual. You might find that one of the cookbooks listed here suits you perfectly. But remember that there are many, many more available and sometimes half of the fun is looking for just the right one.

THE ART OF CHINESE COOKING
Benedictine Sisters of Peking
Charles E. Tuttle Co.
94 pp. $5.95

This little book is probably unique among those listed here. Two Benedictine sisters spent about 20 years in China as missionaries, leaving for Japan by way of Taiwan only when a victory by the Communists became certain in 1949. Hard pressed in Tokyo, they established a cooking school. To their subject they brought both professional background in teaching cooking in the U.S. and long association with their Chinese cook, Ta Shih Fu. From a reading of the book there is no indication of how their cooking school fared subsequently, but their book acquired a life of its own—the forty-third printing was done in 1980.

This book is included for a couple of reasons. One, the recipes are for northern-style cooking, though there are no recipes for mutton or any dishes that include marinated meat—supposedly a northern characteristic. The other thing is that the book is a bit of a curiosity, a period piece. A wok is called a "coolie hat pan" and fresh ginger root is to be obtained by planting it in your garden or flower pot. One salient "trick of the trade," as the sisters put it, is, "Before starting to cook, read each recipe three times." This is indispensable advice when talking about a mode of cooking wherein sometimes 90% of the cook's time involves readying the ingredients for cooking. What if you forgot to plant the ginger?

There is no discussion of methods or techniques, only a brief introduction to ingredients and then about 70 recipes grouped by major ingredient. To appease the western palate, the sisters have concocted some western-type desserts that apparently go well with Chinese food.

If this book has any value in a time when Chinese cookbooks are increasingly sophisticated, it lies in the recipes themselves. They appear to be very simple. But if you have had no experience in Chinese cooking, best first to find a book that will give some clue as to what's going on in terms of technique and methods.

CREATIVE CHINESE COOKING MADE EASY
Flora Chang
Golden Pacific Enterprises
145 pp. $6.95

This is one book you certainly should not judge by its cover. Its unpretentious cover and spiral binding may lead you to assume that it's another low-budget affair put out by a somewhat less-than-professional cook. Not so. *Made Easy* has lots of information that is well organized and clearly presented. It has brief explanations of cutting and cooking techniques, utensils and ingredients, plus about 125 recipes. The recipes are based on Flora Chang's "system," the linchpin of which is the interchangeability of ingredients with certain sauces and marinades. This system appears to be unique and it should point the venturesome cook in the directions of creativity and discovery.

HOW TO COOK AND EAT IN CHINESE
Buwei Yang Chao
Vintage Books Edition 1972
249 pp. $3.95

This is one of the old timers among Chinese cookbooks in the U.S. Originally published in 1945, the third edition came out in 1963, the paperback version only in 1972. Its age shows—there is no mention of food processors, no indication of calorie consciousness, or other characteristics of new approaches and attitudes toward food. In both recipes and method of preparation Mrs. Chao shuns the fancy. As she says in the Preface to this edition, ". . . nothing fancy, but everything folksy, things for folks like you and me."

The strength of this book is its 250 recipes. They are presented in a very straightforward manner and are accurate in terms of proportions and cooking times. And there is a lot of common sense involved here. Mrs. Chao, though not making a point of paying attention to calorie counting, nevertheless is concerned with nutrition. (She was a practicing physician and therefore understands the importance of eating properly.)

Mrs. Chao is also a cultural observer. Having traveled with her husband around much of China and later in Europe and the U.S., she is aware how much Chinese eating habits differ from those of the west. For example, in her delightful Introduction, she notes that westerners are taught not to slurp soup, noodles and the like. The Chinese generally don't recognize this convention. The author says the Chinese approach is purely practical: some foods are best when they're hot, and the best technique for eating them is to draw in air over a narrow opening so as to hasten evaporation and diffuse flavor. "This is why hot soup, hot soup-noodles . . . are best sucked in with as loud a noise as possible." These kinds of observations make for interesting reading, especially in Part I, "Cooking and Eating."

If this book has a drawback, it would be lack of attention to technique. It is not a book for total beginners; on the other hand, nothing here is very fancy, so people with a little background should be able to benefit from it. In the Preface, Pearl Buck says that she thinks this is "a perfect cookbook." That's quite an endorsement. While it may be a bit overblown, it's safe to say that this is as much cookbook for your money as exists on the market.

CHINESE HOME COOKING
Julia Chih Cheng
Kodansha International Ltd.
136 pp. $7.95

Many people both in and out of China think of the Cantonese as the epicures of China. The semi-tropical climate makes available a wider array of fruits and vegetables over longer periods of each year; south China has been a relatively prosperous area over much of the recent past, producing at least a small middle class that has had time and resources to devote to food; south China has had much more foreign contact than other parts of China, which has produced a somewhat cosmopolitan atmosphere; and thousands of miles of coastline have afforded the south Chinese the possibility of adding a wide array of seafoods to their diet.

Julia Chih Cheng is a transplanted northerner now living in Hong Kong. Julia married into a large Cantonese family living in Hong Kong and spent a number of years learning the southern style. This book is the product of that experience.

All the components of a good cookbook are here—discussions of utensils, ingredients, cooking methods and menus—but they are for the most part short and not very informative. For example, the equivalent of only one page is devoted to methods. Another area which receives scant attention is menu planning—three very short paragraphs. The value of this book lies rather in the 24 pages of color photographs. The final form of each of the 100-plus recipes is "tastefully" displayed. This gives the aspiring chef something to aim at and imparts a psychological advantage to novices.

Cantonese food is the style that we find in most Chinese restaurants, so people who generally like restaurant food may like the results of these recipes as well.

These recipes also contain a larger proportion of meat than those of most of the other books listed here—again, something that may appeal to an American palate.

CHINESE COOKERY
Rose Cheng and Michele Morris
HPBooks
192 pp. $7.95

This attractive book has a lot going for it: a diverse assortment of recipes from all over China, a layout which is pleasing to the eye, and lots of color pictures. In fact, the latter alone may be worth the price of the book. Over 80 color pictures serve to give the reader an idea of the finished product, of various techniques, and the appearance of a number of ingredients. There is some interesting, though rather limited, information about Chinese customs and the four major regional styles of Chinese cooking in the early pages.

No cookbook can do it all. The major shortcoming of this book is its relative lack of attention to the mechanics of Chinese cooking, methods and techniques. Only one page is devoted to cooking methods, and then only three methods are discussed. The section on technique, "Getting Ready," is a short two pages and six photos long. That may be okay for the experienced Chinese cook, but it's probably not enough for the beginner. On the other hand, cooks at any level will find inspiration in the color photos.

Chinese Cookery is slick and well written. And it's reasonably priced. It would complement nicely another cookbook that has more information on cooking techniques.

BETTY CROCKER'S CHINESE COOKBOOK
Recipes by Leeann Chin
Random House
96 pp. $7.95

Leeann Chin is a restauranteur in a Minneapolis suburb and is the source of the recipes which appear in this book. Of course, we all know that over the years there have been a number of Betty Crockers and that the name really represents General Mills, Inc. (The various Betty Crockers have become leaner, taller and younger over the years.) The title basically means that the recipes have been tested repeatedly in the kitchens at General Mills.

This book is a reflection of this orientation—a cookbook for American Chinese food as served in many restaurants. How so? Well, for one thing, the dishes have proportionally more meat in them than do those in most other cookbooks. For another, virtually all the dishes in this book would be likely to appear on the menu of a big Chinese restaurant in this

country—nothing exotic, no specialty dishes, pretty much the standard fare. We have included this book for precisely these reasons—many Americans are accustomed to this approach to Chinese cooking, which includes the use of cornstarch, sugar and ketchup; they will prefer the kind of Chinese food produced from these recipes.

This book would probably be useful to a person just starting out in cooking Chinese food. The recipes are quite simple, many American ingredients are used, and the color pictures are helpful. There is a useful picture of about 30 ingredients, occasional illustrations of technique and some sample menus.

THE PLEASURES OF CHINESE COOKING
Grace Zia Chu
Simon and Schuster
240 pp. $4.95

"There is probably no one . . . who has done more to familiarize the public with the food (of China) than Madame Grace Chu. The ability to cook well is an inborn talent, and Madame Chu, although highborn in an age when servants were a commonplace, is possessed of the magic

involved in using the wok, the traditional cooking utensil, to the greater glory of the human palate. In person she has taught hundreds of New York men and women the joys of Chinese cuisine—and her book, simply written and easily understood, will enrich the table on a vaster scale." Thus spoke Craig Claiborne, food editor of *The New York Times* back in 1962 in the Foreword to this book. Yet, more than 20 years later, much of this book can still be of use to people interested in learning about Chinese cooking. Most of its value is in the recipes.

In terms of the phenomenal development of Chinese cooking in this country, 20 years is a couple of eons. So even though the recipes haven't changed much, the method of presentation definitely is a reflection of that early stage. For example, the book is organized by menus out of concern that Americans at that time didn't know how to combine Chinese dishes. Today many parts of this book have an almost quaint ring to them. Hence Mr. Claiborne has to make sure you understand what a wok is in the above quote.

On balance *The Pleasures* has some of the components of a good cookbook: a discussion of ingredients and some minimal attention to cleaver and wok techniques and cooking methods. On the other hand, these discussions are limited. The novice may be reluctant to start in on these recipes with no greater grasp of the process than that presented in the early pages. It's a period piece and should be used as a supplement to more descriptive cookbooks.

MADAME CHU'S CHINESE COOKING SCHOOL
Grace Zia Chu
Simon and Schuster
319 pp. $4.95

Madame Chu is probably the elder statesperson among the limited ranks of those who teach and write about Chinese cooking in this country. As of the writing of this book (nine years ago) she had taught 3,000 students over the course of 22 years. Her early book, *The Pleasures of Chinese Cooking*, continues to sell. Some of her students have themselves become experts in the field of Chinese cooking (for example, Karen Lee and Margaret Spader).

Why write another cookbook? Because, explains Madame Chu, she is now very familiar with the problems Americans face in learning how to prepare Chinese food. "Americans are far more sophisticated now than they were . . . and many, many more Chinese food products are available in their supermarkets and in an ever-growing number of Chinese specialty stores throughout the country. More advanced and interesting dishes can now be made, but new, simple dishes

are always welcome, too. This is why I feel a second volume is needed to round out the first."

The major drawback to this approach of following up the first volume is that Madame Chu now assumes more on the part of readers, devoting even less attention to the basics, techniques and methods of cooking. This is definitely not a book for beginners when it comes to actually preparing the dishes.

One section that would be of interest to people who lack background in Chinese cooking is about forty pages of questions and answers. These are questions that students have asked Madame Chu over the years. The section is more entertaining than edifying, but there's value in dealing with some of the stereotypes that many Americans harbor about the Chinese and their food. And some of it is just plain useless information that's fun to know. One questioner wants to know if there's any truth to the cliché that one becomes hungry an hour after eating Chinese food? (possibly, and if so it's because the Chinese generally eat much more rice with their food). Are fortune cookies really Chinese? (yes and no, seeing as how they were invented during World War I by a Chinese-American in Los Angeles). Does the use of chopsticks for eating help in enjoying Chinese food? (tough call, but basically yes *if* one can master the technique). And so on.

Buy this book if you already have a cookbook or two and want to expand your access to a wider range of recipes. If you are just starting out, best to stick to a book which will afford you a more systematic approach.

HENRY CHUNG'S HUNAN STYLE CHINESE COOKBOOK
Henry W. S. Chung
Harmony Books
145 pp. $10

Henry Chung is a restauranteur in San Francisco whose food has attracted a lot of attention because, apparently, it is very good. Tony Hiss of *The New Yorker* calls it, "the best Chinese restaurant in the world," and in 1977 the mayor of San Francisco issued a proclamation saluting Henry and his wife Diana on the third anniversary of the opening of their restaurant. Later in his introduction Hiss mentions a man from the New York *Times* who rated the Chung restaurant as the very best of the 2,000-odd Chinese restaurants in San Francisco. It doesn't say how many meals he ate in each one to arrive at his opinion.

Mr. Chung makes clear from the outset that the food of Hunan is plentiful and hot. Plentiful because the soil is good, the climate favorable and the people hardworking. Hot because Hunan is far from salt-producing areas and the hotness fills some of the flavor gaps left by lack of salt,

because the weather is hot and humid and eating hot food promotes sweating, and because such spices stimulate the appetite. (This doesn't explain why some areas of the world with these same characterics don't favor hot food, but it's worth thinking about.) But the real message in Mr. Chung's "First Words" is that he absolutely loves his native food. The enthusiasm is infectious.

The 75 recipes in this book do not appear to be very different from those found in many cookbooks, although a high percentage of them calls for hot spices and condiments such as fermented black bean sauce, hot dried red peppers, fresh hot green peppers, and hot pepper oil, plus the old reliables of Chinese cooking, ginger and garlic. The other major difference is that most of the recipes call for deep frying the main meat ingredient before combining it with the other ingredients. This is not a weight watcher's cookbook.

The attractive aspect of Mr. Chung's work is the cultural slant that goes along with it. You will read about his grandmother and the great influence she had over his childhood; about the legendary exploits of Fairy Chow, whose prediction of a major fire enabled Henry to leave Hunan's capital, Changsha, before the disaster; of Chinese geomancy, Chinese weddings, Chinese attitudes regarding the proper times to have sex and the dos and don'ts of pregnancy. We're hard pressed to tell you what these things have to do with Hunan cookery, but they do add to the book by providing peepholes into random facets of life in Hunan. They make this a personal book. Indeed, the title is very appropriate.

THE GOOD FOOD OF SZECHWAN
Robert A. Delfs
Kodansha International Ltd.
124 pp. $9.95

The subtitle of this book is "Down-to-Earth Chinese Cooking." Mr. Delfs gives us 80 standard recipes that are rather simple and do not require much time for preparation. But don't be fooled—the author has provided plenty of background information on ingredients and utensils as well as the food itself. And it appears that he's done his homework, having "consulted with profit" books in both Japanese and Chinese. The book is an outgrowth of his experiences eating and cooking Sichuanese food almost exclusively during a year in Taipei in 1970.

Sichuanese cookery has enjoyed a vogue in the U.S. in the past few years and continues to be very popular. One reason is that the basic ingredients are somewhat familiar to Americans, unlike the more exotic foodstuffs used in Canton, for example. No doubt another reason is that some like it hot. Probably the most obvi-

ous feature of this food is the liberal use of red peppers, fresh ginger, garlic, and the so-called Sichuan pepper, reddish-brown peppercorns that smell a little like pine. Although not all Sichuanese food is hot, most Americans think of it in those terms.

Before talking recipes, Mr. Delfs takes us through an interesting introduction to the flavors and cooking methods. The flavors include sour, hot, sesame/peppery, bitter, sweet, fragrant and salty. It is important to understand the methods because their names incorporate the type and strength of flavoring to be used. Next is a section on ingredients which includes suggestions on how to store them and for how long. The following sections on utensils and methods are sufficient but not very detailed. A short section on serving suggestions is helpful, pointing out the pros and cons of serving hot food and how to balance out the hot foods with not-so-hot ones. Perhaps the best piece of advice here is that beer goes very well with Sichuan-style meals. Tea is fine before or after the meal, but beer is the thing during those moments of truth.

REGIONAL COOKING OF CHINA
Margaret Gin and Alfred Castle
101 Productions
192 pp. $4.95 paper

Mr. Castle sets the tone of this book in the first section, "Discovering China": ". . . the world of imperial palaces, expensive restaurants and professional chefs is far removed from ordinary home kitchens and dining rooms. It is the excellence that has long existed in less pretentious surroundings that deserves discovering." He goes on to say, "The new interest in everything Chinese may have been triggered by the recent recognition of world leaders that China, after all, is part of the planet earth." But he suggests another

reason as well: "People of the western world are finding their food and energy supplies are not without limit and are seeking new ways to solve population, food and energy problems without sacrificing the 'good life.' They know the Chinese people have lived with shortages for centuries and somehow survived. In investigating how this was possible, many find that hidden treasures lie in the regional foods prepared in tiny Chinese kitchens. Using little meat, a wide variety of inexpensive ingredients are turned into real delicacies over small fires consuming very little energy."

Indeed, economy and ease of preparation seem to characterize the 243 recipes in this book. They are Ms. Gin's department. She has chosen recipes from all over China, arranged according to the main ingredient. Within each category she has attempted to represent the major traditional methods of cooking. The result is a kind of "sampler"—a tad of this and a smidgen of that.

The book's only drawback is that it doesn't pay any attention to technique. On the positive side, it is attractively illustrated and has some interesting and insightful information about Chinese history and culture. There is a useful glossary of ingredients at the back. Finally, the price is very right, averaging out to less than 2¢ per recipe. Highly recommended to anyone who has a grasp of fundamental techniques.

THE COOKING OF CHINA
Emily Hahn and the Editors of
Time-Life Books
Time-Life Books
206 and 120 pp. $12.95

This is actually two books, one a large cloth-bound book, the other a smaller spiral-bound containing only recipes. Why didn't they put it all in one book? Everybody else does. But it makes much more sense—the little book stays in the kitchen and the big one should stay by the easy chair or the bedside, even on the coffee table. It's a monumental piece that should be savored slowly and it deserves to be displayed in a place where guests can enjoy it.

In a way, the large book is more a literary piece than a cookbook. A culture is on display and we just happen to be viewing it through the prism of its food. The book is well thought out and organized, but its information is hardly put forward in a mechanical or compartmentalized way; rather, the presentation flows . . . some background here, a quote from an ancient book there, a vignette, a painting, a poem . . . all sorts of indirections ultimately leading the reader in the direction of a greater understanding of Chinese food.

The two books are the product of a joint effort by some talented people. Miss

Hahn is an engineer by profession who has lived around the world and has written several books about China and its people. The consultants were Grace Chu and Florence Lin of the widely known old guard of Chinese cooking teachers. Professional photographers were sent to China, Taiwan and Hong Kong to take the pictures. Got the drift? It was an elaborate effort and the results show. The book is highly recommended.

CHINESE TECHNIQUE
Ken Hom with Harvey Steiman
Simon & Schuster
345 pp. $17.95

The subtitle is "An Illustrated Guide to the Fundamental Techniques of Chinese Cooking." The key word is "illustrated." This book has more pictures than any other cookbook listed here—almost a thousand. Ken Hom aims to teach technique: slicing, shredding, boning, chopping and all the rest. Short of a live demonstration or a full participation class, careful attention to the photos has to be the best way to learn. In fact, the book presents as many techniques as it does recipes—over a hundred of each.

Ken says in his introduction that in order to understand the essence of Chinese cooking it is necessary to make a "cultural mental leap" to understand the material and mental conditions in China that have for so long shaped the culinary habits of that country. He points out one reason China's cuisine is unique: it developed independently of the West. In China there were almost no ovens, a chronic shortage of fuels, an insular culture (although some historians would dispute that assessment), a poor transportation network and a scarcity of arable land. These among other factors led to the development of economical means of cooking food (stir-frying), to the prominence of pork above other kinds of meat (little grazing land for cattle), and to

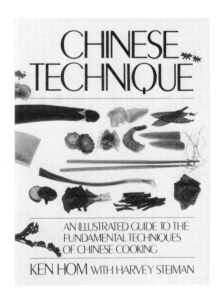

the Chinese penchant for using parts of both plants and animals that we in the West would throw away (a popular snack commonly sold by vendors in Taiwan is braised chicken claws).

Another result of these factors is that Chinese cooking is basically very simple and there is logic to the way that things are done. Tools are few and simple and therefore technique becomes all the more important.

Of course, there is more to the book than presentation of technique. There is a long section on ingredients, and the authors give further information on ingredients when they talk about individual recipes.

The bulk of *Chinese Technique* is subdivided according to the main ingredients of a dish. Headings include vegetables, chicken and other small poultry, meat, fish and seafood, rice dough and noodles, and soups. Again, these recipes are pegged to the "how to" framework. This would appear to allow maximum ease in following the directions.

Chinese Technique is very informative on the strength of the pictures alone. The organization is clear. To use a phrase from the dust jacket, the authors just might have filled in one of the "missing links" to fine Chinese cooking with their meticulous attention to technique.

THE CHINESE MENU COOKBOOK
Joanne Hush and Peter Wong
Holt, Rinehart and Winston
274 pp. $5.95

This book is so entitled because the authors feel strongly that menu planning is more important in Chinese meals than in any other kind of cooking. In western cooking a dinner is generally built around a single main dish supplemented by vegetables and salad and what have you. The quantity varies with the number of people, but usually the number of dishes doesn't change. In Chinese cooking it's the other way around—the quantity of a dish is the same, but the number of dishes changes. One major reason is the nature of stir-fry cooking itself. One just can't double or triple a stir-fry recipe and obtain the same results. From this practical limitation stems the Chinese emphasis on diversity in menu planning.

So how does the beginner plan a meal that is not only good to eat, but manageable in the kitchen and made with ingredients that can be found without unreasonable effort? This book aims to answer these questions. The authors stress balance in their menus, meaning that foods should go well together. And their recipes present combinations of dishes that don't require either too much advance preparation or last-minute fry-

ing. There is attention to structuring recipes to make preparation easier. All the recipes tell approximately how much preparation and cooking time is required. And the authors have tried to choose recipes whose ingredients can be easily found in most places in the U.S.

A lot of this information is basic, but this book is not for the novice alone. If you've done some Chinese cooking and don't need the "how to" information, the book still offers a varied selection of recipes brought together in balanced menus.

INTRODUCING CHINESE CASSEROLE COOKERY
Lilah Kan
Workman Publishing Co.
285 pp. $5.95

Most Americans assume that Chinese cookery is mostly a matter of stir-frying with an occasional bow to steaming, roasting and boiling. Casserole cooking is a new concept to most of us, but the Chinese have employed the method for many years. As Ms. Kan points out, soup or stew usually made with meat was the primary dish of ancient China—confirmed by the discovery of cookbooks found in tombs over 2,000 years old.

The recipes in this book generally call for the meat component to be braised with vegetables or simmered in a sauce. This sauce is a mixture of soy sauce, wine and spices, proportions varying with the dish. The other characteristic of this type of cooking is that the preparation time is short, the cooking time long. This is more like American-style cooking and the opposite of our notions of Chinese cooking. One advantage of this approach is that it leaves more time for attention to the dishes that must be served immediately after stir-frying. Another is with the blending of so many flavors, substitution of ingredients is possible. Indeed, the author encourages imagination on the part of the cook. The recipes are guides, not mandates carved in stone.

The most important piece of equipment in casserole cookery is the pot. Earthenware is the most authentic type, but metal or enamel pots work just as well. Often the clay pots are caged in a net of wire that helps strengthen and protect them. They are sandy-textured on the outside with a smoothly glazed interior. Contrary to what many people think, this kind of pot can be used in top-of-the-stove cooking, and the recipes in this book call for only this method. Ms. Kan feels that putting the pot in the oven is a waste of fuel.

A leading expert in Chinese cookery has a two-word endorsement for the recipes in this book: "They work." Why say any more?

THE KEY TO CHINESE COOKING
Irene Kuo
Knopf
532 pp. $16.95

What is the key to Chinese cooking? Irene Kuo says it lies in understanding the basic techniques, how and why they are used and what they will do to food. That sounds pretty straightforward, but then this remarkable book goes on to describe, clearly and in an organized fashion, the many variations on this theme. This is not just a book of recipes, but a manual from which one can learn about Chinese food and cooking.

If you're going to emphasize technique, it's important to talk about tools. So the first chapters are devoted to tools and cutting, topics that any really good cookbook should cover. Then the author takes the reader, very gradually, through a discussion of the methods of cooking and their seemingly myriad subcategories. The four succeeding chapters deal with cooking in liquid, in oil, with wet heat and with dry heat. The three categories under cooking with oil are stir-frying, shallow-frying and deep-frying. Then under deep-frying we find a discussion of cutting, marinating and coating, sauces, general rules, and some observations on deep-frying itself. Finally we arrive at a number of recipes which employ the techniques and illustrate the points just mentioned.

After a hundred pages of this we come to the Introduction to the Recipes: "Now that you are familiar with the basic techniques and have built up considerable confidence and dexterity by using the recipes in the first part of the book. . . ." Following are hundreds of recipes arranged according to their major ingredients. There is usually a description—so far as this is possible—of what a dish tastes like to assist the reader in meal planning. The author, cognizant of the "everything happens at once" tendency in Chinese cooking, goes to some lengths to point out what can be done ahead of time. In terms of the demands made upon the reader's cooking skill, there appears to be great variety among the recipes.

In the introduction Mrs. Kuo states that "If there is anything the Chinese are perpetually serious about it is food." If that is so, then she epitomizes this quality. This is a big, serious book, well thought out and well presented. The soft pencil illustrations are pleasing to the eye and the section on ingredients is very informative. All in all it's an admirable piece of work.

CHINESE COOKING FOR THE AMERICAN KITCHEN
Karen Lee
Atheneum
363 pp. $7.95

In the Author's Preface Ms. Lee states that for her Chinese cooking began as a hobby but is now a preoccupation. It shows. In the introduction, almost a hundred pages in itself, she covers everything from how to sharpen a cleaver to explaining the characteristics of individual ingredients in detail. (Who would have guessed that "deveining" is inaccurate in describing the process whereby you remove that gritty glunk from a shrimp?) Ms. Lee devotes 11 pages to cutting techniques. There is even a list of six food stores where the staples of Chinese cooking can be telephone ordered. Ms. Lee is nothing if she is not thorough.

For each of the 80 or so recipes in this book there are several suggested substitute ingredients, usually items more readily available to American cooks. Not only does this simplify things, but it also, strictly speaking, raises the number of recipes in the book to several hundred.

THE CHINESE PEOPLE'S COOKBOOK
Mai Leung
Harper and Row
236 pp. $12.95

Mai Leung has a point. Talking about the advent of a greater consciousness of real Chinese food in America, she goes on to qualify her remark by pointing out that ". . . this fine Chinese food represents only half of the rich and manifold Chinese cuisine. What people in the United States commonly learn, enjoy, and think of as everyday Chinese fare is actually substantial dinner and banquet food for formal entertaining. The other half of the Chinese culinary tradition, the colorful daily fare of the Chinese, has not been

discovered by most Westerners." How true. Many Chinese people are confirmed snackers and really don't eat the more formal dish-after-dish meals too often. Rather, they eat the kind of food talked about in this book.

What is it? Well, certainly more than "snacks," which is the most frequent translation of the term *dim sum;* and more than just noodles with their seemingly endless variety. It is all these things plus various kinds of foods from street vendors, special foods customary at certain holidays, and more. These foods are boiled, fried, steamed and braised just like the many dishes in more traditional Chinese cookbooks. And some of them are just as time consuming to make—dumplings, for example. Perhaps the main difference between these and more elaborate dishes is that the ingredients here are slightly less expensive. These are the kinds of dishes that are found near places of public entertainment and in alleys and cul-de-sacs all over China. Often they are temporary stands, erected nightly. Just as often they are established restaurants that specialize in dumplings or noodles or scallion cakes. Tourists usually can't or don't go to these kinds of eateries. Anyway, this appears to be a practical and systematic guide to the "other side" of Chinese cooking. You'll find many delightful recipes here. And in the process of discovering them, you'll gain a fuller understanding of how the Chinese eat.

THE CLASSIC CHINESE COOKBOOK
Mai Leung
Harper and Row
363 pp. $13.95

We're not sure why the word "classic" is employed in this title. Does it mean that the reciples are an array of the greatest hits in Chinese cooking? Or is it meant to contrast with something on the current Chinese cooking scene that is not

"classic"? The blurb on the dust jacket implies that this book is important because it deals with Chinese cuisine as a whole, rather than focusing on one style of regional cooking. Is this connected with "classic"? Hard to say.

It's clear, however, that Ms. Leung doesn't balk at including some relatively difficult recipes. For example, the Eight Precious Jewels Whole Winter Melon Soup probably takes longer to say than it does to eat. But on the whole it's the lists

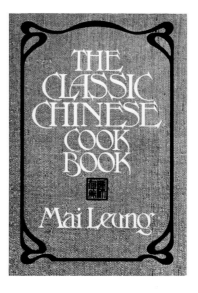

of ingredients that are long, not the steps involved with preparation. The recipes are presented systematically, i.e., they appear to be easy to follow, although there is not a great emphasis on technique. Ms. Leung obviously has gone to some lengths to make Chinese cooking comprehensible. That is certainly the first responsibility of anyone who aims to write a good cookbook.

This book has a somewhat personal air to it. Ms. Leung draws on both her personal experiences as a girl growing up in China and on the mythology that seems to explain and nourish so many aspects of traditional Chinese culture. For example, the discussion of a recipe entitled "Childbirth Ginger" affords the reader some insight into traditional attitudes surrounding the birth of boys vs. girls; the recipe for "My Mother's Lettuce Packages" is a very brief yet moving account of the influence an educated person could have in a village where most were illiterate. The author's attachment to her native culture lends warmth and sincerity to the tone of the book.

105

FLORENCE LIN'S CHINESE REGIONAL COOKBOOK
Florence Lin
Hawthorn Books
344 pp. $8.95

Florence Lin is one of the old guard among teachers of Chinese cooking in this country. She's taught at the China Institute of America in New York for about 17 years (She's still there if you're interested). This book is one of three she has written alone, and she is also a co-author of the Time-Life cookbook mentioned above. It's an impressive record. And this book is a solid part of her achievements.

Mrs. Lin is concerned that her readers learn something about China as well as Chinese cookery. How else would you explain the fact that her first chapter begins with a discussion of Chinese history, complete with a chronology of the dynasties? She goes on to a general explanation of the development of regional cooking styles. Without going into great detail she manages to convey an understanding of the four major regional cooking styles and some sensitivity to their origins. Other preliminary chapters discuss cooking methods and utensils, meal planning and preparation, and Chinese wines and teas.

The balance of the book contains 200 recipes divided into sections on poultry and eggs, meat, fish and shellfish, vegetables, soups and *dim sum*. An interesting and useful feature is the chart that precedes each section. Each dish in the section is described very briefly along with its cooking method and cooking time. A glance at these charts should facilitate meal planning.

This book is everything that a good cookbook should be, but does not attempt to specialize in any particular area of Chinese cookery. It's a good, general cookbook that can be used with benefit by most anyone.

CHINESE GASTRONOMY
Hsiang Ju Lin and Tsuifeng Lin
Jove Publications
208 pp. $4.95

Chinese scholars, unlike their western counterparts, have seldom been reluctant to write serious pieces on the joys of eating. Enjoyment of food has been a legitimate source of concern at all levels of society for at least 2,000 years, as evidenced by the *Nei ce*, or "Regulations of the Household," dating from the Han Dynasty. The Lins, mother and daughter, qualify as modern standard bearers of that comfortable tradition. *Chinese Gastronomy* is a skillful blend of knowledge of the history of Chinese cuisine and culture

with a practical understanding of the hows and whys of Chnese food.

One dictionary defines "gastronomy" as, "Good eating and its lore." In the Introduction the authors apply a more strict definition: the roots of the word mean "stomach" and "rules"—rules for the stomach. "The art of eating has always been a disciplined habit. To eat well requires a sense of fitness (taste) and an adventurous spirit." Later in the book they go on to say that ideally it is the combination of the gastronome's cultivated taste with the technical skill of his cook that leads to the development of excellent cuisine.

That's the tone of the book—the pursuit of excellence in food. At the outset the authors set forth certain criteria as standards of judgment for food. The twin goals are toward flavor and texture, the attainment of both in one dish making it a success. Flavors should blend so as to be undetectable or should complement; putting flavors together is itself an art. "It is rather like creating chords in music, harmony through precise differences." As for texture, the goal is variety. It can be a goal in itself—witness the number of ingredients in Chinese cooking, such as bird's nest or shark's fin, that have texture but no taste whatsoever.

This special approach continues on throughout the book. The authors talk about principles and generally introduce the 140 recipes by way of illustration. It's a good combination because you're learning about Chinese food while making specific dishes. And the book is well organized, especially the chart in the introduction showing how certain methods and ingredients can be used to modify both flavor and texture.

Chinese Gastronomy is a marvelous piece of work. Like the other excellent cookbooks listed here, the reader will learn about the culture and spirit of China through its food. It's a long, gentle journey for the patient reader and cook.

CHINESE REGIONAL COOKING
Kenneth Lo
Pantheon Books
278 pp. $5.95

Kenneth Lo is well known in the West as an authority on Chinese food and has written—are you ready—20 books on various aspects of Chinese cooking. His *Encyclopedia of Chinese Cooking* is a really superb book. *Regional Cooking*, while not so ambitious an undertaking, can nonetheless give you an idea of Mr. Lo's extensive knowledge of Chinese cuisine.

The author divides China into four major regions in order to organize his material. These are the four standard areas of north China, Canton, Shanghai and east China, and Sichuan. Within each section Mr. Lo arranges the recipes according to the main ingredient. The exceptions are the soup recipes which lead off the sections. Each section has about 75 recipes. The index at the back is arranged according to ingredients only. So if you're wondering about a certain dish that has snow peas, for example, that's the place to look.

One reservation about this book is that the author seems to take for granted that the reader will know something about preparation techniques and that he has some knowledge of Chinese cooking. The beginner in Chinese cookery may want more explicit directions, some "handholding." Thus, the Cantonese dish Soya Chicken in Aromatic Oil simply says, "Clean the chicken and chop it through the bones into 18-20 pieces." Well, we all know it's not quite that simple. There are many more examples. In sum, this is a good book with a wide range of recipes, but don't make it your first Chinese cookbook.

"ONE OF THE MOST INTERESTING AND INFORMATIVE BOOKS ON CHINESE COOKING"
—CRAIG CLAIBORNE

CHINESE GASTRONOMY

HSIANG JU LIN & TSUIFENG LIN

WITH A PREFACE BY LIN YUTANG

CHINESE VEGETARIAN COOKING
Kenneth H.C. Lo
Pantheon
185 pp. $4.95

In this book, Kenneth Lo's approach is to keep it simple. " . . . Chinese cooking is like riding a bicycle. Once you can mount a bicycle and stay on it, you can do almost anything with it, even if you do not fully understand the complex relation of forces between one wheel and another." So he sets out to divide Chinese cooking into its components—cutting, heating and flavoring. In Chinese cooking, cutting is determined by two variables, the type of heat being used and the shape of the principal substance to be cooked. Food to be cooked a long time requires little cutting. If the principal substance is noodles, say, then the other ingredients should be shaped in roughly the same fashion. If it's rice, then diced is nice. Mr. Lo then goes on to categorize methods of heating and flavoring. The book is divided under different methods of cooking and then subdivided into different vegetables employed, or into the different main groups of dishes being produced (soups, salads, desserts, etc.).

Mr. Lo does not aim his approach at what you might call "hard core" vegetarians. "This book is dedicated to all lovers of vegetables, but *not* to those who have taken to vegetables because they abhor meat and have to put up with vegetables by default." Thus many of the 175 recipes have a trailer paragraph "for non-vegetarians" telling the less finicky how to add meat-related items from oyster sauce to beef.

THE HONG SISTERS MICROWAVE TO THE ORIENT
Lily Hong Mow and
Mary Hong Saunders
101 pp. $6.00

In the area of Chinese cooking this may be the epitome of "east meets west." This little book seeks to apply the relatively new technology of microwave cooking to the centuries-old art of Chinese cooking. The combination will be welcomed by people who want to add another dimension to the use of their microwave ovens.

The Hong sisters, Chinese Americans, are natives of Stockton, California. Their mother taught them to employ the senses for successful Chinese cooking. Exact measurements of ingredients and cooking times were definitely not a part of the routine. After both had acquired microwave ovens, that approach had to change, and they began to follow recipes faithfully. After gaining some confidence, they began to branch out. In due course they were invited to give demonstrations of microwave application in Chinese

cooking. Observers of the demonstrations continually asked for recipes, which led the sisters to further experimentation and finally to the publication of about 70 recipes in this book.

Probably the most important section of the book is its Basic Cooking Instructions; always check food for "doneness" before the cooking time is up, let it stand for one-fourth the cooking time after coming out of the oven, vegetables can be cooked in plastic bags, etc. But this section is the book's weakness, too—there isn't enough attention paid to methods and techniques. Preparation is the key element in successful Chinese cooking, regardless of how you actually cook the food. And the relation between preparation time and cooking time in Chinese cuisine raises one basic difference between Chinese and American cooking. The Chinese are long on the first, short on the second; for western food, vice-versa. This means that the relative convenience of microwave cooking is much greater in western cooking.

This is a pioneering book and the sisters deserve credit for their work. But if you have a microwave oven, perhaps you should acquire another Chinese cookbook that pays attention to technique and method before you buy this one. Otherwise, even if you follow these recipes with great care, you will not understand *why* you are doing thus-and-such, and this might keep you from experimenting and getting maximum mileage out of your microwave Chinese cookery.

THE PEOPLE'S REPUBLIC OF CHINA COOKBOOK
Nobuko Sakamoto
Random House
288 pp. $6.95

Here we have over 200 recipes from the PRC, translated into English and thoroughly tested for application in the American kitchen. The three origins of the book are worth noting. First is *Treatise on Famous Chinese Dishes*, a series of cookbooks compiled from the results of a government request to chefs all over China to submit recipes of their specialties. These eleven books were used as textbooks in cooking classes for training chefs and their helpers. The series includes recipes from the imperial court as well as many others from virtually every corner of China. The second source is *The Cookbook of Famous Dishes from the Peking Hotel Restaurant*. For many years this restaurant has catered to movers and shakers from around the world. Third, *The Masses Cookbook* was published by the government in 1966. It introduced the "new cuisine" of China, emphasizing nutrition, economy, and ease of preparation. The author spent over a decade translating many of these recipes and adapting them to her American kitchen.

The work is big on technique, using drawings instead of photographs for illustrations. In a way the drawings work better than pictures because the reader can see, for example, through the carcass of a duck how to skewer it properly, or through the skin of a fish to see how it should be boned, or through a steam pot to see how a heat-proof bowl should be placed for the cooking of winter melon.

The recipes are divided into the four major culinary regions of China, the north, east, southeast and southwest. Each section has a preface wherein the author basically does two things. One is to outline some of the salient characteristics of the cuisine of that area. The second is to cite restaurants that provided some of the recipes. So, many of the recipes in this book have a kind of pedigree. Thus the reader knows that the pork recipes in the section for the north, for example, came from the House of Earthen Casserole in Peking, established in 1741 and famous for its earthen pot, four feet in diameter, in which pork is cooked. This sort of background gives the reader an impression of authenticity that other cookbooks often do not impart. Leafing through this book one has a feeling of careful research and attention to detail.

MRS. CHIANG'S SZECHUAN COOKBOOK
Ellen Schrecker with John Schrecker
Harper and Row
359 pp. $14.95

The recipes in this book are for the dishes that a housewife from Sichuan prepared for her family in pre-revolutionary China. Mrs. Chiang learned the recipes at home by watching her mother. Who is Mrs. Chiang? She cooked for the Schreckers for a year when they were in Taipei. (John did advanced work in Chinese language.) They had been in Taipei for a year in 1961 and on the basis of that experience had decided that the food in Chinese restaurants in America was not really authentic Chinese food. They returned to Taipei for another year's stay, and during that time they "found" Mrs. Chiang and eventually brought her to America to continue in her capacity as cook and cultural informant. This book is the happy result of that confluence of events.

Why "happy"? Because it's a very solid book that deals exclusively with an important regional cuisine of China. The Schreckers' high standards no doubt contribute to the authoritative quality of the book. They say repeatedly that their chief concern is with the *zhen wer*, the true taste of Chinese cooking. It was this concern that turned them off Chinese cooking in the U.S. and also that attracted them to Mrs. Chiang. In addition, the Schreckers obviously understand Chinese culture. Their observations enrich the book by helping the reader understand why things are done the way they are. For example, soup served at the beginning of a meal fills one up too fast, so do as the Chinese do and serve it at the end. The section on menu planning is as clear and complete a presentation of the topic as exists in any of the books listed here.

This book has a warmth and personal tone seldom found in any book, let alone a cookbook. The Schreckers have combined the skills of Mrs. Chiang with their appreciation and knowledge of Chinese food. It's a fine combination for anyone who doesn't care for bland Chinese food.

THE BOOK OF TOFU
William Shurtleff and Akiko Aoyagi
Ballantine Books
433 pp. $2.95

People avoid eating meat for a number of reasons which generally can be grouped under economic, health, ecological and spiritual headings. Meat is expensive; red meat, especially, is known to be heavy in cholesterol and large quantities can aggravate the heart-related problems; it might not be ecologically sound to derive our protein from animals; and, finally, animals have a way of being a lot more like us than plants, hence the problem of taking life is uppermost in some vegetarians' minds.

The authors of this book explore all these meat-related considerations and make a case for substituting tofu for much of the meat that we eat. They begin their presentation by showing how tofu is

a worthy replacement. Tofu is very cheap. (And, in the six years since this book was written, it has become widely available in the produce sections of American supermarkets.) It is very low in calories and saturated fats and is cholesterol-free. Soybeans produce over 33 percent more protein than any other known crop and twenty times as much usable protein as can be raised on an acre given over to beef cattle or raising their fodder. The authors claim that from the body's point of view the usable protein contained in one-half cup of soybeans is no different from that contained in five ounces of steak.

The book covers the several different types of soy-derivatives products (soy milk, fermented tofu, etc.), employing them in a total of over 250 recipes. The recipes are both western and eastern, mostly Japanese—it so happens that the authors did their research in Japan. But, of course, tofu was originally a product of China and is widely used in Chinese food. (There are an estimated 150,000 tofu shops in China.) Hence much of what the authors say is applicable to Chinese cooking. A look through virtually any of the cookbooks in this section will make that clear.

Shurtleff and Aoyagi bring an almost poetic philosophy to their task. Consider that Shurtleff, writing in the Preface, attains an almost lyrical quality in his reverence for tofu: "As our work neared its completion, both Akiko and I realized that perhaps our finest teacher had been tofu itself. Like water that flows through the worlds, serving as it moves along, tofu joyfully surrenders itself to the endless play of transformation. Pierced with a skewer, it sizzles and broils above a bed of live coals; placed in a bubbling, earthenware pot over an open fire, it snuggles down next to the mushrooms and makes friends; deep-fried in crackling oil, it emerges crisp and handsome in robes of golden brown; frozen all night in the snow under vast mountain skies, it emerges glistening with frost and utterly changed. All as if it knew there was no death to die, nor fixed or separate self to cling to, no other home than here." That's pretty heady stuff, but it's also an indication of the enthusiasm and dedication of the authors. This is a good book which deserves attention even if you're not considering giving up meat. These recipes will certainly broaden any cook's repertoire and will increase the nutritional value of his final product.

CHINESE DIET COOKBOOK
Charmaine Solomon
McGraw Hill
126 pp. $9.95

With the proliferation of books in the area of Chinese cooking, it's becoming important to adopt a "slant," a specific ap-

proach which gives the work an identity. This book has a slant and a "sub-slant": A diet book which concentrates on a specific kind of diet, low carbohydrate. Attention is given to grams of carbohydrate rather than to calories. The author says that reducing intake to about 80 grams of carbohydrate per day will lead to a weight loss of about four or five pounds a week, tapering off as you reach your weight. That's quite a claim.

The author generally tries to use standard Chinese recipes, deleting or making substitutions for ingredients that are heavy with carbohydrates. This means that you can't go back to the pot for another bowl of rice—it has about 18 grams of carbohydrate in each half bowl. And no heavy sauces, for sure. Other examples include reducing the amount of water chesnuts or almonds in a dish. The book has only a handful of deep-fry recipes.

Successful dieting is, of course, more than just the implementation of a single new approach or gimmick. The author tacitly recognizes this fact by giving some tips that will aid in the diet effort. They include using small plates or bowls; using chopsticks (because they'll slow down your rate of intake); eating only one dish at a time; and cooking no more than is needed for one meal. These are some of the many small adjustments that can contribute to the success of any diet. But regardless of your approach, the only real key is to cut down on the amount you eat. As long as that is understood, then the approaches offered by one book or another can be seen as variations on a theme. And, for Chinese food lovers at least, this particular theme might prove to be a most attractive one.

CHINESE COOKING FOR BEGINNERS
Huang Su-Huei
Wei Chuan's Cooking (dis't.)
103 pp. $5.95

CHINESE CUISINE
WEI CHUAN COOKING BOOK
Huang Su-Huei
Wei Chuan's Cooking (dis't.)
237 pp. $12.50

These books offer the epitome of authenticity in Chinese food. At least that's what Nina Simonds says, and she should know—she translated them from the original Chinese into English. They present a wide range of main dishes, 355 in *Cuisine* and about 90 in *Beginners*. Nina also says that the recipes are surprisingly easy to follow and that they work well. Assuming that's what good cookbooks are all about, these are very worthwhile books.

What does it mean to say that the recipes are authentic? Well, certainly one thing is that the range of ingredients reflects Chinese rather than American tastes. For example, one section deals with viscera, including duckling gizzards and pork stomach. In the seafoods section, we find squid, jellyfish and sea cucumbers. For venturesome types whose tastes range far afield, *Cuisine* presents a number of recipes that you simply won't find elsewhere.

The recipes in *Beginners* don't have quite the range and, generally, are easier to prepare. But don't be misled by the title—there is plenty here to interest the accomplished cook.

Both books have many color pictures, somewhere around 220 in *Cuisine* alone. If you're just starting out, try *Beginners* first before even considering the big book. Neither contains much in the line of cultural information or material on techniques and methods but the recipes are the important thing.

CHINESE SNACKS
Huang Su-Huei, ed.
Wei Chuan's Cooking
187 pp. $12.50

This could well be *the* book for Chinese snacks, what with 203 recipes, each one accompanied by a large color picture of the finished product and four smaller ones illustrating technique at various stages in the preparation. The recipes are presented systematically and appear to be relatively easy to follow.

Looking over the table of contents, you could easily wonder where "cuisine" stops and "snacks" start—so many of these dishes look like they would comprise the better part of a meal in themselves. The contents are grouped into noodle snacks, rice snacks, soups, rice, noodles, congees and processed foods. But it's not terribly easy to guess what types of dishes appear in the sections. For example, under Noodle Snacks are listed various steamed buns, fried and steamed dumplings, and cakes. Why these dishes should be grouped under noodles is not

clear. So you're probably better off looking at the individual entries in the table of contents and browsing through the book itself, looking at the pictures.

This book is a trove of ideas and could serve nicely as your standard reference in the area of *dim sum*. If you're completely new to Chinese cooking though, you may also want a cookbook that teaches the *dim sum* basics.

THE MODERN ART OF CHINESE COOKING
Barbara Tropp
William Morrow and Co., Inc.

Barbara Tropp has high standards when it comes to Chinese food. What else could you say about a person who feels that there are only four good Chinese restaurants in San Francisco? She feels strongly that most Chinese restaurants in this country belong to the "glop and goo" category, using too much cornstarch, sugar, MSG and the like. Her aim both in this book and in her classes is to introduce people to "real Chinese cooking," bringing together classic Chinese recipes and modern western kitchen tools such as the food processor.

What does "real Chinese cooking" mean? Well, partly it's technique, something largely overlooked by all but a handful of cookbooks. Another component is taste. Barbara aims at "light, sane and healthy flavors." And she puts great stress on the art of Chinese cooking. Authentic Chinese cooking means having good cooking sense, understanding the philosophy behind Chinese cuisine. Proper balance in the flavors is needed, what the Chinese refer to as yin and yang.

Finally, Barbara tries to present her readers with recipes that represent the range of Chinese cuisine. Here again she feels that only a few of the hundreds of Chinese cookbooks on the market even begin to suggest this range; the great majority simply rehash recipes that most people have seen before.

CHINESE COOKING
THE EASY WAY
WITH FOOD PROCESSORS
Dee Wang
Elsevier/Nelson Books
208 pp. $8.95

It doesn't take much culinary experience to know that a major part of Chinese cooking involves cutting, chopping, dicing, mincing, shredding, and on and on. Everything is bitesize or smaller. If you live around Chinese people, you know that often your first clue that suppertime is coming around is the low and monotonous sound of cleaver hitting cutting board. And it's not all that much fun. That's why the food processor is a significant contribution to Chinese cookery.

Dee Wang says of the food processor, "This versatile machine can take over much of the work of knife or cleaver and do many jobs in seconds that might otherwise be difficult or extremely time-consuming." Fair enough. Hence every recipe has directions for employing the food processor. This book is for busy people who want to learn how to cook Chinese food.

Mrs. Wang has put some thought into making her recipes appealing and nutritious. She has included recipes from each of the four major types of Chinese cooking. She is adamant about not using MSG; has tried to reduce the level of animal fat wherever possible; and suggests very few dairy products. Her rules of thumb are to use a maximum of four ounces of meat per serving, to cook with corn oil, and consistently to serve low-cholesterol meals.

GREAT ASIA STEAMBOOK
Irene Wong
Taylor and Ng
97 pp. $4.95

When Americans think of a Chinese meal, they tend to imagine stir-fried dishes such as sweet and sour pork or chicken with cashews. And often these dishes come with a heavy sauce. Few Americans associate steam-cooked dishes with oriental cuisine. *Great Asia Steambook, A Practical Guide to Asian Styles of Steam Cooking,* sheds some light on the possibilities of steam cooking; it is the first definitive work on the subject.

Steam cooking has many advantages, especially to weight- and nutrition-conscious Americans. It preserves the natural vitamins and flavors in foods, adds no fat, generally takes less than an hour, and saves money by consolidating all cooking above one water-covered heat source.

Ms. Wong's book has discussions on steaming equipment, steaming procedures, food preparation, recipes and menus. It contains steam cooking recipes from southeast Asia, Japan, the Philippines and Hawaii as well as China.

CHINESE VILLAGE COOKBOOK
Rhoda Yee
Yerba Buena Press
92 pp. $4.95

The author spent much of her childhood in her father's native locale, a small village in Guangdong Province near Canton. Her experiences during this period of her life are the inspiration for this book. Many of the recipes are from that area. It is this background that, selectively recounted, gives the book much of its charm. Ms. Yee talks about the village after disposing of questions about utensils in a nicely illustrated chapter. Then, very gradually, she begins to weave into her story some recipes, first breakfast menus. She goes on to talk about the local teahouse, presenting a number of recipes for *dim sum* dishes in the process. Then more narrative about being a child in a Chinese village, followed by more recipes. And so it goes. There really isn't a story line as such, but by the time you're finished you have absorbed some vivid impressions about life in a Chinese village, and may even have the feeling that you know Rhoda Yee. It's a special, very personal book.

Another attractive feature of the book is the photographs. The photographer, Spaulding Taylor, is a partner in Taylor and Ng, the San Francisco retail, wholesale and publishing firm. The pictures are utilitarian where they have to be (cutting technique), evocative (a Chinese village), and just plan frivolous (close-up

of the mug of a cow). They are a very tasteful blend and they complement the text nicely.

You will enjoy the warmth and humor in this book. It has a personality and is informative about things other than food.

DIM SUM
Rhoda Yee
Taylor and Ng
92 pp. $4.95

"Dim sum" in Chinese literally means "dot heart." A more poetic rendering would be something like "heart's delight." For the uninitiated, *dim sum* usually are bite-sized amounts of filling inside a dough wrapper which is usually deep-fried, baked or steamed. There's bound to be some sauce that goes with them. The most familiar *dim sum* to Americans is egg rolls, but in fact there are hundreds of types. Rhoda Yee has done us a great service by writing a book about them.

In traditional China, where the author spent her first 12 years, the teahouse was the place where people congregated to socialize for both business and pleasure. Long-established teahouses would have menus of several dozen items, each one by our standards more or less a "snack." Put several of them together and you have a meal. With that in mind Ms. Yee gives us eight suggested menus at the end of the recipe section. But initially your goals are going to be more modest; you'll want to try out a number of the individual recipes first.

As in Ms. Yee's other book, *Chinese Village Cookbook,* recountings of the author's childhood experiences in and impressions of China mix with the strictly food-related information. The chapter entitled "Festivals and Legends" provides a good example. Accompanying the five recipes are explanations of the origins of that *dim sum.* It's a lively mix of food and culture, one that may have you reading rather than rolling the dough.

Utensils and Methods
The Right Stuff

To cook the way the Chinese do you're going to need more than Grandma's crockery bowls and a set of Revere Ware. Of course, you can improvise here and there with western utensils, but you'll find that having authentic equipement makes a big difference in Chinese food preparation. By the same token, you will need to perfect a few special methods of food handling that are unique to Chinese cooking. Chinese cookbooks spend a good bit of time introducing the novice to special utensils and techniques. Here we've included some information that we think will be particularly valuable in making sure you've got "the right stuff."

CLEAVERS

Most writers of Chinese cookbooks advocate owning two cleavers. One, relatively thin and lightweight for slicing, light mincing and chopping, looks something like a knife, but the blade is wider and shorter. The other cleaver should be three to four inches wide and eight or more inches long. It may weigh as much as two pounds and is to be used for hard mincing and chopping. There is much more hacking, chopping and mincing in Chinese cooking than in western cooking, and the ability to use these items with facility is important.

As is the case with spatulas, most people recommend that you buy carbon steel cleavers. This means a cleaver can rust, but the metal is harder and maintains a sharper edge longer. Despite the ominous size and weight of these instruments, don't make the mistake of assuming a slightly dull cleaver is safer—this attitude can make you careless. A very sharp edge will tend to encourage you to pay attention to business.

You should have a small abrasive stone with a rough side and a smooth side for sharpening your cleavers. The rough side will do the bulk of the sharpening, the smooth side will give the blade the necessary fine honing. Remember that the cleaver should be dry when you do this and that a few drops of water or oil should be sprinkled on the rough side of the stone first.

Big as it is, the cleaver is a precision instrument. It should be gripped in slightly different ways depending on how you're using it. A slight motion like that of mincing does not require anchoring of the blade, hence you should hold your entire hand on the wooden handle. Cutting requires a lot of blade control, so slide the hand forward, squeezing the blunt top of the blade between the index finger and thumb. For chopping the hand should also be forward, but the index finger should be wrapped around the neck of the blade, allowing for both control and the increased wrist action which will generate the force to cut through bones. Experiment. The cleaver is the most used tool in a Chinese kitchen and it's best to be thoroughly familiar with it.

CHOPSTICKS

Chopsticks are the item that we most frequently associate with Chinese food. They are certainly the simplest and probably the most ingenious eating utensil devised by man. Just when the Chinese began to use them is not clear, but we have evidence of their use about 3,400 years ago. Scholars surmise that at that time most people ate with their hands and that the use of chopsticks began among the nobility, perhaps as a status symbol.

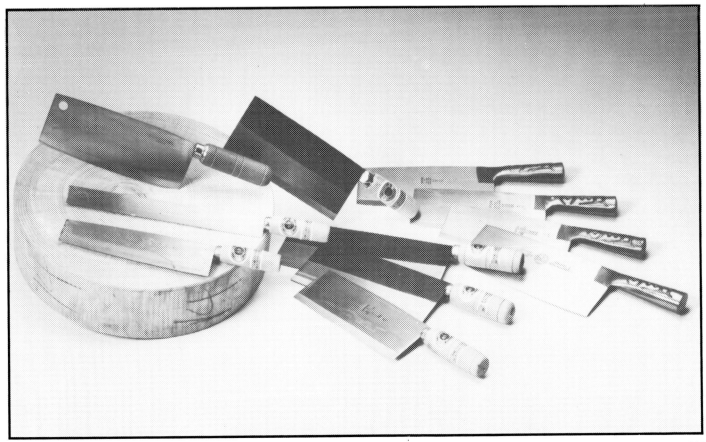

Chopsticks usually are about 10 inches long, square on the top half for more secure holding and round on the bottom. Chopsticks are made from many materials, from bamboo to precious metals. From both a practical and an economic standpoint, bamboo chopsticks are best—they are not nearly as slippery as other types and are much cheaper. Bamboo does not absorb the flavor of food. Lacquered wooden and plastic chopsticks are also available, but they tend to be a bit more slippery. Chopsticks are made of ivory, jade and silver as well, but both ivory and jade can warp and silver conducts heat—and, of course, all three types are very expensive.

HOLDING CHOPSTICKS

A lot of oldtimers will tell you that good chopstick technique is simply learned and that it is pointless to try to explain how it is done. Well, the people who learn that way are usually Chinese children between the ages of two and five and they have had ample opportunity to witness their elders using the sticks. For the rest of us a little theory probably wouldn't hurt.

Chopsticks should be held about three-fourths of the way up the stick on the square ends. The whole idea is to create a pincer movement. In order to do this, one of the sticks should be stationary, this being the bottom one. The top stick should be movable. In this way, in effect, you're creating a pair of tongs. When mastered, you'll be amazed at how simple the motion is.

First, take one stick and put the top part of it in the crook of your thumb, the bottom part resting on the inside end of your ring finger. The thumb and that ring finger should be fairly rigid throughout, but not so much that tension accumulates in the hand. This is the stationary stick against which the top one works. You make sure it's stationary by pressing the

middle of the thumb and the ring finger toward the stick. Now, simply grasp the other stick as you might a pencil, between the tip of your thumb, the tip of the index finger and the middle joint of the third finger. Don't try to pick something up at this point, rather only try to manipulate the top stick while keeping the other immobile. When the two ends are together they should form about a 30 degree angle. You'll find that you can begin to manipulate the top stick simply by varying the pressure of the middle and index fingers. Be sure that the ends of the sticks are even. Unless the two ends are flush, no amount of practice will allow you to become proficient with the sticks.

Many people wonder why all the fuss about using chopsticks. After all, the Chinese themselves often use porcelain spoons. Well, if you feel that way, perhaps it won't make any difference. But many people find that they have a psychological edge in their attitude toward eating Chinese food when they master the use of chopsticks. It's more fun and, even if you're a natural with the sticks, using them tends to establish a leisurely pace at which you consume your food.

If you've never used chopsticks, it's a good idea to practice a bit before making an attempt to use them at your next Chinese meal. Such first attempts often

fail because of the scrutiny they receive from others and because the stomach often doesn't cooperate in terms of patience. So try it at some less critical time. We suggest you try picking up peanuts. Stage one is when you can pick up a dry-roasted peanut with relative dexterity and transfer it to the mouth without mishap. Stage two is when you can do it with a peanut that has some oil on it. Stage three is when you can pick up two peanuts side by side. At this point you're destined for stardom.

Finally, it's important to make sure that the sticks are straight. Experts can deal with warped sticks, but anyone below that level is well served to make sure the sticks are in good shape.

CHOPSTICKS AND THE DISHWASHER

Only bamboo chopsticks should be washed in the dishwasher. Plastic can warp or crack in the hot water and ivory will discolor. The main problem in using the dishwasher is in making sure that the chopsticks don't fall through the racks and get into the machinery. One way to prevent the possibility is to punch holes in the bottom of a metal can, put the can in the silverware section upright and the chopsticks in the can. Another way is to lay them flat in the top section, tied together at the square end rather tightly. When in doubt, just rinse them off and then soak the food handling end in some boiling water for a few minutes.

CHOPPING BLOCK

A traditional Chinese chopping block was made of hardwood at least 15 inches in diameter and six inches thick. Though this size block is hard to find these days, don't pass up an opportunity to have a cross-section cut or to buy someone's old one—a block of this thickness will raise the level of the action, a blessing to many taller cooks who must spend a lot of time chopping.

A good chopping block is at least 12 inches square or in diameter and two inches thick. It's going to be absorbing blows from a heavy cleaver, and a thinner or smaller one is likely to slip under the pressure of sustained heavy chopping.

Be sure to clean the block with hot, soapy water and some kind of abrasive brush or pad. Whether it's a tree cross-section or a board, be sure to oil it every week or two to avoid cracking. Every month or so it is a good idea to pour salt over the wood and leave it there overnight. This will cut down on the bacteria population and help get rid of stains.

STRAINERS (SKIMMERS)

This utensil is not unique to Chinese cooking, but it's very useful. The Chinese version is in the shape of a large, shallow ladle and usually has copper mesh with a wooden handle. It is used to scoop ingredients out of hot oil or for turning them. It is also good for removing things like wontons from boiling water. Finally, it can be very useful when you suddenly decide that a sauce is not thickening properly and you want to remove the other ingredients from the wok.

SPATULAS

The Chinese spatula is about the size of its American counterpart, but it is a little heavier and the blade will not bend. The right-hand, or leading edge of this spatula should be slightly convex so as to fit the contours of your wok. A steel spatula is best because a stainless steel one will scratch your wok. But, of course, this means that you should dry it immediately after washing to prevent rust. A new spatula should be scrubbed with soapy steel wool to remove the grease.

Many Chinese use a ladle spoon in their other hand when the cooking action gets heavy. It can be used to ladle water, stock, oil or sauce out of the wok. Many woks are sold together with the ladle and spatula. Don't automatically assume, however, that these utensils are indispensable. You may find that chopsticks, because they are lighter and more maneuverable, are easier to use. In any case, the important thing is to find a combination that works well for you—these tools are basically extensions of the hand and it's important to be able to use them with maximum dexterity.

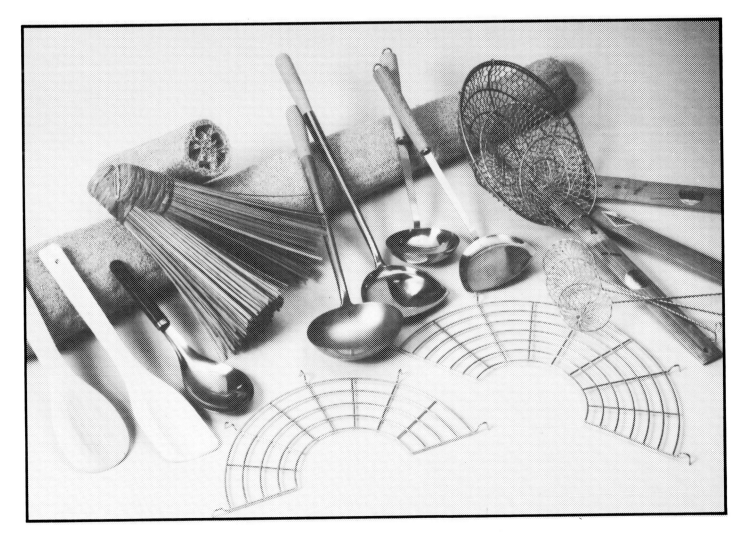

HOW TO BUY A CHINESE WOK
(With Thanks to Margaret Spader)

In Chinese markets, the wok, ring, and lid are priced separately; but a number of mail order firms offer the complete set for prices ranging from $10 to $25. The authentic one is made of light-weight iron. It heats evenly and holds the heat, but will rust in places of high humidity. If not used frequently, it's a good idea to store it in a plastic bag, protecting it from excessive moisture.

New aluminum woks are available and they heat evenly and quickly but don't retain heat like a heavier metal. The domed cover or wok lid is usually made of aluminum. Be sure to get the size that fits your wok.

When you shop for a wok, it's a good idea to take the grid from a top burner on your gas range with you. Some rings that fit under the wok are not large enough to fit over a grid and V-shaped notches have to be cut. The notches should be cut big enough to provide air for the gas burner. Some rings already have holes or notches cut in them for that purpose. Be sure they are big enough to allow adequate air for the burner.

Cleaning and Seasoning Your Wok

A new wok is coated with grease to keep it from rusting. That coating must be thoroughly removed before you start to cook. Wipe the wok with a paper towel to remove the heavy film. Then:

1. Place the wok on the ring and fill it with boiling water. Let it soak for 30 minutes. Wash in warm, soapy water and use a stiff brush to remove any coating that adheres.

2. When the surface is smooth and clean, rinse well, wipe with a paper towel and place over a low flame to dry. This will take about a minute.
3. Using a paper towel, rub vegetable oil on the surface of the wok. Keep the heat low so you can keep up rubbing action. Don't let oil sit in the wok. Heat about ten minutes. Repeat the oil treatment. Heat ten minutes more.
4. Use a fresh paper towel and wipe out the wok, removing excess oil. It is now ready for use.
5. After cooking in the wok, soak it in hot water and clean as you would an omelet pan. Never use detergents or abrasives because they will remove the seasoning and cause foods to stick to the surface. Use a stiff brush if food sticks, or steel wool without soap.
6. Always dry the wok thoroughly over low heat.
7. At the seashore or in humid climates, store the wok in a heavy plastic bag to keep moisture out.

STEAMERS

There are two basic types of steamers. One is the traditional bamboo steamer, and the other is the more modern metal steamer—usually made out of aluminum. Both work very well, and each has its own attractive features, so it's really a matter of personal preference. An aluminum steamer usually consists of a pot, one or two trays and a lid. This is a self-contained unit because the pot holds the water that provides the steam. The bamboo steamer does not come with a pot. Its trays and lid must be used with a wok or other vessel to hold the water that will

become steam. The aluminum steamers retain heat longer, do not absorb food odors and, of course, do not split or warp. Thus, the aluminum steamers always fit together perfectly—an important factor, especially in very humid climates. So what can be said for bamboo steamers? Well, they're pretty for one thing, and they sort of appeal to the "natural" and "authentic" sensibilities we sometimes attach to ancient cooking methods. Using the bamboo steamer is sort of like frying chicken in the old, blackened, cast iron skillet instead of using the electric frypan.

If you decide on the more romantic bamboo steamer, be sure to season it before putting it to use. Simply soak the racks thoroughly and then set up the steamer as if to start cooking. Let the steam run through it for about an hour, periodically pouring a little water down through the racks. When not in use, always keep a bamboo steamer out where air circulates and use cooking oil on the individual pieces if they warp a bit and are hard to fit together.

Miscellany

WOK TALK
c/o The Chinese Grocer
209 Post St.
San Francisco, CA 94108
(415) 982-0125

Wok Talk is, to our knowledge, the only Chinese cooking newsletter in this country. It is ". . . published bi-monthly (every other month) . . . for the interest and edification of Chinese food lovers." That's the way they say it, and it's comforting to realize that someone else has trouble with "bi-" and "semi-."

The newsletter is available for $9.50 per year, $15 for two years. If you enjoy Chinese cooking—or even if you're just getting started—you'll find it stimulating and informative. Or it would make a great gift for that Chinese cook in your life.

COOKING METHODS

STIR-FRYING

Stir-fry, of course, is the cooking method most of us associate with Chinese food, and it is uniquely Chinese. Stir-fry uses a very high heat for a short period. This helps seal in flavors and juices and pre-

serves much of the nutritional value as well as crunchiness of vegetables. Stir-frying calls for a lot of action in a very short period of time—meaning that it's important to be well prepared and organized, and that the cook's vigilance is of utmost importance.

The first step in stir-frying is to heat your wok, usually for a minute or so until it is very hot. Only then do you add the

oil, swirling it around until it covers the surface of the wok. The oil should be hot, but not smoking, in a minute or less. Then you turn down the heat and add ginger, garlic and scallions. The hot oil will draw the flavor out of these seasonings. Then add the vegetables or meat. In a very short time everything will be cooked, and it's important to keep your eye on the color of the ingredients—with such high heat, and because the pieces are small, things are easily overdone. Often the meat is put in until 80% done, the other ingredients partially cooked, and then everything thrown together in the final minute or less of cooking. The key to successful stir-frying is to make sure that everything in the wok comes into contact with the hot oil in the bottom of the wok. The more ingredients, the more important to maintain a rhythmic scooping motion with the spatula.

It's easy to overcook food, at least initially. The cook must be alert and ready to react quickly. Overcooking will toughen the meat and take away the bright color and crunchy texture of the vegetables.

DEEP-FRYING

The Chinese think favorably of deep-frying, even prize it, because of the textures it can produce. But the effect is lost if the oil is either not hot enough or too hot. Not hot enough means the food will absorb too much oil and become soggy and greasy, and the residues from meat, especially, will cloud the oil. If it is too hot, the cooking will be uneven, the outside of the food being done while the inside is not yet cooked enough. So oil temperature is very important. One way to test the temperature of the oil is to drop a piece of scallion into it. If the heat is right, the scallion will twirl around quickly and sizzle. If there is little sizzle and no spin, the oil needs to be hotter. If the oil is smoking, it's too hot. Another problem with deep-frying is splattering oil. Always slide the food in gently and make sure there is no water on it. Remember that oil can be used repeatedly.

STEAMING

Traditional Chinese stoves were basically walled compartments for the fire with an opening on top. There was no place where food could be baked, as we understand the process. Steaming is the Chinese equivalent. The wet heat of steaming has long been used to "bake" bread, cakes and dumplings. In addition, it is often used as the first step in a two-step cooking process. Steaming softens and

moisturizes the food, while a second step such as deep-frying will put a tasty and textured crust on a dish.

The big attraction of steaming is that it adds no flavor of its own, so it brings out the delicate flavors of the original ingredients. They lose few of their original juices. And it is an ideal cooking method for calorie-conscious Americans. Steaming is an especially good way of cooking fish.

RED COOKING

Food is covered and cooked very slowly for a long period of time. The simmering liquid usually contains a certain amount of soy sauce and sherry, the mix being brown or black. Red, however, is an auspicious color in China and therefore the process is referred to as red cooking. During the cooking process seasonings are put into the liquid, which is usually used as a sauce when the dish is done. Often, in braising, the meat is stir-fried before being put into the simmering liquid for a much longer time. Whole fish are often cooked this way and the effect can be out of this world.

WHITE COOKING
(clear simmering)

Similar to red cooking, except no soy sauce is used. The liquid can be used as a clear soup. Most white-cooked dishes are of meat and fish. A very low fire should be used after the dish first boils. It's probably best to skim the pot after that initial boiling of duck or pork, especially.

White cooking brings out the best in a good cook and can show up a poor cook because there is nothing to mask less-than-desirable flavors. An advantage to white cooking is that it yields a main dish and a soup.

MAKING CHILI PEPPER OIL

Chili pepper oil is an important item in the kitchens of those who aspire to cook hot food. Here's how: heat a cup of oil in a small saucepan until very hot, then turn the heat low and add either 10 dried chili peppers, or three tablespoons of powdered chili, or ¼ cup of crushed chili pepper flakes. Stir for about a minute. Then turn off the heat and let the mixture cool. Again stir it very well, then strain the oil.

THE CHINESE STOCK POT

Chinese stocks are produced in much the same way as western stocks. But besides boiling bones and scraps together for a prolonged period of time, the Chinese often add other items, such as the inedible parts of shrimp, for the sake of variation in flavor. For really high class stocks, sometimes they will add small amounts of ham or beef. Two ingredients added to most stocks are ginger and scallions, which can cut the gamy or fishy smell that the other ingredients might have produced.

In China stocks are divided into three grades. The *secondary stock* is produced from only a chicken carcass or pork bones, simmered in water with a few slices of ginger root and perhaps scallions for two hours and more. Salt is usually the only seasoning. A *primary stock* is similar, but usually has some lean pork and soy sauce for seasoning. The very *best stock* will have some finely minced chicken, about a quarter pound for each quart of stock, added for four or five minutes before being filtered off. This will add the sweet and fresh element mentioned above.

Of course you can make a clear stock using only the chicken. Many Chinese cooks prefer this stock because it is much lighter and therefore allows the flavors of other ingredients to come forth.

"SHAKE-ON SEASONING"

Tsang and Ma International, among many other excellent Chinese culinary supplies, offers a unique group of shake-on seasonings. These complete seasoning mixes were formulated to create authentic regional flavors. They take the worry out of using many spices or sauces in combination.

There are five flavor combinations. *Indo China/Coconut Curry* is a distinctive but mild curry and coconut flavor for use in seafood, meat, or vegetable dishes. *Japan/Teriyaki* is a blend of soy flavors, especially good on broiled meats. *Szechuan/Hot & Sour* is a completely balanced seasoning for use in Szechuan-style cooking. *Polynesia/Lemon Luau* is a delicate blend of lemon and smoke flavors for polynesian dishes. *Peking/Mongolian Fire* is a very hot seasoning used for delicious Mandarin style foods, mongolian beef, and spicy oil dip. These regional seasonings are available through Tsang & Ma International, 1306 Old Country Road, Belmont, CA 94002.

Mongolian Grill.

The Joy of Not Cooking

If sweating it out over a hot wok is not exactly your idea of a good time; if your attempt to follow Chinese recipes results in great piles of what is best described as "former foodstuffs"; if your Chinese cooking school teacher urges you to drop out and enroll in a remedial home economics night class at the local high school; or if you're just in the mood to enjoy an evening out of the house you should seriously consider making reservations at a good Chinese restaurant. The experience will be unique and, if you enjoy the food, one you'll want to repeat often.

Listed below you'll find some of the very best Chinese restaurants in the United States. Many of them are famous and some are practically landmarks. Of course, New York and San Francisco have a great number of excellent Chinese restaurants because of their thriving Chinatowns. But, there are superb Chinese restaurants all over the country. Certainly all of the ones listed here are well worth a visit.

CALIFORNIA

The Mandarin
430 N. Camden Dr.
Beverly Hills, CA 90210

Featuring the recipes of Cecilia Chiang. A very elegant presentation of the four classic cuisines.

Kee Joon's Cuisine of China
433 Airport Blvd.
Burlingame, CA 94010

Just outside San Francisco. Gorgeous interior with such specialties as Manchurian beef and sizzling rice soup.

Fung Lum Restaurant
1815 Bascom Ave.
Campbell, CA 95008

Very fine Cantonese food. No reservations for less than eight.

Jade West
2040 Avenue of the Stars
Los Angeles, CA 90067

Opposite Century Plaza Hotel. Moderately priced.

Shanghai Winter Garden
5651 Wilshire Blvd.
Los Angeles, CA 90036

Authentic Chinese cuisine in simple setting.

Panda Inn
3472 E. Foothill Blvd.
Pasadena, CA 91107

Fine Szechwan cuisine. Spring chicken with peanuts and sizzling rice soup are specialties.

Asia Gardens
772 Pacific
San Francisco, CA 94108

Inexpensive Cantonese food in Chinatown.

Empress of China
China Trade Center—Top Floors
838 Grant Ave.
San Francisco, CA 94108

Fabulous view of the heart of Chinatown. A myriad of the finest delicacies. Fabulously decorated with antiques.

Harbin Manchurian Cuisine
327 Balboa St.
San Francisco, CA 94118

Garden decor. Northern cuisine features lion head meatball, Mongolian lamb and cashew chicken.

Imperial Palace
919 Grant Ave.
San Francisco, CA 94108

All regions of cuisine represented.
Excellent *dim sum.* Peking duck and
lobster imperial are specialties. One of
the most elegant and exclusive Chinese
restaurants in U.S.

Kan's
708 Grant Ave.
San Francisco, CA 94108

Formerly the restaurant of the late and
beloved Johnny Kan. It was first of the
truly superb Chinese restaurants in
Chinatown. Elegant Cantonese food.
Peking duck and winter melon soup are
unsurpassed.

The Mandarin
900 N. Point St.
San Francisco, CA 94109

A wonderful restaurant in Ghirardelli
Square. Mongolian fire pot, sweet and
sour fish, and smoked tea duck are
excellent. Interesting desserts.

Sun Ya
823 Clay
San Francisco, CA 94108

Inexpensive Cantonese in Chinatown.

Madam Wu's Garden
2201 Wilshire Blvd.
Santa Monica, CA 90403

Traditional Chinese food exquisitely
presented in a garden setting. Peking
duck, beef in ginger, hoisin sauce and
black bean sauce are excellent.

COLORADO

The Yuan Palace
7555 E. Arapahoe Rd.
Denver, CO 80232

All four cuisines are represented, plus an
unusual Mongolian barbecue.

DISTRICT OF COLUMBIA

Empress
1018 Vermont Ave.
Washington, D.C. 20005

Award-winning cuisine, moderately
priced. Mandarin and Szechwan
specialties.

FLORIDA

Tiger Tiger Teahouse
2235 Biscayne Blvd.
Miami, FL 33139

Rather expensive Szechwan, Mongolian
cuisine. Jin jo shrimp and cashew
chicken are wonderful.

HAWAII

King Tsin
1486 S. King St.
Honolulu, HI 96814

Mandarin cooking in intimate surroundings.

Mandarin Palace
Hotel Miramar
2345 Kuhio Ave.
Honolulu, HI 96815

Very Americanized but good value. Interesting buffet. Bean curd specialties.

Wo Fat
115 N. Hotel St.
Honolulu, Hawaii 96813

Elegant downtown restaurant with authentic Cantonese specialties.

ILLINOIS

Abacus
2619 N. Clark St.
Chicago, IL 60614

Gourmet cooking from the four classic regions. Hunan shrimp and Peking duck are excellent. Interesting desserts.

Chiam
2323 S. Wentworth
Chicago, IL 60616

Exotic atmosphere and moderate prices in Chicago's Chinatown.

House of Hunan
535 N. Michigan
Chicago, IL 60611

Hunan, Szechwan and Mandarin cuisine in a Hong Kong/Victorian setting. Willow beef and shrimp with pine nuts are very special.

Austin Koo's House of Hunan
1233 E. Golf Rd.
Schaumburg, IL 60195

Suburban branch of House of Hunan in Chicago. Excellent staff, spicy and refined Szechwan cookery.

MARYLAND

Mandarin House
3501 St. Paul St.
Baltimore, MD 21218

Authentic mandarin cuisine.

MASSACHUSETTS

Lucky Gardens
282 Concord Ave.
Cambridge, MA 02138

A restaurant with a devoted following. Szechwan and Hunan specialties. Great dumplings. Fairly inexpensive.

MICHIGAN

Ah Wok Restaurant
41563 W. Ten Mile Rd.
Novi, MI 48050

Mandarin/Szechwan cooking. Authentic and beautifully presented. Rice paper shrimp a specialty. Best Chinese restaurant in Detroit area.

MINNESOTA

The Nankin
20 S. 7th St.
Minneapolis, MN 55402

Excellent Cantonese food.

Szechwan Star Restaurant
3655 Hazelton Rd.
Minneapolis, MN 55435

More expensive, but very excellent service and cuisine. Unusual Chinese smorgasbord.

MISSOURI

Imperial Palace
103rd & State Line
Kansas City, MO 64114

Rather expensive. Features a multi-course Chinese feast.

NEBRASKA

House of Genji/House of Cathay
8809 W. Dodge Rd.
Omaha, NB 68114

Two restaurants in one building. Japanese on one side and authentic Chinese on the other.

NEVADA

Great Wall
(no address available)
Las Vegas, NV

Authentic Chinese food with Peking duck as specialty.

NEW YORK

NEW YORK'S CHINESE RESTAURANTS
Stan Miller, Arline Miller, Rita Rowan, and James Rowan
Atheneum
216 pp. $4.95

It must have been fun putting this book together—the authors and friends touring restaurants in New York's Chinatown sniffing and tasting their way through 80 restaurants and then writing up the results of their "research." It sounds like a burden most of us would be willing to bear for a while.

The authors used four rating criteria: the freshness and quality of the original ingredients, the contrast of the colors and textures of a dish, the final blending of a dish, and the speed with which the freshly prepared dish was brought to the table. Care is taken to point out that other variables—which can have a great effect on the overall success of a restaurant outing—were not included in the rating system. They include the decor, the service and the assault on one's sensibilities from the jukebox, etc. It appears to be a fair system, wisely factoring out the subjective elements that weren't directly related to the quality of the food.

The book has some other chapters that will be of interest to the tourist and the hardened New Yorker alike. There is discussion of the regional cuisines of China, which will be valuable to people who have not had exposure to different types of Chinese cuisine. The section describing Chinatown itself is very interesting, though all too brief. The suggested walking tour is a must for visitors.

Eighty of the 100 or so restaurants in Chinatown are evaluated, but New York City is estimated to have over a thousand Chinese restaurants, so the title is a bit misleading. But it's a handy little book, especially for those of us who tend to think of Chinatown in New York as an impenetrable maze.

China Royal
17 Division St.
New York, NY 10002

Large restaurant with a variety of Cantonese dishes at reasonable prices. Chinatown.

David K's Cheng Kuo Yuan
1155 Third Ave.
New York, NY 10021

All four classic cuisines. Very authentic. Chicken with walnuts and orange beef are specialties.

Foo Joy
13 Division St.
New York, NY 10002

Very plain but very grand cuisine. Fukienese cuisine is unusual and very good. Chinatown.

Happy Garden
12 Bowery
New York, NY 10002

Good service. Wide variety of excellent traditional favorites. Chinatown.

Hong Fat
63 Mott St.
New York, NY 10013

A favorite with many New Yorkers. Very inexpensive. Chinatown.

OKLAHOMA

Hoe Sai Gai
5201 N. Shartel
Oklahoma City, OK 73118

Mixed menu but some good Cantonese dishes. Moderate prices.

Oregon

Jade West
122 S.W. Harrison
Portland, OR 97201

Rather expensive, but excellent Chinese food.

PENNSYLVANIA

Lotus Inn
1010 Race
Philadelphia, PA 19107

Traditional cuisine at moderate prices. Features a 90-minute dinner.

TEXAS

Peking Palace
4119 Lomo Alto Dr.
Dallas, TX 75219

Empress hot shrimp and Szechwan steak are wonderful here.

Moon Garden
4675 Montana
El Paso, TX 79903

Cantonese with some American dishes. Interesting decor.

China Garden
1602 Leeland
Houston, TX 77003

A Houston favorite for many years. Inexpensive Chinese fare.

Timmy Chan
2606 Fanin
Houston, TX 77002

Some polynesian food mixed in with traditional Chinese. Pleasant atmosphere with moderate prices.

Uncle Tai's Hunan Yuan
1980 S. Post Oak Rd.
Houston, TX 77056

All Hunan cookery. Very high style with very good staff. Contemporary elegant decor.

WASHINGTON

Hong Kong
Chinatown
Seattle, WA

Moderately expensive. This is Chinatown's oldest 1st class restaurant.

Peng's
219 E. 44th St.
New York, NY 10017

Some call this the best Chinese restaurant in NYC. Dragon and Phoenix (lobster and chicken) is a favorite here.

Pearl's Chinese Restaurant
38 W. 48th St.
New York, NY 10036

An elegant celebrity hangout. Art deco decor. Lemon chicken is excellent.

Sam Wo
39 Mott St.
New York, NY 10013

Unobtrusive restaurant with terrific Cantonese food. Inexpensive. Chinatown.

Shun Lee Dynasty
900 Second Avenue
New York, NY 10017

All cuisines available here. Szechwan is very good.

Ordering from the Chinese Menu

Jokes about ordering in Chinese restaurants (one from Column A, two from Column B) abound in the United States probably because the Chinese approach to restaurant dining is not completely understood by most westerners. In the west, and particularly in America, ordering from the menu is a private affair. Each person fends for himself by ordering the drink, appetizer, entree, vegetable, and dessert he plans to eat. The Chinese meal is, or should be, a much more communal effort.

When an order is delivered in a Chinese restaurant, the waiter generally places the dishes randomly in the center of the table. He's not doing this because he's forgotten who ordered what; he's doing it because the diners are supposed to share the various dishes—that's the whole idea behind a Chinese meal. The order should be made with this in mind. The "one-from-Column-A" approach is designed to help the novice combine suitable dishes. This, however, is slowly going out of fashion. Generally speaking, the diners should order one dish per person. Soups and appetizers may be added depending on how hungry the group is. An order for a hungry group of four might include two appetizers, two soups and four entrees. If the party includes some light or hesitant eaters, drop the soups, the appetizers or one of the entrees.

The Chinese enjoy making their orders as varied and interesting as possible. Americans sometimes want to order the same thing. For instance, two people out of a party of four might want to order lobster Cantonese. Strictly speaking, asking for two orders of lobster Cantonese is not in the "Chinese spirit" of things. Of course, it would be possible to allow the two who want the lobster to taste it first and perhaps share most of it, but the better idea is for the party to decide together on four different dishes and to enjoy them all equally. The Chinese go so far as to making sure that the dishes don't even resemble each other in style or ingredients. Thus a good Chinese order for four might be something like: lobster Cantonese, barbecued spare ribs, chicken with walnuts, and sweet and sour cabbage.

Lest the diners become too abashed by all of this "communal" business, they may be assured of having their very own plates, rice bowls, and tea cups. And, desserts in most Chinese restaurants in America are usually served western-style with each person ordering separately.

If you want to get as much of the Chinese eating experience as possible, it might be interesting to ask the waiter to make a selection of dishes himself. It is often difficult for Americans to know what dishes truly "harmonize." Tell the waiter that you'd like to eat "ho-ts'ai" (harmonized dishes) for a certain price ($20, $30, $40 or whatever) and then tell him that you'd like to eat as much like the Chinese do as possible. You'll very likely be pleased with the selection you get. (Remember to tip the waiter accordingly for this special service.)

Key Words on the Chinese Menu*

Gai (Chi)—Chicken
Yu (Yü)—Fish
Har (Hsia)—Shrimp
Loong har (Lung hsia)—Lobster
Gee yook (Chu-jou)—Pork
Opp (Ya)—Duck
Ngow yook (niu-jou)—Beef

Ding—Dice
Kew—Chunks
See—Shredded
Soong—Minced
Sub gum—Mixed meat and/or
　　　　vegetables

*Alternate spelling in parenthesis

Four Classical Cuisines

PEKING AND NORTH CHINESE (MANDARIN)

Many very famous dishes originated in Peking as a result of the fact that, for many centuries, it was the imperial city. During the Ming and Manchu dynasties in particular, thousands of chefs from all over China were hired to work for the emperor in Peking. The *haute cuisine* of this area, notably fu yung of chicken (chicken velvet) which is finely minced chicken and egg whites, was developed for the imperial palate. But northern Chinese cooking is also influenced by Moslem and Mongolian cookery. Thus the "hot pot" and the use of lamb and mutton are widespread in northern cuisine. Another characteristic of northern Chinese cooking is the heavy use of soya paste, garlic and Chinese cabbage.

SHANGHAI/FUKIENESE

The abundance of rice and seafood have most influenced the cooking of east China. Rice is made into rice wine in the east Chinese provinces and therefore many dishes involve a wine-based marinade. Rice is also mixed in many recipes. Eight Precious Duck is a dish that features a duck stuffed with eight different ingredients including rice. And, of course, the seafood dishes are numerous and excellent. The soups of Fukien Province and Shanghai are quite famous. Especially noteworthy are fish head soup and three-shred soup. If one characteristic predominates in east China coastal cuisine, it is the use of fresh vegetables. The emphasis here is on a fresh rather than a spicy taste.

SZECHWANESE

The cuisine of western, inland China is best known for its liberal use of hot and spicy ingredients—onion, pepper, chili, garlic, ginger, sesame, and aromatic vinegars. There is also a tendency for Szechwanese foods to be chewy in texture. Vegetables and meats are often stir-fried until dry. Much of the cooking in this area, though quite refined, is based on peasant cooking sensibilities. It has an earthy quality mainly developed around use of native herbs, tree fungi, nuts, mushrooms, and a wide variety of bamboo shoots. With no coastal area, fish do not figure much in Szechwan cuisine. Beef is a bit more popular here than in other parts of China, though pork is also much admired. A great deal of the flavor of Szechwan cuisine may have originated in the fact that the population was somewhat isolated and had to be concerned with preserving food. The use of pickled, dried, smoked and salted foods no doubt set a standard of flavoring in Szechwan that has been carried down through the centuries.

CANTONESE/SOUTH CHINESE

Canton (Kangchow) is only one city in the large southern coastal area, but its name has been applied to the whole range of southern Chinese cuisine. Needless to say, it is the food of Canton that most of the rest of the world thinks of as being Chinese. When the last dynasty in China (the Manchu) collapsed, many of the chefs of the Forbidden City or imperial capital of China fled to Canton. Here a cuisine of high standards and international distinction developed. Because of the almost tropical climate and growing season, and as a result of the international sea trade in the nearby ports of Hong Kong and Macao, the cooks of Canton employed the most extensive variety of ingredients in all China. They are famous for intricately blended flavors, typified by such ideas as using fish to flavor other meats—oyster sauce with beef, or chicken with shrimp sauce. It is in Cantonese food that we see a trend toward the exotic, again with a myriad of combinations—lemon duck, pork and chicken liver, pork ribs and plums. Pigeon, frog, lobster, and dog all find their way into the Cantonese kitchen. Almost every imaginable cooking method is used as well. And, like the French, their sauces are made with exquisite culinary precision. It's little wonder that the cuisine of Canton is known and relished all over the world.

Chinese Spirits

Intoxicating liquors in China are basically grain distillates. Rice wine, or "yellow wine" as it is known in China, is a rice distillate and is the most popular. Shaohsing is generally considered the best of Chinese rice wines. It is sometimes called Shaohsing Daughter because, in times past, when a daughter was born in the city of Shaohsing, the family was supposed to begin distilling the rice wine that would be served on the girl's wedding day.

Rice wine is not at all similar to wine made from grapes. It is quite strong and is sometimes compared to cognac or sherry. It is usually rather thicker in consistancy than grape wine and is often gulped from small cups, the effect being a little bit like knocking back schnapps. The flavor is quite sharp and unfamiliar to many western palates. It produces a light-headed, intoxicating result quickly, but the effect wears off almost as fast as it is produced. It is not meant to be sipped along with dinner. However, if wine is ordered at a Chinese restaurant, appetizers of some kind should be eaten with it. The Chinese do not drink without eating.

There are also some fruit distillates which resemble liquers. Plum wine, tiger tendon, and quince and pear wine are the most famous. An unusual green wine called "snake wine" is just that. It is made by placing a poisonous snake in high-proof alcohol and allowing it to sort of "brew," sometimes for several years.

In many American Chinese restaurants, beer and western wine are served. Beer is very good with the spicier dishes of the Szechwan and Hunan variety, and dry whites are usually quite nice with Cantonese dishes.

Chinese Fast Food

Like so many other nationalities, the Chinese have added generously to our great American lifestyle. In the area of food, Chinese take-out is by now an established piece of Americana. To be sure, the Chinese in China buy food "to go"—ready-to-eat noodles and rice dishes are frequently sold from carts on the street. Some even call Chinese food the original fast food because some of it can be prepared so quickly. But American Chinese take-out has developed a character all its own. Many Chinese food establishments, especially on the east coast, do nothing but a take-out business, and many sit-down restaurants all over the country have facilities for take-out orders as well.

Certain "Americanized" Chinese dishes are particularly popular and lend themselves well to the take-out business. Happily, Peking Duck and other gourmet masterpieces are generally not available. Here are a few of the most popular all-American Chinese dishes you will find to take out.

CHOP SUEY

Today, not many serious Chinese restaurant patrons in America would order chop suey as the gastronomic centerpiece of a Chinese meal. But at one time chop suey *was* Chinese food in America. Chop suey (which means "odds and ends" in the Cantonese dialect) did not originate in China at all. It was invented right here in the United States. Chinese laborers, so the story goes, cooked it up for lunch

alongside the new transcontinental railroad tracks they were laying. It does seem like a sort of mix between Cantonese cuisine and a wild west, campfire stew. And, of course, it was served over rice, which must have vaguely reminded the Chinese of home. Anyway, supposedly it was the best thing that the Chinese railroad cooks could come up with considering conditions in "the new world."

After the tracks were laid, many of the Chinese railroad cooks took up making and serving chop suey to the American public, who, of course, loved it. Their restaurants, which were even called "chop suey houses," were the modest forebears of the Chinese restaurant industry in America today. Although chop suey is still served in some restaurants and is a popular take-out item, its preeminence on the Chinese menu is a thing of the past.

CHOW MEIN

Also popular as a take-out item, this dish is often thought of as just another kind of chop suey. Chow mein, however, has a long and distinguished past that reaches as far back as the ancient cuisine of China. Basically, it is a vegetable and meat mixture served over fried noodles. If prepared properly with fresh vegetables and *real* fried Chinese noodles (not the American canned variety that resembles a crunchy, beer snack), chow mein can be quite good.

EGG FU YUNG

This is probably another Chinese-American invention and was perhaps first served as an alternative to chop suey. Egg fu yung is really a sort of omelet. Sauteed chicken, shrimp or other meat, and vegetables are added to an egg mixture, which is then cooked like a pancake. A gravy-like sauce is usually poured over the egg pancake. It's easy to see the sort of east/west compromising that went into an early Chinese-American dish like this one.

MOO GOO GAI PAN

This is a very popular but relatively simple stir-fried dish usually made of chicken breast, button mushrooms and sweet green peppers. A bit of cornstarch or water chesnut powder is used to glaze the chicken and vegetables as they cook. Although most Chinese food gourmets would never dream of ordering this dish, it remains an American eat-in and take-out favorite.

EGG ROLLS

Generally speaking, Americans eat egg rolls much as the Chinese do, that is as a sort of appetizer or snack. Egg rolls are called "spring rolls" in China and are really a teahouse snack or *dim sum*. The quality of egg rolls varies greatly in U.S. restaurants. One of the favorite kinds is made with shrimp, bean sprouts, celery and mushrooms. The meat and vegetables are chopped finely and mixed with other ingredients to make a kind of filling. This filling is then wrapped inside a very thin square of dough called a "wrapper" and deep fried to a golden brown. The freshness of the filling ingredients and the relative toughness or tenderness of the fried wrapper make all the difference in the quality of the egg roll. Many Chinese restaurants sell egg rolls to take out. They are a welcome addition to the hors d'oeuvre tray at cocktail parties especially when served with homemade Chinese dips.

WON TON SOUP

Won tons are like tiny dumplings or ravioli usually filled with a ground pork mixture. The won tons are boiled until thoroughly cooked and then added to a chicken broth-like soup. Won ton soup seems to come one of two ways in Chinese restaurants, either rich and flavorful or bland and watered-down. Of course, the former is the more desirable. A good won ton soup taken out in a paper container can make a great lunch all by itself and is truly one of the great delights of take-out Chinese food.

EGG DROP SOUP

This is a very simple thickened chicken broth soup to which beaten eggs are added. The eggs are poured slowly into the hot broth in a narrow stream so that they are cooked in thin strands. This is usually a rich and hardy soup and, if ordered to take home, can be heated and reheated without being ruined. Though it's a plain soup that can easily be made at home, it never seems quite as satisfying as when it comes from a favorite Chinese restaurant.

Chinese Slow Food

The items below are not so slowly as they are carefully prepared. These are some famous dishes that often appear on Chinese restaurant menus. Needless to say, the fact that they are widely known does not guarantee their quality in every Chinese restaurant. But these dishes have all contributed to the excellent reputation Chinese cuisine has gained in this country. What should be slow about this food is the enjoyment of it. Don't rush through a well prepared Chinese meal. Remember, since ancient times the Chinese have sought to perfect food preparation and presentation. The texture, flavor, cut, and color have all been taken into account in the development of each dish. Think about that and you'll find you're enjoying your meal even more.

PEKING DUCK

Really, a Peking duck is just a roasted duck, but it's the quality of duck and the method of roasting and serving that have made this such a famous dish. Ducks are specially bred in China for use in Peking's famous duck restaurants. In the U.S., Long Island duckling is most often used. The birds are very carefully prepared before roasting. After being killed and dressed, they are hung up to dry out for at least half a day and sometimes longer. While they are hanging, they are twice coated with sugar water. When they are ready for roasting, they are hung on poles by the neck and placed in a high-heat, kiln-like oven. As a result, the birds come out very crisp and yet succulent. The skin and the meat are usually "peeled" from the carcass and served with shredded onions and cucumbers and a piquant duck sauce. Many restaurants request that Peking duck be ordered in advance. Also, do not order Peking duck if you have only an hour to eat. It is best enjoyed as part of a leisurely evening meal.

FIRE POT

The fire pot, also called "hot pot," is an invention usually credited to the Mongols of northern China. It is usually a brass pot with a central funnel or burner. The funnel is filled with hot coals and the surrounding bowl is filled with stock. The boiling stock serves to "cook" the small pieces of meats and vegetables which are dropped into it by the diners. It is reminiscent of, but absolutely nothing like, the electric fondue fun pots of the fabulous '60's. Mongolian hot pot is a dish that usually features lamb, cabbage, spinach and noodles. Chrysanthemum fire pot, so named because it's usually served in the autumn, boasts a wide variety of meats and vegetables. The hot pot is a traditional dish of Peking and northern China and makes an enjoyable eating experience, especially with a group of good friends. Not all Chinese restaurants offer "hot pot" dishes and those that do may request reservations ahead of time and a minimum number of guests at the table.

DRUNKEN CHICKEN (AND FRIENDS)

The cuisine of Shanghai and east China is influenced by the fact that it's in the main rice producing area of China. The abundance of rice results in an abundance of rice wine, so several of the most famous dishes from this area are made with wine and therefore called "Drunken Chicken," "Drunken Shrimp," "Drunken Spare Ribs," and the like. Drunken chicken is made by boiling a chicken, chopping it up and then soaking it in a wine-based marinade. It is allowed to sit and chill for a period and is then served cold. There are a number of dishes referred to as "drunken" on some menus. When they

are cold dishes, such as drunken chicken, they are usually meant to be eaten as the first course of a larger meal. These dishes are certainly a great way to start things off.

SWEET AND SOUR PORK

Although it is unclear whether sweet and sour sauce first appeared in the north or the south of China, this famous and popular dish is a Cantonese or south Chinese specialty. Other dishes, too, are prepared in the sweet and sour tradition—shrimp, cabbage, chicken, etc. But, sweet and sour pork is best known in American Chinese restaurants. It is usually prepared by deep frying batter-coated pieces of pork and serving them with a thickened sauce usually made with a mixture of sugar, soy, lemon or vinegar, tomato sauce and condiments. In some restaurants stir-fried vegetables such as green peppers, bamboo shoots, onion and the like are added. An even more "Americanized" version may include carrots, pineapple and who knows what. Popularity is not good for any dish. It usually results in too many variations on the theme. A very good Chinese restaurant, however, will also make a very good and probably authentic sweet and sour dish. It's good to remember that some Chinese refer to the dish as "one pork and two flavors." Tasting the two flavors in a skillful balance is the true test of sweet and sour cookery.

SZECHUAN BEEF

Beef is a bit more popular in Szechuan Province and west China because there are more beef cattle. The beef, however, is often herded a good deal and is usually tough. As a result, it is generally shredded and dry-fried until it is chewy or simmered for a long time until it is tender. Because it shows up in so many variations, "Szechuan Beef" is practically a generic term on the Chinese menu. You might find it steamed or dry-fried, sauced or plain in the average American Chinese restaurant. Of course, Szechuan peppercorns are almost always used to spice the beef or to flavor the sauce that might accompany it. A favorite sauce is one made with black beans. Hoisin sauce, soya, or aromatic vinegar can also be used with the beef to establish the characteristic Szechuanese hot and sour flavor. Many other dishes (pork, fish, vegetables) are also prepared in the Szechuan style and are seasoned with the peppery and aromatic Szechuanese condiments.

BIRD'S NEST SOUP

This widely known but rarely tasted soup is a chicken based soup that features chicken velvet (chicken fu yung) which is essentially a mixture of whipped egg whites and finely minced chicken, and the gelatinous seaweed nests of the Chinese swift. It is a delicate and highly prized soup and is often served, topped with slivers of ham, at "big deal" banquets in China. Genuine bird's nest soup is not common in Chinese restaurants throughout the United States. However, if you find yourself in a restaurant of exceptional quality and bird nest's soup is among the offerings, it should not be passed up.

SIZZLING RICE SOUP

Here's a dish that proves that we sometimes love to hear what we eat. Kellogg's Rice Krispies has always known this and some Chinese American restaurants have literally made an art out of preparing and serving this soup. A delectable hot broth made with chicken or pork shreds, wine, shrimp, and a variety of fresh vegetables is poured over deep-fried rice squares. The rice sizzles and pops and makes a great show for the diners, and the soup itself makes a splendid addition to any meal.

HOT AND SOUR SOUP

This is a wonderful, savory soup made with stir-fried pork or chicken shreds, usually including leeks, peas, mushrooms and bamboo shoots in a thickened chicken stock. The delight in this soup is again the delicate balance of the flavors. It is spiced with pepper, vinegar, soy and chili pepper oil. This is a good soup to have on a cold winter's night.

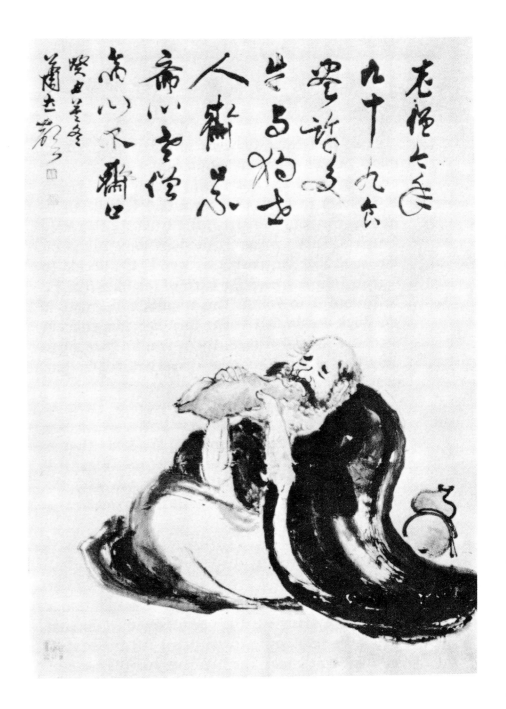

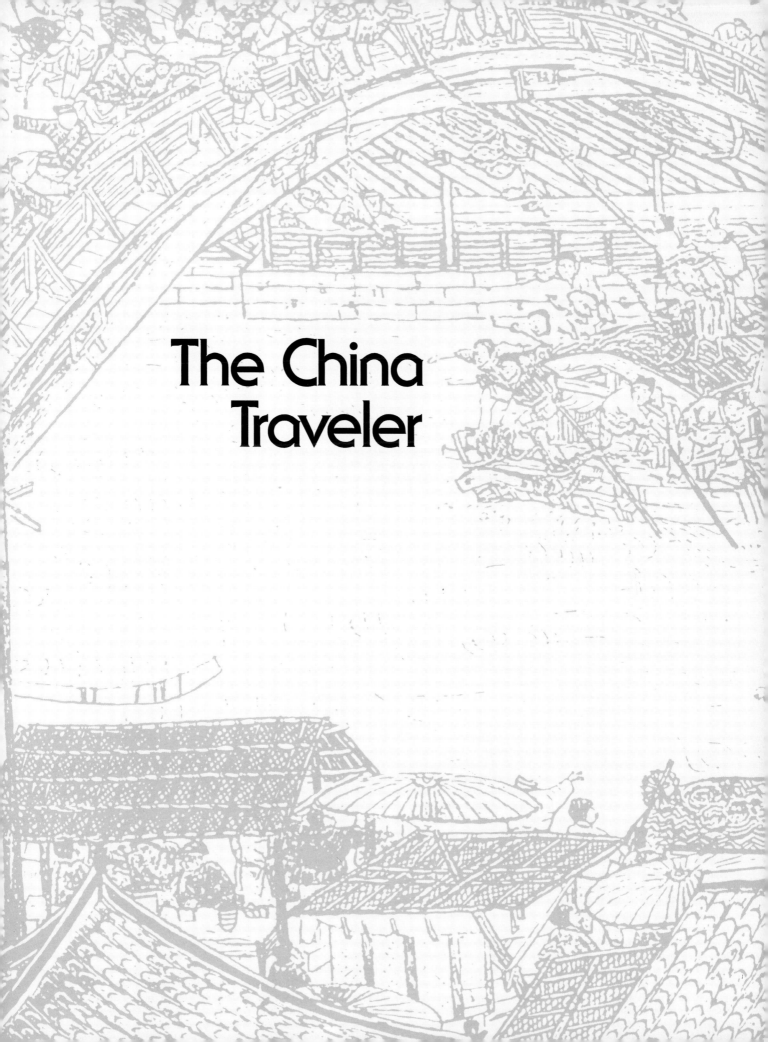

The China Traveler

At Home and Abroad

In many respects, the idea of traveling to China has about the same effect on Americans as it must have had on the friends and relatives of Marco Polo. "It's so far away!" "What is there to eat?" "They're so *different* over there!" "Do they even allow anybody in?" "It's impossible to understand anything they say or write!" "It's so mysterious, it's scary!"

A surprising number of the reservations Marco must have had before taking off are still being expressed by those who would like to go to China. Well it may be hard to believe, but China has changed a lot since the 14th century. The "Mysterious East" is not quite so mysterious anymore. The industrial revolution, modernization, and the world wars have affected China, too. And now that the United States recognizes the People's Republic of China, trade and travel, particularly, are increasing.

The major steps toward opening China to worldwide tourism were taken in the middle and late 1970's. But social disruption and economic difficulties, dating back to before World War II, had rendered China's tourist facilities outmoded and inadequate by modern standards. The Chinese were determined, however, to build a thriving and up-to-date tourist business. In the last few years, their progress toward this goal has been impressive.

The Chinese government began by establishing the China International Travel Service (CITS) to organize travel in China. The service has proven to be an efficient and well organized group, genuinely interested in promoting tourism, and determined to constantly upgrade its own expertise. Nor has CITS been mired in bureaucratic red tape to the point of becoming indifferent or closed entirely to new ideas. Should you decide to go to China, CITS is the organization that will see to your hotel accommodations, your domestic travel arrangements in China, and will provide the itinerary and the tour guides for your group while you are there. Traveling to China is still not as easy as going to Europe or the Caribbean. The visas are usually issued as a group document rather than individually stamped in your passports and must accompany the group on entry to China. Your itinerary is still limited to basically what the Chinese want you to see. And accommodations are still not quite up to par. But, *everything* is getting better all the time. And one thing *is* just as true as it was in Marco Polo's time—China is still one of the most fascinating and awe-inspiring places on the globe to visit.

On the next few pages, you'll find some interesting information about travel in China. There are some reviews of selected tour groups and guidebooks to China. You'll find some interesting tips about travel in China and about China's most interesting tourist spots. For those of you who still can't quite muster the courage (or the cash) for a trip to mainland China, there's a section at the end of this chapter about visiting China without ever leaving the continent. It's a short tour guide to some of North America's best known and best loved Chinatowns.

So, if you're planning a trip abroad or a trip nearer home, you can capture some of the magic of Cathay. China's not as "distant" as it seems!

Travel Bureaus and Tour Agencies

KUONI TRAVEL, INC.
11 E. 44th St.
New York, NY 10017
Tel. (212) 687-7190

This travel bureau arranges a number of tours to the People's Republic of China. However, since it operates in connection with two eastern air carriers—Philippine Airlines and Korean Air Lines—it tends to offer tours that include places outside of China. You may visit several places in the PRC but you may also find yourself in Bangkok, Singapore, Tokyo or Manila as "gateway" or "exit" cities. This might be just what you're looking for. On the other hand, the better part of three days of your tour spent in Manila might be a waste of time if you're really interested only in China. Frequently tours are organized around an air-carrier's home city. Japan Air Lines, for instance, will probably want to make sure that part of your "China Tour" includes the great "gateway to the Orient" city, Tokyo. Philippine Airlines makes sure that you usually hit the "crossroads city of the Orient," Manila. This is an important factor when choosing your tour. Don't get stuck in Tokyo or Manila or Seoul or Bangkok unless you want to.

Kuoni offers what might be a very fascinating 23-day tour (16 nights in China) which includes a cruise on the Yangtze River from Chongqing (Chungking) to Wuhan. The tour also includes Guilin (Kweilin) and Guangzhou (Canton). It ends with two-and-a-half days in Hong Kong. Prices for Kuoni tours seem quite reasonable and all depart from either San Francisco or Los Angeles.

LOTUS TOURS
444 Madison Ave.
New York, NY 10022
Tel. (800) 221-4566
In New York:
(212) 832-7830 (For Public
information &
reservations)
(212) 758-3662 (For Travel Agents
information &
reservations)

Among a number of interesting tours of the Orient, Lotus Tours offers a "Capital Cities" tour of China. In seven days and six nights, the traveler sees Shanghai, and Peking. It departs from Hong Kong weekly. Someone already in the Orient can pick it up from Hong Kong. It's a convenient add-on mini package for business people or "round-the-world" travelers. You can join this tour from the east or west coasts as well, but it is less appealing because the expense of traveling from New York or California for only seven days in China seems quite high.

Twice a year Lotus offers a special tour for the hearing impaired. The tours have a bilingual guide, but they also have a professional sign language interpreter assisting in the communications. People on the tour have some contact with deaf people in China, including a visit to a school for the deaf in Shanghai. According to Lotus, deaf Americans have slightly less trouble communicating with Chinese counterparts because of similarities in the signs the groups use.

Lotus also makes up special itineraries for groups of people who share specific interests—art, archeology, medicine and the like. Tours by Lotus come well-recommended and are sometimes fashioned to include stops in Bangkok, Bali and Singapore. At present, they offer seven different China itineraries from which to choose for varying lengths of stay and interests.

SOCIETY EXPEDITIONS
723 Broadway East
Seattle, WA 98102
Tel. (206) 324-9400

The China tours offered by Society Expeditions have names such as "Archeological Expedition and Inner Mongolia," "Archeological and Yangtze River Expedition," and so forth. They're not kidding either! The tours offered by this organization are adventurous, exotic and

erudite. They are directed toward the traveler with an adventurous and investigative spirit. The tours specialize in art, architecture, archeology, and natural sciences. A "reading list" is sent to each tour member after booking is completed, and lectures are given as part of the tour.

One of the most exciting and interesting tours that Society Expeditions offers is its expedition to China's "Silk Road" cities. The itinerary begins in Peking with the expected sights—Forbidden City, Great Wall, etc.—then takes the traveler to Sian (Xian), the ancient capital of China with its archeological bonanza on the site of China's first emperor's grave. The more than 7,000 life-sized terra-cotta figures here were buried with the emperor over 2,000 years ago. From here the tour proceeds to Dunhuang (Tunhuang) famous for its caves of Buddhist art; Lanzhou (Lanchow), an ancient trading center with Moslem bazaars and mosques of unusual Moslem/Chinese architecture and design; and Urumqi (Urumchi) in the remote Sinkiang Province with a visit to a Kazak tribal camp near Mongolia. Not much time will be scheduled for browsing through souvenir shops on these tours. They are designed for the tourist interested in exploring and learning. They cannot be described as "econo-tours" either. A good deal of effort seems to go into planning these unusual tours and they are, therefore, not cheap. Needless to say, these tours are not for everyone. But, for the discriminating tourist with adventure and discovery in mind, these tours seem made to order.

LINDBLAD TRAVEL, INC.
P.O. Box 912
Westport, CT 06881
Tel. (203) 226-8531

This firmly established and well respected travel organization operates a great number of innovative and altogether interesting tours to China. Lars-Eric Lindblad is President and inspiration for this successful travel company. He has made certain that as new areas of China open to the west, Lindblad tours are arranged to include these areas as quickly as possible. For that reason, Lindblad offers a Tibetan tour that *really* explores Tibet. On this 18-day tour, seven full days and nights are spent in Tibet. Needless to say, you see a lot more than the Potala Palace and downtown Lhasa! It's certainly one of the best of the Lindblad tours and perhaps the best of its kind in the world. In like manner, Lindblad offers an in-depth tour that includes Inner Mongolia, the cities along the "Silk Road," and the Tian Shan (Tian Mountains). And its Yangzte River tour is truly a *river* tour, offering a view of life and scenery along over 1,800 miles of the river. The M.S. *Kun Lun*, formerly a Chinese government ship used to entertain dignitaries and heads of state, takes the traveler on a 14-day cruise (with several stops at cities along the river) between Nanjing (Nanking) and Chongqing (Chungking). It's quite an excursion!

Among the unique tours offered by Lindblad are the "Coastal Voyages." These tours are made aboard M.S. *Lindblad Explorer,* a small cruise ship with accommodations for fewer than 100 passengers. These friendly, comfortable cruises make extensive tours of the famous cities on China's coastal waters—Guangzhou (Canton), Shanghai, Dalien (Talien), Tianjin (Tientsin), Hong Kong, and many more.

Lindblad has added two new China tours to its 1984 itinerary. Seven-day cruises are offered aboard the M.S. *Goddess*, also along the Yangtse River. The *Goddess* was specifically designed as a tourist vessel and offers a great many amenities including 30 outside cabins, each with private facilities and all fully air-conditioned and heated. These 7-day cruises can be incorporated into longer itineraries, ranging from 18 to 29 days in length.

Also new for 1984, is a 27-day "Splendors of China" land tour. This tour includes visits to all three of China's great centers of Buddhist Art: The Mogao Grottoes at Dunhuang; the Longmen Caves at

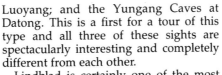

Luoyang; and the Yungang Caves at Datong. This is a first for a tour of this type and all three of these sights are spectacularly interesting and completely different from each other.

Lindblad is certainly one of the most experienced and professional tour organizations around. Their tours are planned with the traveler in mind and they approach each itinerary as a voyage of discovery. In China, at least, that's just as it should be.

U.S.-CHINA PEOPLES FRIENDSHIP ASSOCIATION
110 Maryland Ave. NE
Washington, D.C. 20002
(800) 368-5883 Tours Information

USCPFA is the oldest China tour operator in the U.S. It is a non-profit educational organization. It offers approximately 90 tours per year. The tours are either 19 or 22 days long and all make a first stop in China in Beijing (Peking) and leave China from Guangzhou (Canton). But there's plenty of variety in between, and "special itineraries" are available on some of the tours. For example, you can arrange to take a couple days out from your stay in Kunming (capital of Yunnan Province in the southwest) to visit Hsi Shuang Pan Na in the rough hill country, populated by China's Thai National Minority.

The USCPFA begins its tours with a one-day orientation program. This includes a program of films, lectures and travel tips, plus a reception for tour members on the evening before departure. The organization claims that the main purpose of its tours is to ". . . provide an educational experience in the context of travel. Through this . . . we hope to strengthen friendship between the people of both countries, to increase our understanding of the Chinese people and society, and to further exchange between our two countries in the areas of culture, the arts, science and technology, and among students." This philosophy has led the Friendship Association to sponsor tours of China for special interest groups such as project and engineering managers, junior and senior high school principals, and professionals in the fields of labor relations, human resource management, and so on. People on these tours spend some of their time with their professional counterparts in China. If this kind of approach appeals to you, USCPFA is the tour operator to contact. The tours are very well planned and the tour groups are kept small (maximum of 34 passengers per group). It is also possible for groups, institutions, and qualified individuals who wish to organize exchange and travel projects of their own choosing to make necessary arrangements through USCPFA.

CHINA HOLIDAYS
30 S. Michigan Ave. Suite 502
Chicago, IL 60603
Tel. (800) 621-2267
In Illinois: 346-9767

China Holidays seems to have a very close connection with China International Travel Service (CITS) of the People's Republic of China. The tour brochures state that "all tour arrangements while in China will be under direct control of CITS" and that "alterations to these tours cannot be considered." Well, of course, CITS is in control of *all* tours inside China, but most tour agents do not make a big deal of the fact. There seems to be a kind of bureaucratic smack to some of the statements in the China Holidays material, but they do seem to offer some very good tours at most reasonable prices. They appear to be "no frills" tours but you certainly can be sure that you won't be "taken" by this organization. The itineraries are varied and everything is included. In most cases, you'll fly directly into China, not through a "gateway" city, and you have the option of staying over in Hawaii on your way back at no additional air fare expense.

The tours offered by China Holidays range from 15 to 27 days in length and can include as many as ten different cities including some exotic ones such as Lhasa (Tibet) and Hohhot (Inner Mongolia). Many tours begin or end with a three-day stay in Hong Kong. One thing for sure, you'll get your money's worth with China Holidays.

SPECIAL TOURS FOR SPECIAL PEOPLE, INC.
250 W. 57th St.
New York, NY 10019
Tel. (212) 586-6577

The Special Tour people put out a nifty little handbook or, as they call it, ". . . a comprehensive guide to help you decide when, where and how to visit China and get the most out of your trip." Obviously they think that once you've studied the various points they suggest for consideration, you'll choose one of their tours. It's a solid approach, though, and they may well be on the right marketing track with it. Why? Because they really do offer something special.

Very simply, Special Tours aims at putting people of the same background into tour groupings. One "given" exists in all tours of China. That is that you *must* go in a group. Special Tours tries to take this "requirement" and turn it into an "advantage." Each tour has what they call a "professional focus" and this focus varies from the very specific (Society of American Archivists) to the more inclusive (ornithology, cuisine, art, archeology).

Each group is led by a specialist in its field of interest and much of the sightseeing or visiting of factories, communes and offices is pegged to the collective interest of the group. It's a way for the independent traveler to be placed with a group with like interests. As the brochure points out, travel companions can have a large influence on the outcome of a tour.

Special Tours apparently feels confident enough about what they offer to suggest that the prospective traveler study competitive tour brochures carefully and take a hard look at the details. And then let them know early of your special interest. But you won't be excluded from Special Tours if you have no special interest. There are "General Interest" tours organized as well.

INTER PACIFIC TRAVEL-IN-CHINA
485 Fifth Avenue
New York, NY 10016
Tel. (800) 221-3594/5
In New York: (212) 953-6010

This organization is an authorized agent of China International Travel Service (CITS). That means that its relations with CITS are very good. Certainly one thing can be said for Inter Pacific Tours, they go just about everywhere in China currently open to Western visitors. There are tours to ancient Chinese capitals, tours to Inner Mongolia, Tibet, Yangzte River as well as the more standard tours of Beijing, Canton, Shanghai, and the like.

There are 17 different tour programs and more than 33 varied itineraries with over 400 departures per year, including China, China and the Orient, China-Japan, China-Russia, and the Orient alone. It appears that Inter Pacific offers genuine value in that it is constantly researching the various changes that are constantly occurring in China in order that it may offer its clients the very best accommodations available. Prices are reasonable for the services offered.

ACADEMIC TRAVEL ABROAD, INC.
1346 Connecticut Ave., N.W.
Washington, DC 20036
Tel. (202) 785-3412

Academic Tours can boast of clients such as Friends of the Nelson Gallery, Kansas City, Mo.; American University, Washington, DC; National Conference of State Legislators; and, Princeton University Alumni. This organization caters especially to educational and cultural institutions. It helps museums, professional organizations, schools and universities arrange for travel with an educational focus. The Asia Department of Academic Travel concentrates on tours to the People's Republic of China. These tours are designed so that tourists can gain some understanding of the institutions that are important to modern China: agricultural communes, factories, schools, nurseries and neighborhood health centers. Academic Travel appears to be unique in this respect.

Another interesting feature of Academic Travel is the arrangement of tours on a thematic basis. For example, tours are based on such themes as "The Cradle of Chinese Civilization" which concentrates on ancient cities of Xian (Sian) and Louyang (Loyang) and on the archeological sites nearby. Another tour, "Historic Cities of China," goes to the cities of the central and southern regions, the heart of "medieval" China. "Xinjiang and Northwest China" tour visits remote areas such as the site of the famous Mogao Buddhist grottoes and Urumqi (Urumchi), modern capital of the Xinjiang-Uyghur Autonomous Region and ancient caravanserai of the famous Silk Road.

Obviously Academic Travel is not for the ordinary "holiday" traveler. The organization concentrates on institutional travel with emphasis on the educational value of the tour. Their philosophy is very nicely summed up in one of their brochures: "We feel deluxe accommodations may not always be necessary, but deluxe educational arrangements are a must."

CHINA TOURING CENTER
Simone Travel Bureau, Inc.
2112 Broadway, Suite 500
New York, NY 10023
Tel. (212) 496-1900

The China tours offered by this organization cannot be booked through a travel agency but must be purchased directly from Simone Travel Bureau, Inc. This company specializes in serving professionals and "highly sophisticated world travelers." (That sounds as if it might leave out some of the "fun" people.) But Simone says that her tours are a "social experience where friendships are made"

and that her organization takes pride in the repeat business and referrals they've received over the years. There are also 29 cities in China which Simone Travel can arrange visits to on an individual basis, without a group. These trips include private chauffeured cars and a guide.

There are a number of tour categories offered by Simone. One group of tours is directed toward medical and dental professionals. Another group concentrates on Chinese arts and crafts, particularly aimed at those interested in buying Chinese porcelains, silks, lacquerware and the like. There is also a tour for archeology buffs and one unique tour that is organized around the Chinese performing arts—opera, ballet and musical performances are integrated into the regular sightseeing tour. Simone even offers a special tour for Jewish travelers. Although kosher food *per se* is not available in China, the traveler may order from a vegetarian and fish menu daily and there is no traveling or sightseeing on the Sabbath.

Although these special interest tours are practical and well thought out, Simone offers a tour that is perhaps *the* unique way to visit China. It is a Moscow to Peking tour that includes a trip by train from Irkutsk, Siberia through Ulan-Bator, Mongolia to Beijing and on through China. This excursion begins and ends in the U.S. with stops in London on the way to Moscow and Hong Kong on the way home. Although the time spent in China is less than on some of the other tours, it certainly offers a different perspective—imagine arriving in China without crossing the Pacific!

GLOBUS-GATEWAY TOURS
Los Angeles, CA
(Make all arrangements through your travel agency)

Globus-Gateway tours claim they can offer you prices so low that they cannot be matched elsewhere without loss of quality. So it probably would pay to look into them.

Now and then travel organizations will advertise special deals, "supersavers" or whatever, to popular vacation spots around the world. These agents usually cut costs by booking charter flights at group discounts and by making deals with little known hotels and tour guides in the host countries. The price of the tour is surprisingly low, but the risk is usually fairly high. The flight will be as safe as any, but when the weary traveler finds himself spending the first night of the "Vienna Dreams Holiday Tour" in a run-down dump called the Hotel Fritz, he may be less than completely satisfied with the bargain tour.

Great China International Tours has advertised some "supersaver" vacations to China. But you are in less jeopardy with trips to China than you might be with other destinations for one very simple reason. Once the traveler enters China, he is treated absolutely equally whether he flew first class on Pan American's Champagne 747 or was shipped stand-by on Harry's East-Meets-West Freight Transport and Air Bus. It doesn't matter because CITS, the PRC's official travel association, handles the booking of all hotels and the conduct of all tours inside China. So, in effect, no matter how irresponsible your U.S. travel agent might be (and this does not refer to Great China International Tours) it will not affect your travel inside China.

Great China International Tours are very popular because the price is very right. The tours are usually booked soon after the newspaper announcement is made. They are generally routed through Narita, Japan, but there is no touring provided in Japan. The stops in Japan are simply shower-and-sleep stops before and after the China tour.

Always check out the company you're dealing with on "super-saver" excursions. Deceit is not completely unknown in the travel industry.

Currently, they are offering a number of tours to the Orient, many of which include China exclusively or with other main areas of interest. Their "Heart of China and the Fabled Yangtze" tour features a 7-day cruise through the Yangtze River Valley aboard a deluxe cruise ship, the MV *Three Gorges,* China's newest and most luxurious tourist vessel.

They also offer a very comprehensive tour, "China in Depth." This is a 25-day tour which uses Tokyo as its stopover. Eighteen complete days of the tour are spent in China; it includes eight different cities with plenty of time spent in each. You depart via Hong Kong.

Other tours which include China are their "China Triangle" tour, which includes three major Chinese cities with stopovers in Tokyo and Hong Kong; "Ancient Routes through China and the Orient," which includes stops in nine different cities of China as well as Tokyo, Hong Kong, Bangkok and Singapore. This is a 31-day tour.

number of days spent in the PRC. Join a tour that begins and ends in Hong Kong and spend 16 full days in China or take a tour that does not include Hong Kong—land in Beijing (Peking) and depart from Guangzhou (Canton). Kuo Feng will also customize a tour for a group. It appears to have access to just about every location and facility that China has made available to the Western traveler. Kuo Feng has organized tours for the North Carolina Art Society, New York County Lawyers Association, and the American Chinese Medical Association. In addition, Kuo Feng has arranged the Columbia University Study Tours to China. They also handle individual travellers to China.

Kuo Feng arranges departures from New York and San Francisco. The flights are booked with Pan American and Japan Air Lines. The prices for the tours are quite reasonable, especially those that begin and end in the PRC. The addition of Hong Kong seems to add a significant expense to all tours to China.

KUO FENG CORPORATION
Travel and Tours
2 E. Broadway
New York, NY 10038

Kuo Feng was among the first tour operators in America to be recognized by CITS and therefore has logged in some fairly impressive experience at handling tours to China. Kuo Feng visits 22 locations in China—20 cities, the Yangtze River area, and Tibet. These locations are offered in a number of itineraries with a good many departure days. Kuo Feng tours are generally 18–21 day tours. One impressive thing about these tours is the

PERCIVAL TOURS, Inc.
One Tandy Center Plaza
Fort Worth, TX 76102

Percival Tours has been in the American travel industry for over a quarter of a century. At present, they offer a 19-day "China Highlight" tour which includes five of China's major cities via Hong Kong.

China is also included in their "Orient Mystique" tour along with South Korea, Thailand, Bali and Japan. This is a 22-day tour in which seven days are spent in China.

PACIFIC DELIGHT TOURS, INC.
(Must be booked through your travel agency)

These tours, available through travel agents all over the U.S., are offered by an organization that has close and personal ties to China. Their brochures put it this way: "For many of us at Pacific Delight Tours, China is our homeland and so naturally it is of personal importance to us that you gain the utmost pleasure and satisfaction from your China Experience."

The tours offered are fairly standard,

with Hong Kong used as the "gateway" city. The tours seem quite economical and are offered on a number of departure dates. Part of the break on the price seems to be that these tours are based on a "non-affinity group" rate which is obviously more economical.

These tours offer the advantage in the number of days spent in China as compared to "gate-way" or "exit" cities. These tours are *truly* Chinese. Twenty itineraries, ranging in duration from 17 to 26 days, offer a great deal of choice and diversity. Each itinerary highlights various aspects of China and its life, such as a 24-day grand tour highlighting the famed centers of ancient Chinese civilization; a 19-day grand tour highlighting the Yungang Grottoes and Inner Mongolia; and a 13-day grand tour highlighting the ancient Buddhist cave sculptures and monasteries. Truly interesting tours from people who have a genuine knowledge of China.

OLSON-TRAVELWORLD, LTD.

This is another organization that works exclusively through professional travel agents. Travelworld is also a "deluxe" touring organization. Their approach to the "cost" situation is put this way: "In developing our Travelworld tours, we assume that our guests are interested in only the very best available. We also assume that our guests know that you get what you pay for." Snob-city? Well, not completely. Travelworld is very conscientious about the comfort of their travelers, but they also emphasize the human aspects of travel, encouraging personal contact with the people of the various regions of China and in other countries throughout the Orient. And, according to their brochure, some accommodations are also chosen because they are "unique" or "exotic" not because they are luxurious.

An interesting claim that Travelworld makes is that their guests are not restricted to the CITS *table d'hote* hotel meals. Travelworld claims that its guests may visit an "outside restaurant in each region of China visited, featuring the special delicacies of the area." That sounds like great fun.

Travelworld books through Pan Am and uses Tokyo and Hong Kong as "gateway" cities. The tours are not inexpensive—they include a number of special services and, as a result, are priced at the high end of the scale. Travelworld also includes China on some spectacular "round-the-world" excursions. One 34-day around-the-world tour visits Japan, China, Thailand, Nepal, India, Egypt, and Greece. Another tour adds stops in Africa and lasts for 44 days!

HEMPHILL/HARRIS TRAVEL CORP.
Los Angeles, CA

Hemphill/Harris has been in the tour packaging business for over fifty years. There are many advantages to this kind of experience. The connections made throughout the world are quite valuable when arranging the best of accommodations in the preferred areas of the world. That is probably why Hemphill/Harris specializes and takes great pride in deluxe touring. Needless to say, these tours are not for the economy-minded traveler. The tours by Hemphill/Harris are posh. Where possible, they assure the traveler of deluxe hotel accommodations. In China, of course, no tour group has control over where CITS makes hotel accommodations. Hemphill/Harris does, however, have access to Beijing's State Guest House, and will book as many travelers there as possible. You can be sure that, as more deluxe accommodations become available in China, Hemphill/Harris will be there. In addition to deluxe hotel accommodations, Hemphill/ Harris has one of the most attractive meal plans available anywhere. While in China, of course, three meals per day are served *table d'hote*. But outside China, Hemphill/Harris reimburses the traveler for any meal eaten anywhere—hotel, room service, restaurant, Kentucky Fried of Singapore—wherever you wish to take your meals, the check is paid by Hemphill/Harris. Now that's deluxe!

Hemphill/Harris tours always include cities outside China. They book through Japan Air Lines, so a Japanese sojourn is very often a part of the tour. There are a number of "grand tours" of the Orient that include China. One fabulous 35-day tour includes such cities as Tokyo, Kyoto, Manila, Bangkok, Katmandu, Delhi, Bombay, Singapore, Bali, as well as major cities in China—Beijing (Peking), Shanghai, (Wuxi) Wuhsi, Suzhou (Soochow) and Hong Kong. This tour, like so many by Hemphill/Harris, would be the travel experience of a lifetime!

CLUB UNIVERSE
Los Angeles, CA
Phone (213) 484-8910

This travel organization is the largest in the western U.S. It is famous nationwide and for some very good reasons. Club Universe guarantees its departure dates, and works to bring the traveler interesting itineraries at the best prices possible. The price of the tour is also guaranteed for the 75 days preceding departure if the tour price is paid in full 60 days prior to the departure date. In these wild days of airline and travel price hikes, this means more than it might appear at first glance. As a result of these policies, Club Universe is a very successful organization.

Club Universe books through Pan Am so that a great number of China tours arrive and depart from cities in the PRC. The variety of the intineraries and the frequency of departures offered by Club Universe almost demand attention, at the very least for comparison shopping purposes. There are also a number of tours of the Orient that include China, one of which is a 31-day tour that begins with visits in New Zealand, Australia, Bali, and Hong Kong, and ends with 12 days in China. One of the attractive things about this excursion is that for the China part of the journey the traveler has a choice of ten different itineraries that can include as many as five different cities. And the price for all this is very competitive.

It's in the basic China tour itineraries, however, that Club Universe really shines. It offers tours called "China Express," "China Explorer," and "China Journey" that are basically devoted to touring China and Hong Kong. Some do stop in Tokyo for a day or two but the variety of tours in China and the low cost make these China journeys quite attractive.

Club Universe does not advertise "pampering" aspects of its tour packages. It is a straight-forward approach—so many dollars for so much travel. Club Universe apparently expects that the traveler will add something of his own to the basic tours offered. To some travelers, that's just the attitude a tour operator should have.

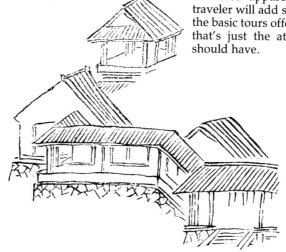

Chinese Cuisine Tours

Various organizations and individuals have organized cooking or culinary tours to China within the last few years. Although the sponsors may change from year to year, the tours seem to depart on a fairly regular basis. They are often advertised in the travel sections of newspapers, in cooking magazines, or through Chinese cooking schools in the larger cities.

To give you an idea of what these tours are like, here are brief descriptions of four recently organized cooking tours of China.

1. Nina Simonds, a well-known Chinese cooking teacher and writer for *Gourmet* magazine, has organized cooking tours to Taiwan and Hong Kong. One tour included ten three-hour demonstration and participation classes featuring two by master chefs from Szechwan Province and Shanghai. Also there were a number of wonderful meals planned in Taipei and Hong Kong. Two of the most interesting were a Chinese vegetarian banquet prepared at a Buddhist temple outside Taipei and a seafood dinner aboard a boat restaurant in Hong Kong's floating community of Aberdeen. This tour was recommended for serious students of Chinese cooking because so much of the time was spent in cooking classes. Nina Simonds can be reached at the following address: P.O. Box 363, Manchester, Massachusetts 01944.

2. Lillian Chen was born in Peking and educated in the United States. She is a teacher of Chinese cooking, language and culture and has organized culinary tours to China. Ms. Chen's tours concentrate on cooking in the PRC. She has chosen special menus at famous restaurants in Beijing (Peking), Shanghai, Hangzhou (Hangchow), and Guangzhou (Canton). She also conducts cooking classes, lectures, and interviews with cooks along the way. Naturally, sightseeing is also included on these tours. Great Places Travel Consultants, 208 E. Washington St., P.O. Box 7670, Ann Arbor, Michigan 48107 organized Ms. Chen's recent tours.

3. Singapore Airlines in conjunction with Andersen Travel Orinda, Inc., Orinda, California 94563 organized the "Ken Hom in Hong Kong" cooking tour. Ken Hom is a well-known cooking instructor on the West Coast. His recent book, *Chinese Technique*, is a landmark publication in Chinese cooking. The Ken Hom cooking tour of Hong Kong is fairly typical of tours arranged around a famous cook. It featured five instructional sessions, seven special restaurant meals with demonstrations of various Chinese techniques, and daily discussions of Chinese culture and culinary history. The tour offered several add-on packages to the PRC, but these trips had nothing to do with cooking, or with Ken Hom for that matter.

4. The Oriental Cooking School of Baltimore organized a "Tour of Culinary China." This kind of tour is handled like a special interest or "affinity group" tour in the PRC. There are no cooking classes *per se*, but the idea is to visit as many food and culinary related locations as possible. This tour included several cities and restaurants, but more importantly it was to include visits to farms where Chinese vegetables are cultivated; to oyster and soy sauce factories; to a typical commune home kitchen; and, to a professional *dim sum* kitchen. Often on such tours it is hard to predict exactly what will be seen. Despite the best laid plans in the United States, the tour in China is completely in the hands of CITS. This tour was organized by Travel Guide Agency Ltd., 311 N. Charles St., Baltimore, Maryland 21201.

Bicycle Tours in China

A fairly recent development in Chinese tourism has been the introduction of extensive bicycling tours of China. One of the great advantages of this kind of tour is that the traveler is biking alongside the Chinese people. Bike traffic can be awesome in China's cities. The bicycle is the primary source of transportation and is a major mode of commercial conveyance—bike jams are not unknown in China. But the best thing about a bicycle tour is seeing the cities and the countryside from a Chinese point of view. And, if it is possible at all for a Westerner to feel free-spirited in China, biking is probably the only way.

Bicycle tours in China are organized by China Passage and coordinated with the All-China Sports Federation (ACSF) of the People's Republic of China. China Passage, 302 Fifth Avenue, New York, NY 10001 (tele. 212-564-4099; toll-free 800-223-7196), is associated with Eurasia Press and has been organizing bike tours of China since 1977. The tours are now arranged with five different itineraries, so that the biker has a choice of areas to visit in China. The itineraries include Mongolia, the Yangtse River Valley, East China (Shandong Peninsula and Shanghai), the China Coast (Fujan Province), and South China (Guandong Province). Sometimes an "extra city" is added to the end of the tour by flying the biker to a distant city for a day or two before he returns to the U.S. For instance, if the biker has been touring the Yangtse River Valley in the area of Shanghai, he might fly to Xian in northwest China for a last two or three days of sightseeing.

The basic itinerary for a bike tour of China includes 18–26 days in China plus 2–3 days in either Hong Kong or Japan. Total cycling distances average 350 miles, averaging 27 miles per day but with no leg of the journey necessitating more than 50 miles cycling per day. All tours are accompanied by bilingual Chinese guides and by experienced bicycle tour leaders from the U.S.

Naturally, one cannot see quite as many of the cities of China on a bike as on a train or bus tour, but what is seen is seen "up close and personal." Meals and social gatherings are often enjoyed with local people along the way, and seeing the countryside from a bicycle is an unmatched pleasure. The camaraderie that develops among the tour members adds a great deal to the experience as well.

Air transport for the traveler and his bicycle, plus a limited amount of luggage, is included in the price of the tour. Oddly enough, the price of this kind of tour is not much different from a conventional bus and train tour of the PRC. Of course, the point is not in saving money, it is in the joy of seeing China in a very special way.

Free information is available from:

China Passage, Inc.
302 Fifth Avenue
New York, NY 10001
(212) 564-4099 or toll-free (800) 223-7196

Major Cities and Places of Interest in China

Beijing (Peking)

Transportation Note

It took a long time, but in January of 1981 the United States and the People's Republic of China at last agreed on terms for direct commercial air service between the two countries. CAAC (Civil Aviation Administration of China) is the official airline of the People's Republic of China and now has more than two flights weekly to and from China (Shanghai and Beijing) and the United States (San Francisco and New York). This breakthrough isn't going to make much of a difference to most people going to China. Why? For starters, you need a visa. Tour operators usually have an allotment of visas and they help you secure one, usually in the form of a group visa, from the PRC authorities in Washington or in New York. Secondly, Americans who wish to tour China do it with a group and a charter flight is usually arranged, with other groups included on board. The CAAC office insists that it is possible, in principle, to simply board the plane, visa in hand, and go to China. But the reality is that travel and hotel reservations are necessary; even the most intrepid loner would probably not be able to enter the tourist orbit. Frequent travelers, such as business people, will take advantage of the new CAAC service. But regular tourists will stick with the tour operators and fly whatever airline that operator books.

Civilization in the area of modern Beijing goes back several thousands of years. As a city, it has been the capital of China for most of the last two thousand years. The Ch'in dynasty (221–206 B.C.) built the Great Wall to protect Beijing from northern invaders and in the 15th century, the Ming Dynasty redesigned and organized it into the city we know today. Modern Beijing is a bustling capital of over 8.5 million people. The great Tian An Men Square in front of the entrance to the Forbidden City or Imperial Palace now serves as an architectural memorial to the glory of Chairman Mao and the revolution. Directly in back of the Forbidden City is the lovely Bei Hai Park with its towering White Dagoba. North of the city are two exceptional sights. At Badaling, the Great Wall can be seen snaking its way among the hills and valleys north of Beijing. And in the northern suburbs of Beijing lie the Ming Tombs which provide interesting insights into perhaps the best known Chinese dynasty. Excellent shopping, restaurants and the world-famous Beijing Opera are also highlights in this remarkable city.

Guangzhou
(Kwangchow/Canton)

In many ways, Guangzhou has been China's "window on the west." It is located on the Pearl River delta, some 100 miles northeast of Hong Kong on the southern coast of China. International trade has traditionally put the population of Guangzhou in close contact with the Western world. Known to most Westerners as "Canton," it is the site of the internationally known Chinese Export Commodities Fair. But this lush tropical city, best known for its exquisite (Cantonese) cuisine, also has a long history of unrest and revolution. It was here, in the 1920s, that the Canton Uprising gave impetus to the rise of communist power in a rapidly crumbling Chinese empire. Guangzhou's tourist attractions include a stunning monument to the revolutionaries, the Sun Yat-Sen Memorial Hall, the ancient Temple of the Six Banyan Trees, and some of China's most beautiful parks. Bai Yun Shan (White Cloud Mountain) is a lovely mountain resort just outside Guangzhou and offers a fabulous panoramic view of the city, the Pearl River, and the entire delta area.

The Chinese call the Yangtse, "Chang Jiang," which means "long river." It is perhaps China's most famous river and certainly one of the longest in the world. But few people are familiar with the spectacular gorges of the Yangtse. There are three main gorges: the Qutang Gorge, a narrow gorge with two chains of steep cliffs which face each other and act as a kind of valve controlling the flow of the entire river; Wu Gorge, perhaps the most scenic because of the mist-clad "Twelve Peaks" of the Wu Mountains which line the banks of the Yangtse here; and Xiling Gorge, the most treacherous because of its rapids and dangerous reefs. There are a number of ancient legends that imbue this stretch of the Yangtse with mystery and romance. The great attraction, however, is the striking natural beauty of the gorges. The two-day boat cruise of the Yangtse Gorges departs from Chongqing (Chungking) in Szechwan Province and continues along the river to Wuhan in Hubei Province.

Tai Shan (Mount Tai)

Located in the mountains of central Shandung, this 4,950 ft. peak is the most sacred of the five sacred mountains of Taoism. The ascent to the top of Tai Shan can be made on foot in about four hours.

The paths and stone staircases combine to make a journey of about six miles. The climb is sometimes difficult, but it is continually rewarding as each turn reveals new and more beautiful vistas. Beginning with the giant stone portal at the entrance to the path, the visitor also sees a number of lovely old pavilions, temples, and other sacred structures along the way. There are rest stops along the paths and one can buy snacks and drinks in many of them. It is possible to spend the night at the top of Tai Shan. The accommodations are rather Spartan, but it allows the traveler a spectacular view of sunrise the next morning. A cable car is planned for Tai Shan in order to facilitate the ascent, but without following the ancient footpaths, much of the inspiration of this sacred mountain cannot be fully appreciated.

Wuxi (Wuhsi)

Tourists, both Chinese and foreign, come to Wuxi mainly because of its location near Tai Hu Lake. It is a resort city with an ancient past. A portion of that past can be captured on an unusual boat trip along the ancient Grand Canal. The canal in Wuxi, which is part of the ancient canal connecting Beijing and Hangzhou, was completed in 610 A.D. The excursion along the canal allows the visitor to see the people and scenery of Wuxi from a very interesting perspective. Tai Hu Lake is the main attraction in Wuxi, however. Along the shores and on the islets of the lake, are a number of beautiful gardens, pavilions and pagodas, as well as natural wonders such as the Cave of Returning Clouds. Wuxi is also known and beloved for two famous products—silk and hand-painted clay figurines. The figurines, which have been produced in Wuxi for over 400 years, are mainly fashioned in a folk art style and represent contemporary literary and political characters.

Nanjing (Nanking)

Situated along the lower reaches of the Yangtse River and near the Purple Mountains, Nanjing is one of the most beautifully located of China's major cities. Nanjing is a very old city dating from about 2400 B.C. Its fame and present layout, however, are mainly due to the establishment of Nanjing as the imperial capital of the early emperors of the new Ming dynasty in the late 1300s. (The later Mings moved the capital back to Beijing.) Nanjing has many very well preserved ancient structures including sections of the original city wall, several gates, and the ancient drum and bell towers. Nanjing is also the site of the Dr. Sun Yat-Sen Mausoleum. The Nanjing Museum is worth a visit for its wide and varied collection of artifacts dating from the time of Peking Man, and the Zijin Shan Observatory located in the Purple Mountains is especially fascinating to those interested in both ancient and modern astronomy.

Guilin (Kweilin)

The strange topography of traditional Chinese landscape painting with its strangely shaped trees and steep limestone escarpments, comes vividly alive in Guilin. This small city is situated along the Lijiang (Li River) in the midst of the most fantastic karst landscape in all China. Steep hills rise perpendicularly from the ground and nearly all of them have underground channels and caverns. This region has long been a source of inspiration for the artists, poets and photographers of China. The five-hour boat trip down the Lijiang is a must for tourists. Also interesting are Seven Star Park and Reed Flute Cave. During the war with Japan, 99% of the city of Guilin was destroyed and Reed Flute Cave became home for over 5,000 refugees.

Lhasa

In the Tibetan language "Lhasa" means "the sacred place." Buddhism, or the Tibetan interpretation of it, reigned supreme in Lhasa and literally made the city what it is today. Here, the Dalai Lama lived and presided in theocratic autonomy until 1955. The current Dalai Lama resides in India, and sacred Lhasa is now open to tourists. The Potala Palace, a 1,000 room fortress and once the residence of the Dalai Lama, plus several important religious buildings including the magnificent Jokhang Temple and Drepung Monastery are architectural treasures of Tibetan Buddhism. The Norbulingka, the summer palace of the Dalai Lama, is also open to visitors. It is located a short distance west of Lhasa in a 100-acre garden. Here one can see the last Dalai Lama's bedroom exactly as he left it when he departed for India in 1955. The trip to Lhasa is not for everyone. Because of its extremely high altitude (12,000 feet above sea level), medical examinations for respiratory sufficiency are necessary before entering Tibet.

Xi'an (Sian)

The ancient city of Xi'an reflects more than any other Chinese city, the continuity of civilization in China. Its history dates back more than 3,000 years. It was the capital for several ancient dynasties and for the first emperor of the Ch'in dynasty (221–206 B.C.), Qin Shi Huang, who is credited with unifying China and connecting various segments of the Great Wall. It is his tomb that became the astounding archeological discovery of the 1970s. Hundreds of life-sized pottery figures were buried with the emperor and are now being excavated in the most gigantic archeological project in China's history. Because of its long imperial history, Xian is one of the most historical cities in all of China. Nearby is the Huaqing Hot Springs resort. Once an imperial retreat, it is now open to the public. It was at this resort that Chiang Kai-Shek was kidnapped in 1936 by his own generals in order to force him to cooperate with the communists against Japan.

Shanghai

This is a relatively "new" city by Chinese standards. Early records indicate that it was established as a fishing village during the Sung Dynasty (A.D. 960–1279). Today, with 10.8 million people it is China's largest city. As a result of colonial exploitation, Shanghai became known as a "paradise for adventurers." Foreign business thrived in the port of Shanghai throughout the late 19th and early 20th centuries. Piers and dockside facilities at the peak of colonial dominance rivaled the best in the world, and money poured into the city. Today, it is a major industrial city of the People's Republic of China, but its lively mercantilism is still in evidence. Small shops and independent vendors crowd the streets, and it is still China's most cosmopolitan city. Services for tourists in Shanghai are probably the best in China because of its long association with foreign travelers. The Bund, formerly a boulevard of colonial mansions, clubs and banks, is now the location for several PRC corporation headquarters, hotels, and Friendship (international trade) Stores. The beautiful gardens and parks along the Bund are well kept and are now open to all. The Shanghai Museum houses an excellent collection of Chinese art, and Shanghai's famous Mandarin's Garden, with its beautiful pools, pavilions and grounds, is a magnificent sight.

FODOR'S
PEOPLE'S REPUBLIC OF CHINA
1982

by John Summerfield
Fodor's Modern Guides, Inc.
514 pp. $12.95

Eugene Fodor is a kind of legend in the travel guide business. He is the creator and the inspiration for the well-known travel guide series that bears his name. The Fodor guides, which now number over 60 titles, are generally published and revised annually so that the factual information they contain is usually pretty accurate. This guide to China was written by John Summerfield who, the back cover tells us, was "a long-time resident of Beijing and still visits China frequently." Of course, a lot of the facts and figures are submitted by the Fodor organization which includes writers, editors and field correspondents all over the globe.

Fodor guides are meticulously organized. Each guide has a complete table of contents and a good index. This guide to the PRC is no exception. After a rather personal and wholeheartedly enthusiastic endorsement of travel to China in the Author's Foreword, the highly organized Fodor form takes over. Headings and subheadings are used extensively so as to categorize each bit of information. The first section, entitled "By Way of Background," is 33 pages long and touches on such subjects as geography, population, agriculture, industry, religion, philosophy, dress, greetings, morality and gifts! This background information is meant to instruct the traveler. It is straightforward and to the point. In discussing the rather strict code of morality in China, for instance, the guides suggest that "as a visitor you should avoid any frivolous or flirtatious display of affection towards the opposite sex." Nuff said! That's the Fodor style.

There's another section that's common to all Fodor guides. It's called "Facts at Your Fingertips." Here are all of the dollars and cents charts (plane fares, bus fares, hotel room charges, etc.), plus all the information currently available on visas, tour guides, train schedules, embassies, vaccinations, liquor, tipping, shopping, hovercraft timetables (for those into hovercrafting), and so forth. Fodor guides shine with this sort of stuff because the information is continually updated.

An interesting and unique section is called "The Chinese Scene." This section has detailed information on specialized aspects of life in China. It's the kind of stuff hardly anyone would expect to find in a guidebook. It includes discussions of ethnic and language diversity in China, and a long section on what is called "Creative China," in which all the arts and crafts of China are detailed. The Chinese political system is examined in surprising detail and Chinese history and cuisine are reviewed. The largest part of "The Chinese Scene," however, is a section called "Doing Business in China." It's an extensive guide to business dealings with the Chinese. It even includes a sample sales contract and insurance policy, plus an "unofficial" translation of the 15 articles of China's law on foreign investment. Only in Fodor's!

The remainder of the book, except for a short supplement on Chinese language which lists useful words and short phrases in English, Pinyin, and Chinese characters, is devoted to travel information on 25 cities and regions in China. Beijing, Guangzhou and Shanghai are given the full treatment. In fact, the section on Beijing is nearly 100 pages long. In addition to the description of tourist attractions, there are city and site maps, hotel and shopping guides and extensive restaurant information. The other 22 entries average about 5 pages each. Most have maps and all have the characteristic Fodor section called Practical Information. Here, the size and location of the area is described, the best time to visit, transportation to and around, approximate cost, highlights for tourists, plus shopping, hotel, and restaurant information is detailed. Complete, up-to-date, practical and highly organized information are a standard of the Fodor series. The number of places discussed is limited, but the information, if somewhat dryly presented, is complete and conveniently arranged for quick reference.

CHINA COMPANION

by Evelyne Garside
Farrar Straus Giroux, New York 1982
276 pp. $7.95

This book is subtitled "A Guide to 100 Cities, Resorts and Places of Interest in the People's Republic." That's an accurate description of the contents, too. There's not much supplementary travel material here. A thirty-page "Introduction" suffices to explain all traveler's aid matters plus the history, geography, customs, religion, politics and culture of China. Ms. Garside spends a minimum amount of time on general travel information. Less than half a page is given to the question of how to get to China, and only one page is devoted to what to bring on the trip. There are several maps but no photographs in the book. The text concentrates almost exclusively on describing 100 cities and regions of China that may be visited by the Western tourist. There is a very brief table of contents, but

an excellent index. There are also appendices and a select bibliography at the back of the book. The appendices include a climate of China and rainfall chart, and a pronunciation guide with some useful but very basic Chinese words and short phrases. The bibliography concentrates mainly on books about contemporary or at least post-revolutionary China.

Of the 276 pages in this guidebook, 222 are devoted to detailed information about places to visit in China. This information is divided into three sections based on three geographical regions: 1) the northeast and north, which includes Beijing and environs, plus Shandong, Shanxi, Henan, and Hebei Provinces; 2) the south, which covers the lower Yangtse, Shanghai, Guangzhou, and Guangxi Province; and 3) the southwest and border provinces—Yunnan, Sichuan, Tibet and Inner Mongolia. This arrangement is good in terms of getting China geographically organized, but it is rather cumbersome as far as quick reference is concerned. The problem is that it's hard to find a city such as Suzhou (Soochow) without knowing what region it's in. And, even then it won't be in any alphabetical order within the appropriate regional section. The only way to find Suzhou or any city or sight quickly is to use the index. Happily, the index in this book is quite complete and has been cross-referenced by Wade-Giles to Pinyin spellings.

The average entry for a city or region of interest is from three to seven pages long. It generally includes a map with a reasonably detailed legend, a discussion of the geographical location, the history of the place, and finally, a very detailed listing of the major places of interest (tourist attractions) in the immediate and neighboring areas. The listing of places of interest is generally very straightforward, one site briefly described in its relative location to the others. Often, however, a site of particular importance will be described in a separate paragraph set off in reduced typeface.

The major tourist cities get a great deal more attention. The section on Beijing and its environs is 40 pages long. It features several maps and structural diagrams, hotel, and shopping information, plus a detailed examination of the Forbidden City, the Summer Palace and the Ming Tombs. In addition, the Beijing section contains a detailed restaurant guide to the city. A similar restaurant guide is provided for Guangzhou.

For sheer numbers of places detailed, it would be hard to find this guidebook's equal. If it has a shortcoming at all, it is that the presentation of this information often gives way to a dispassionate cataloging of places and palaces. The author keeps herself out of the descriptive text almost entirely, thus offering an objective but somewhat less than stimulating reading experience.

THE MORROW TRAVEL GUIDE TO THE PEOPLE'S REPUBLIC OF CHINA
by Ruth Lor Malloy
Quill, New York 1982
379 pp. $12.50

Although this guidebook presents useful information about visiting the various cities and regions of the PRC, its great value is as a guide to planning a trip to China. The first ten chapters of the book are devoted to what might best be described as background or preparatory information about traveling to China. In the first chapter Ms. Malloy discusses the where, when, and how of making a trip to China. She talks seriously about the tour business as it relates to Chinese travel, and explains how to choose a tour group. Another chapter is all about planning an itinerary, budgeting for expenses, and preparing ahead for practically any exigency. An entire chapter is given to discussing (in detail) what to take on a trip to China. Another chapter entitled "Getting There" is entirely devoted to the various modes of transportation to the People's Republic of China. Other chapters provide purely background information on such topics as food, hotels, local customs, domestic transportation, shopping and the like. In the middle of the book is a 125-page chapter called "Destinations." Here, Ms. Malloy discusses the cities and sights in China. Some are given short shrift—Lhasa gets less than a full page, Nanning gets about a third of a page. The more important tourist cities get greater attention—Guangzhou, about seven pages plus a map; Shanghai, about the same; and, Beijing gets a 15-page spread plus a map. The remainder of this fairly large book is devoted to additional background or other information about travel to China. There are some special hints to business travelers and a page or two just for Overseas Chinese travelers. There is a chapter about Chinese history, a chapter composed entirely of addresses and telephone numbers (mainly for CITS offices, hotels, and foreign business or government offices), and a chapter of quick reference information such as yuan-to-dollar and distance-between-cities charts, Pinyin/Wade-Giles spelling comparisons and the like. There are few maps and fewer photos. There is a complete table of contents but, unfortunately, no index.

An interesting feature in the last part of the book is a long chapter called "Useful Phrases." This is not a pronunciation guide, but rather a translation of English phrases into written Chinese characters. Supposedly the traveler can communicate with a Chinese speaking person by pointing to the Chinese characters below the English phrases. There are appropriate responses for the Chinese person to point to as well. It might be more reliable

than trying to actually speak Chinese from a phonetic phrase book, but it seems a rather awkward process. Anyway, it's an interesting idea, and the variety of phrases is considerable. There are collections of phrases relating to such diverse activities as visiting a factory, taking photographs, and attending the theater.

Even though only about a third of this book is related to actual sights and activities in China, this book is really valuable because of all the background information it contains. Ideally, this book should be read before going to China or even before *deciding* to go to China. It's best when it's describing what the traveler should expect and when it's preparing the traveler to get the most out of the trip. One chapter is particularly exemplary. It's called "What Is There to See and Do?" but it's not about the Great Wall or the Beijing Opera. Rather it's a personal discussion of how to enjoy such simple things as taking a walk alone, visiting a school, or shopping in a public market. It encourages and instructs in the matter of asking political questions of the Chinese and it explains something about how to identify traditional Chinese designs—the dragon, clouds, the phoenix—in the ornamentation of buildings and in various arts and crafts in China. It explains relaxing in the Chinese garden, watching Chinese TV, and even suggests things to look for while on a long bus or train ride. Much of this information, of course, reflects the author's personal persuasions and preferences. But it nevertheless represents a source of stimulating and illuminating ideas about the intellectual and spiritual approach to travel in China that is lacking in most guidebooks.

CHINA TRAVELER'S RESOURCE KIT
Distributed by China Books and Periodicals, Inc.
San Francisco $10.95 (price may vary)

This is a unique travel kit. Inside a sealed plastic baggie sort of thing is packed two fold-up maps (one of China and one of Beijing), a pocket-sized Chinese phrase book, a booklet called "Introduction to China," a 224 page "American's Tourist Manual," and 10 postcards. China Books and Periodicals, Inc. has close ties with the People's Republic of China and as a result, has included in this kit some things that are either printed or supplied by agencies of the PRC. The materials in the kit range fairly widely in quality and usefulness.

The fold-up map of China is about 18 inches square and is based on what must have been public access information from the U.S. Government. Of course, since China itself is rather private about what it claims as its borders, complete accuracy is not to be expected. This map, however, is crudely made and the printing is not very good. So, the amateurish look and the difficulty of reading the map properly are problems. The larger Beijing city map is designed around a base map from CITS (the state travel agency in China). Although some of the major tourist sites are pictured, the basic purpose of the map seems to be to point out locations of restaurants and cafes in Beijing. The printing of this map is a bit better than the one of all China, but its presentation is so cluttered that it seems a bit imprecise and is also hard to read.

The 10 postcards included are printed in China. They're not exactly "polychrome deluxe" but they're pretty in a quaint sort of way and would be nice to send or to keep as souvenirs. The little booklet called "Introduction to China," however, is a British publication, put together by the Anglo-Chinese Educational Institute. It's not exactly a "fun" read. It's a rather dry synopsis of contemporary Chinese history, very British and very serious-minded.

The little pocket phrase book is a product of the Foreign Language Press in Beijing. Upon investigation it proves to be one of the most valuable pieces of this travel kit. It begins with a complete key to pronunciation of the English phonetic hanyu pinyin spelling of Chinese words. It then proceeds to list a number of key words and useful phrases in English, Pinyin, and simplified Chinese characters. This little booklet called "Say It in Chinese" can really help you to do just that!

The largest book in the travel kit is the *American's Tourist Manual for the People's Republic of China.* Of the 224 pages in this manual, about 100 are devoted to describing some 48 tourist spots. The descriptive material for the three largest cities—Beijing, Guangzhou, and Shanghai—is fairly extensive and city maps with fairly good legends are included for each. The rest of the cities, with very few exceptions, are treated in about a half a page each. Guilin (Kweilin), one of China's most "touristy" cities is handled in 13 lines! There is no restaurant, hotel or shopping information given for Guilin. Only two specific sights are mentioned: "The Lungyin and Luti Caverns are

found in this area." That hardly does beautiful Guilin justice. And, unfortunately, there is not much organization to what material is presented. All the information is lumped together without subheadings. No "Places to See" section or "Hotels and Restaurants" section, so the book is not much good for quick reference. There is a one-page index which is practically useless, and there is no table of contents at all. In addition, the writing style seems odd, almost as if imperfectly translated from Chinese. And, it often sounds more like a geography text than a travel guide. A good deal of the information here came directly from Lüxingshe (CITS) which probably accounts for some of the stiff, bureaucratic tone. There is, however, a lot of interesting supplementary travel material provided in this book. There are floor diagrams for some hotels, the airport in Beijing, and the Canton Trade Fair. There is also an interesting Chinese menu guide meant to help the traveler in ordering Chinese food.

THE OFFICIAL GUIDEBOOK TO CHINA: 1984

Edited by China Travel and Tourism Press

Hippocrene Books, New York 1984
365 pp. $10.95

This is the third edition of a guidebook that is expressly sanctioned by the PRC's China International Travel Service (CITS or Lüxingshe). The guidebook is unique in that it is written for the American traveler in clear American prose, but with every detail checked, and with much material submitted by Chinese travel experts. The book is very much up-to-date with regard to the cities and regions that are open to the Western tourist. Over eighty cities and regions are described. There are perhaps more city maps, site maps and photographs than in any guidebook to China that is currently on the market. There is a very complete table of contents and an extensive index cross-referenced by Wade-Giles to Pinyin. Of the 365 pages, 224 are devoted to the tourist information about the cities and regions. The remainder of the book is supplementary information about China and particularly about travel in China.

The first section of the book is called "Introduction to China." It's a brief introduction. A little geography, a little history, a bit of culture and that's it. Almost all of the rest of the book is specifically directed toward travel in China. The second section, "Visitor's Information," explains a good deal about entry and exit red tape, public services (postal, medical, etc.), currency, transportation, cuisine and shopping. There's also an interesting few pages on arts and crafts and the native products of China.

Section 3 is all about the three major cities—Beijing, Guangzhou, and Shanghai. The section on Beijing is quite extensive and includes a city map, four site maps and 13 photos of famous sights in Beijing. The sections on Guangzhou and Shanghai are shorter, but the information and photos are equally interesting. Unfortunately, the city maps for these three large cities have been reduced to fit on a single page. And, since they do not have legends, they are a little hard to read. All three sections, however, have good restaurant, hotel and shopping information.

The fourth section is the largest section in the book. It covers some 80 additional cities and regions that are of most interest to the China tourist. Most of these entries are accompanied by photos, maps or both. The information under each city or region is divided into sections: "Places of Interest," describing the tourist sights of the area; "Hotels"; "Restaurants"; and "Shopping." Of course, not all of the places described have hotels, restaurants and shopping for foreign tourists. But, where appropriate, the information is presented. In addition, an interesting bit of background information is given about each city or geographical area described. This guidebook, although not a personal account of China travel, has many interesting minor details about the legends, the mythology and the spiritual life of China and the Chinese. These details give an added dimension to the travel notes throughout the book.

The last section of the book is an appendix that groups all sorts of things together. There is a railroad map, a list of places that accept American credit cards, a list of antique stores; and there are the typical money conversion, rainfall, temperature, and distance between cities charts. There is a Helpful Hints section, too, which really is helpful. And, some restaurant menus are reprinted with a price guide given for each. This edition also contains a new feature, The 100 Most Popular Dishes and the restaurants in which these dishes can be ordered. It also updates the information on new hotels built recently.

All in all, this guidebook presents quite a lot of information in a very organized and readable format. It's a good buy, too!

Dictionaries for the China Traveller

"I Say 'Kwangchow' and You Say 'Guangzhou'"

Guangzhou used to be Kwangchow, but it's always been known as Canton. It's not as mixed up as it seems. "Guangzhou" and "Kwangchow" are just different English spellings or "romanizations" of the name of the same Chinese city. "Canton" is another name for Guangzhou, but it's a name that Westerners gave to the city. Not all Chinese cities have Western names, but almost all of them now have two different spellings. The old British spelling system is called "Wade-Giles." It was developed in Britain in the 19th century. The Wade-Giles system uses lots of "Kw's," "ch's," "chow's," and "-king's"—Kweilin, Chufu, Hangchow, and Nanking. It is still the best-known system among English speaking people. However, the Germans also developed a system for romanization, and other phonetic transliterations of the Chinese sound can be found. The Chinese decided to clear up the discrepancies (and create total confusion into the bargain) by coming up with their very own system of romanization. Their system is called the Chinese Phonetic Alphabet System or Pinyin. It has a very different look. Many of the "kw's," "ch's," "-chow's," and "-king's" were thrown out and replaced with "qu's," "zh's," "-zhou's" and "-jing's"—Guilin (Kweilin), Qufu (Chufu), Hangzhou (Hangchow), and Nanjing (Nanking). There are other differences, too, and the phonetic alphabet has to be studied carefully before a Westerner can hope to pronounce Chinese words that have been romanized by the Pinyin method. In the long run, however, it will probably prove to have been a good idea to standarize the system of spelling.

As a tourist in China, you will see Pinyin being used all over. It's a good idea to get a phrase book, if only to learn how the Chinese spell certain things in English. It's nice, for example, to know that "Chongquing" is just good old "Chungking" in Pinyin.

BERLITZ CHINESE FOR TRAVELERS
Macmillan Publishing Co. Inc., New York
192 pp. $4.95

Berlitz is sort of the Jack LaLane of language studies. Its schools for foreign language are popular nationwide and have a good record of accomplishment. This book is like a very abbreviated Berlitz course in Chinese. It begins with a short grammar lesson and a simplified guide to pronunciation. This book doesn't get into the intricate sounds of the Chinese language. It keeps things simple. The words and phrases are grouped into usage categories. The categories are color coded by a strip of color along the edge of each page—brown means words and phrases about hotels and eating out, green means traveling, sightseeing and etc., red means medical, and so forth. It's a handy idea and partially makes up for the fact that the index in this book is only two pages long—all in English. Don't look in the index for a quick word translation. If you use this book you really need an English/Chinese dictionary, too.

One outstanding feature of this book is the supplemental information given with each section of phrases. It's almost like having a little travel guide in your phrase book. For instance, before the section on food-related words and phrases, there are four pages about Chinese cuisine including some information on banquet dining and even a bit about using chopsticks! There's another special feature. It's the Berlitz version of the "point to the Chinese characters" method of communicating. There is usually a little box in each section with questions and answers printed in English and in Chinese characters. You can simply point at your question and supposedly the Chinese speaking person will point back the correct response. This is great for travelers who feel odd or unsure or both about actually speaking in Chinese. The book is a handy shirt-pocket size and is easy to read.

SAY IT IN CHINESE (MANDARIN)
by Dr. Nancy Duke Lay
Dover Publications, Inc., New York
187 pp. $3.00

Dr. Lay is an instructor of Chinese at the New School for Social Research in New York City. She states at the outset that this little book is not meant to instruct the reader in Chinese grammar. It's just a phrase book. But it turns out to be a very good phrase book. Dr. Lay doesn't fool around much with explaining why the Chinese say things this or that way. She gets right into the phrases. She does give a rather detailed explanation or pronunciation. The Yale system or romanization is what she uses. It's a very complete and maybe a bit complicated phonetic spelling system for Chinese words. But if you're serious about learning and using some Chinese and you're determined to sound as authentic as an occidental can, this is the book for you.

Say It In Chinese has a number of special features, too. Dr. Lay has bracketed words and phrases that can be substituted easily. The idea is that you can use this book with an English/Chinese dictionary and expand your communication possibilities. For example, an entry like this: "I want a room with [a double bed]," means that "a double bed" can be substituted with literally anything you can find in the dictionary. Thus, "I want a room with a view," "I want a room with a closet," "I want a room with a floor show," all become possible! Another excellent feature is the English to Chinese index in the back of the book. It's almost like having a dictionary in the phrase book. It's an index of words with translations and page references to phrases using the words.

The phrases and words are arranged in categories—transportation, foods, laundry, health, hotels, shopping, etc. Here again, the index is helpful because who knows whether the word "soap" is under health, laundry or shopping? There's also an interesting section on common signs and public notices. It's a handy size and it has a sewn binding which usually means a degree of durability. It's a good book and a good value!

Reading Up On China

Books Pertaining To China

It's always a good idea to read as much as possible about a place before visiting it. With China, this is particularly true. Most of us learn very little about the arts or the history of China in school. Our Western European origins tend to influence our educational point of view a great deal. We might read something about Marco Polo, or Genghis Khan; stumble across something about the invention of gunpowder, or see "The Good Earth" or "The World of Suzy Wong" on TV. But more than that usually requires special study.

A bit of reading can certainly set things right. Listed below are some books, fiction and non-fiction that will help fill some of the gaps. There are also some reviews of Chinese magazines in English and some suggestions about how to get hold of them.

NON-FICTION

China Yesterday and Today, Molly Joel Coye and John Livingston. Essays by China experts. Bantam 1979

China: A Short Cultural History, C. P. Fitzgerald, London 1961

China's Three Thousand Years: The Story of a Great Civilization Louis Heren, MacMillan, 1974

Ancient China, Edward H. Schafer, Time-Life 1967

The Rise of Modern China, Immanuel C. Hsu, Oxford University Press 1975

Fanshen, William Hinton, Vintage 1966 Metamorphosis of a feudal village into a modern communist community.

The Arts of China, Michael Sullivan, University of California Press, 1978. Overview of the various arts in China from prehistoric times to present day.

Red Star Over China, Edgar Snow, Random House, 1938 The classic account of the rise of Mao in China.

FICTION

The Good Earth, Pearl S. Buck A favorite American romanticiation of life in pre-revolutionary China by a woman who truly loved China and the Chinese.

Dynasty, Robert S. Elegant Historical novel that follows events in China from 1800s to the present.

Taipan, James Clavell China and Hong Kong are brought to life in this novel about pre-revolutionary China.

Spring Moon, Bette Bao Lord The history of a Chinese Mandarin family from 1892 to 1972. Translates the upheaval of a society to personal terms.

Nobel House, James Clavell This recent best-seller is about economic rivalry in Hong Kong during the 1960s. A facinating insight into modern Hong Kong.

Magazines For The Traveller To China

PEARL
Adasia Limited
G.P.O. Box 8455
Hong Kong

This is an interesting magazine for travelers. It is *very* "Hong Kong" in format and presentation—colorful, slick, and commercial. There are lots of ads. Most have to do with tourism in and around Hong Kong. The magazine is obviously heavily financed by the tourist industry, especially the ferry and hovercraft companies that provide transportation between Hong Kong and Kowloon and Guangzhou (Canton). A lot of the pictures and articles in the magazine, however, are concerned with travel in mainland China. Certain cities and tourist sights are featured in each issue. Moreover, there is a lot of supplementary information—bus schedules in various cities, currency info, temperature charts and, of course, hovercraft schedules.

You can subscribe to this magazine by writing to the above address. It's rather expensive—$23 for a one-year subscrip-

tion (6 issues). That might not be so bad if it includes postal charges. Once in Hong Kong you'll probably be offered a number of complimentary copies of *Pearl.* They're usually given free with your room at the hotel, with tickets at the travel office, and, naturally, when you board the hovercraft!

CHINA: SIGHTS AND INSIGHTS
P.O. Box 82615
North Burnaby Postal Station
North Burnaby, B.C.
Canada V5C 5W4

This relatively new magazine (premier issue, April 1981) is a bi-monthly put out jointly by the China Travel and Tourism Administrative Bureau and a private company in Hong Kong. There's lots of different kinds of information in the first issues. Here's hoping that the editors continue to maintain their high standards and diversity.

The very first issue started out with some straight talk from Lu Hsuchang, the Vice-Minister of the Import and Export Commission of the PRC. Mr. Lu pointed out that tourism in China is still relatively new, which explains ". . . why the Chinese are still inexperienced and have thus been unable to provide high standards of service." He goes on to say that complaints about pricing and service have been numerous, and that the Chinese tourist industry is trying to do something about these problems. He also says that the major problem facing the tourist industry in China today is the shortage of accommodations of an international standard, especially in peak seasons. The piece ends with the obligatory assurances of great strides in the future. On balance, it's refreshing to know that high-echelon administrators are aware of these problems and are willing to talk about them publicly.

Much of the first issues was given to articles about tourist sites and activities in and around Beijing. Lots of color pictures, perhaps a little short on text. But then, the aim of the magazine is to whet the reader's travel appetite. That it does. The cliche about a picture vs. a thousand words in this case is true.

There are also some short articles about goods and services with which the tourist may come in contact. An introduction to Chinese liquors, and a "Shopper's Guide" section affords some idea of the range of merchandise available in Beijing stores for tourists. Another section, "For the Collectors," discusses Chinese scenic stamps and Tianjin carpets, the best that China has to offer.

This is a fun magazine for the prospective visitor. It has almost no advertising, but it makes you want to buy your ticket right away. It may take a while, however, to figure out how there could have been a "reader's column" in the very first issue! You can subscribe to *China: Sights and Insights* by writing to the above address. The initial subscription offer was $13.50 for 6 issues (1 year) and $25.20 for 12 issues (2 years).

GUOZI SHUDIAN
China Publications Centre
Chegongzhuang Xilu 21
P.O. Box 399, Beijing, China

A number of foreign language periodicals are published in China specifically for distribution abroad—especially to Europe and America. You can receive a catalog of these periodicals by writing to the above address. Or, if you know a good bookstore, newsstand, or travel agent that deals in foreign periodicals, you may be able to get a catalog through that outlet.

It's worth looking into, particularly if you're planning your trip in advance—like a year in advance. Reading a Chinese magazine or two, or even better subscribing to one, will give you some new insights into the country.

A variety of magazines are available, and although they may be somewhat more alike than different, it provides a degree of choice. *Beijing Review* is a Chinese news magazine with distinct political overtones. *China Pictorial,* a picture magazine, is also political, but deals more with culture, industry and history. *China Reconstructs* is basically a magazine about socialism in China. There are special interest publications, too: *Chinese Literature, Women of China, China Sports, Social Sciences in China* (a catchy title), plus journals of medicine, science, and even a quarterly periodical called *China's Screen* about the Chinese motion picture industry! Naturally, there's a lot of gratuitous praise for the socialist system in all of these magazines. But they do present an interesting look at Chinese society as perceived or portrayed by the Chinese themselves.

Once You're There

Travel Notebook

"Some of the News That's Fit to Print"

So you've finally decided to make the trip of a lifetime. After two days in Beijing you find yourself missing something. Finally, after another day or so, you realize what the problem is: you haven't heard a thing about the outside world since you stepped foot in China.

That's when it's time to find yourself a copy of *China Daily*, first published on June 1, 1981. It is the first English language newspaper in the history of the PRC, and is available Tuesday through Saturday. *China Daily* is designed to fill a need for foreign residents and visitors to China. The publishers seem to think that the paper will also be of interest to officials and business people who want to learn English in order to do their jobs more effectively. Americans, in their language naivete, may think of that as a remote possibility, but it's a good bet that each copy of the paper is seen by many more Chinese than foreigners. The Chinese, at least a good many of them, seem obsessed with learning English.

So what's in this paper? News, mostly international, with some, but not enough, domestic stories and some sports. Perhaps the most useful part of the paper for tourists is on the second-to-last page. It's a column called "What's On." Here you'll find notices of movies, drama and exhibitions that may be of interest. In sum, it's not the *International Herald Tribune*, but the *China Daily* seems to be part of the permanent scene.

"Shopping Around"

Friendship Stores and Sailors Clubs are not social organizations for singles in China. They are the stores set up by the Chinese for trade with foreign visitors. Located all over China, you'll find the best ones in the large and coastal cities. The stores carry almost identical lines of merchandise throughout China and the pricing structure is standardized from store to store. (Central planning'll do that every time!) You can find quality Chinese handicrafts, jewelry, jade and fabrics here, as well as certain western products such as American cigarettes and liquor. If you want to shop in one of the Chinese stores with the Chinese, go to one of the General Department Stores. The prices are reasonable and you'll get a good idea of what the Chinese have to choose from

in their stores. It's also fun to visit the Chinese arts and crafts department stores and, of course, the wonderful Chinese antique stores. And, you don't have to be worried about being ripped off. The Chinese are incredibly honest and the authenticity of antiques is strictly controlled. All genuine antiques over 100 years old carry an authorized red seal of authenticity.

One word of caution. You'll see some lovely ivory items in China. But the United States, because of ecological considerations, does not allow ivory into this country. So, forget about bringing back ivory pagodas or ivory chessmen. Obey the law—and save the elephants!

"Studio 53½"

Rock music and Western-style night life are certainly not a part of the China scene as yet. But, recently in Beijing a few discos have been allowed to open their doors for the amusement of Western tourists. The Minzu Palace Disco located in the Palace of Minorities (where else?) is the best known. It's called "Studio 53½" by foreign residents in Beijing. The latest Western disco tapes are interspersed with some live 1940s swing sounds. Foreign cigarettes and cocktails are available at the disco as well, and sometimes the dancing is allowed to continue as late as midnight or 1:00 AM!

In China these wild goings-on might be just short of scandalous. Westerners, however, will find China's discos about as "hot" as an all-Pat Boone sock hop at the local "Y." But it's fun to "get crazy" in Beijing and dance the night away—even if the best you can muster is a sort of rusty funky chicken.

"Hairdos & Don'ts"

Do expect to find that barbers and hairdressers have set up shop in most of the larger hotels in Beijing, Shanghai, and Guangzhou.

Don't expect Vidal Sassoon and "unisex hair design" to be lively topics of conversation around the old hairdryers.

Do bring some of your own hair care products (favorite shampoos, conditioners, etc.) for the operators to use on your hair if you feel certain that you will need an appointment while in China.

Don't be disappointed if you cannot find fashionable cutters, colorists, or stylists in China. Most barbers and hairdressers in China are not schooled in the latest high-fashion styles.

Do expect the attendants to be extremely helpful and polite.

Don't expect to pay much. Shampoos, cuts, and sets are very inexpensive in China.

"Coke Is It!"

Coca-Cola, probably the most famous American product ever made, is now in China. And, as everywhere, it's made a big hit. Having Coke available is an unexpected travel pleasure for Americans in China. Not only is it something familiar, but many tourists find the beverage situation in China a bit restrictive.

Most tourists do not want to take the chance of getting sick on the water, and although bottled water is available, it is not always around when you want it. Foreign liquors (scotch, gin, vodka, rum etc.) are available in most Friendship Stores. Wine of all sorts—even California wine—is also common in the foreign trade stores. Local beer is pretty good; "Beijing" and "Tsing Tao" are popular brands. Coffee is not appreciated much in China so you're unlikely to get a good cup in a restaurant or hotel. (Bring your own jar of Taster's Choice, Folger's Freeze Dried or another good instant to mix yourself.) Hot water is plentiful—you generally receive a carafe or thermos of it in your hotel room every day. But, soft drinks are limited in choice in China. There are some lemon and orange flavored beverages available, but if you really want a soda—Coke *is* it!

"*Lüxingshe* (It doesn't mean 'Luxembourg' in Chinese!)"

"Lüxingshe is the Chinese name for CITS—the Chinese International Travel Service. Without Lüxingshe there would be no travel in China. The organization was created by the government of the People's Republic especially to deal with foreign tourism in China. Lüxingshe makes all hotel reservations in China, arranges all ground transportation and domestic air travel for visitors, and trains and assigns the bilingual tour guides who accompany all groups traveling through China. The sights and sounds of the People's Republic of China are still some-what restricted, and access to some areas is very carefully controlled. Lüxingshe makes certain that whatever control of foreign tourism the government deems necessary will be exercised. But, it would be unfair to think of Lüxingshe personnel as a group of plain-clothes cops. They're a professional tour group, interested in making your visit to China a success.

"Taxi!!!"

Success in the taxi game in China depends upon following three basic rules. First of all, be sure to allow plenty of time. Do not decide to call a taxi a few minutes before you hope to depart. You will usually be disappointed. Second, ask someone who speaks Chinese to help you. Taxi drivers do not speak English. If you call for a taxi on the telephone yourself, be prepared to speak in your very best Chinese. The hotel clerk is the best bet. He knows the taxi situation and will be able to get you one sooner than practically anyone. If you have a number of stops to make, have someone write the stops down in Chinese for you. Third, and perhaps most important, do not let your driver go. If you are going back to your hotel or to another destination, have the driver wait. You will be charged for the wait, but it is relatively inexpensive—even if the driver waits for a couple of hours or so. And since hailing taxis in China is not especially easy, it's better to have your driver wait. Your fare is basically figured on the model of the car you're being driven in, and the distance you travel. If your itinerary includes a number of stops, it is also possible to get the driver to set a price in advance. On a Beijing trip recently involving several stops and approximately four hours of time, the fare was set at 26 *yuan*, approximately $13.00 American, a bargain.

Incidentally, one delightful feature of Chinese taxi travel is that drivers will not accept tips. Don't try it either. Tips will be rejected and may even be taken as insults. This will leave you feeling awkward and possibly crass.

China in North America

Not everyone can afford to take a trip to China. Not everyone *wants* to take a trip to China. But there is a way to see something of China without leaving North America. You can visit one of the famous Chinatowns in the United States or Canada.

Although there are Chinese populations in practically every major city in North America, only a few have what can be called *true* Chinatowns—that is, communities where the culture, style of life, and even the "look" of communities in China have been transplanted to the new world. There are five main Chinatowns that are worth visiting because of their ethnic authenticity. They are located in San Francisco, New York, Seattle, and Los Angeles in the United States, and in Vancouver, British Columbia in Canada. What follows is a brief description of what you may expect to find and enjoy in each of these unique communities.

San Francisco

For many people, Chinatown and San Francisco are practically synonymous. It is the best known and largest Chinatown in North America. Located a few blocks north of the central downtown (Union Square) district, it is an integral part of the urban scene in San Francisco—it has been since the beginning of the town itself.

In the late 1840s and early 1850s, settlers began to flock to the western coast of America in search of gold and the good life. The Chinese came, too. They were much like all the other new inhabitants except that they kept their native style of dress and an unusual hairstyle—the queue, a long pigtail of braided hair. This behavior seemed to increase prejudice against the Chinese and locked the immigrants into an imitative lifestyle within the larger "Americanized" communities. Thus were born the Chinatowns of North America.

San Francisco's Chinatown is bounded on the south by California Street, on the west by Mason, on the north by Chestnut and on the east by Kearny. Grant Avenue is the "Main Street" of Chinatown. The best way to approach Chinatown is from the south at Bush Street and Grant Avenue. Here you'll see the beautiful Dragon Gate, a gift of the government of Taiwan, inscribed with a plea for justice on earth by Dr. Sun Yat-Sen. This gate leads you along Grant Avenue to the very heart of Chinatown. Stockton Street runs parallel to Grant Avenue one block to the west. It's the commercial street most used by

the Chinese in Chinatown and in some ways it's more interesting than Grant Avenue. Some of the finest Chinese restaurants in the United States are here in Chinatown. There are also some excellent retail stores that specialize in goods imported from Taiwan and the PRC. There are theaters and galleries including the Chinese Culture Center at 750 Kearny Street, and interesting food markets of all descriptions. Also, you'll want to visit Portsmouth Square, a terraced garden full of activity. It's literally Chinatown's front yard.

There are two interesting tours of Chinatown. One is called the Chinese Heritage Walk. It takes place at 2:00 PM and leaves from the Chinese Culture Center, 750 Kearny Street (3rd floor, Holiday Inn), Tel. 986-1822. It's very popular and three-day advance reservations are required. However, you may telephone to check on other Chinatown walks that may be offered as well. Ding How tours offers a night tour of Chinatown with dinner optional. They usually pick up at the hotels. Call for a schedule at 981-8399. Ding How is located at 753½ Clay Street.

In addition to the everyday color to be found in Chinatown, you can see some spectacular color if you can arrange to come during one of the two major Chinese events. One is the Double Ten (October 10th) celebration of the anniversary of the Chinese Republic. The other is the Chinese lunar new year celebrated in late January or February. As a participant, they're both very special events that you will never forget.

To read more about San Francisco's Chinatown, pick up a copy of CHINATOWN *San Francisco* by Richard Reinhardt with great photos by Peter Perkins. It was published by Lancaster-Miller Publishers, 3165 Adeline St., Berkeley, California 94703.

New York

In August of 1847, an exhibition junk named *Kee Ying* was docked in New York harbor. Before it left on its return voyage to China, a few of the sailors jumped ship and took up residence in New York. These sailors may have been the first Chinese in New York and may well have been the first citizens of New York's Chinatown. But most of the Chinese who settled in New York after the *Kee Ying* set sail came via California. These early immigrants settled in a tiny triangular area bordered by Mott, Doyers and Pell streets in Lower Manhattan. Today that triangle is the heart of a much larger Chinese community known in New York as "Chinatown."

Early Chinese immigrants to New York were ninety-nine percent male. Unlike other immigrant groups in New York, the Chinese did not come to stay. They were "sojourners" who came to make money and return to China to buy land. Many of them did stay though, and Chinatown in New York became an established fact. For some time, there were restrictions on the number of Chinese immigrants that were allowed into the United States. National origin quotas were abolished in 1965, however, and many Chinese (15,000 to 20,000 a year) now immigrate to America. One-third of those settle in New York. That makes New York's Chinese population larger than any city's in the United States. Although the majority come from Hong Kong and Taiwan, an increasing number are coming from the People's Republic of China. Chinatown is home and workplace to most of these new citizens, but since space is always limited in Manhattan, the Chinese have fanned out into all the boroughs of New York. There are many jobs available to incoming Chinese in the bustling restaurant business in Chinatown. But the garment factories located there provide the greatest source of immigrant employment.

Tourism is a big deal in New York's Chinatown. New Yorkers and out-of-towners alike can feel like tourists in Chinatown. It is by far the most exotic neighborhood in Manhattan, and probably the only one in which you might actually feel as if you're in another country. The streets, the buildings, the people, the shops, the sounds and smells—all seem foreign to an average American. That is probably the great delight of this Chinatown. It has that teeming, oriental urban reality that one associates (probably thanks to Hollywood) with Shanghai or Canton.

Mott Street is still the main drag in New York's Chinatown just as it was in

Seattle

The first settlers in Seattle made their living largely by supplying San Francisco and the rest of California with lumber. Business was good in the late 19th century because of the rapid growth of the population in California and would remain healthy as a result of a continued building explosion on the west coast (not to mention a rebuilding explosion as a rsult of certain memorable fires and earthquakes)! But chopping down trees and turning them into 2×4's does not a great city make. As late as the 1890s Seattle's population was only about 20,000. But, in 1897, everything changed. In that year, the steamship "Portland" docked in Seattle. Aboard was one million dollars in gold, fresh from the Yukon. Seattle suddenly found a new purpose in life. She became "the emerald city" built on the boom in Alaskan trade and travel. The brash and burly logging town would never be the same.

Seattle's population jumped to over 200,000 in the first years of the new century. Among the new settlers came the Chinese, and, as in San Francisco and Vancouver, they settled in the heart of the city and created a little town within the town. Nowadays Chinatown is in what is called the International District in Seattle. That's probably because it includes Japanese and other east Asian businesses and residents as well as the Chinese. It is not quite the "pure" Chinese community one finds in New York or San Francisco, but it is interesting and very enjoyable in its own way.

The International District is located roughly between Yeslerway on the north, Interstate 5 on the east, Dearborn on the south, and 4th Avenue on the west. Chinatown tours begin at the Kobe Park Building. You can go on walking tours with some offered that include lunch. There are a number of stores and restaurants in the district that attract customers from all over the city. Tourists will find them excellent as well. You can see fine exhibits of Asian folk art at the Wing Luke Memorial Museum at 414 8th Avenue South. Hing Hay Park, with its colorful Chinese Pavilion, is a must. It is often the site for martial arts exhibitions and Chinese folk dancing. Chinese New Year is, of course, celebrated here annually. And a colorful Chinese community parade in the International District takes place in July as part of Seattle's annual citywide SeaFair—a great time to visit Seattle!

the 1860s. Turn south on Mott Street from Canal Street and you'll pass all kinds of bright and exotic shops and restaurants. Then simply wander around the narrow, winding streets. You'll soon get the feel of life in this unique Chinatown.

There are a number of cultural activities and festivals that take place in Chinatown or are sponsored by the Chinese community. The Yeh Yu Chinese Opera Association presents classic Chinese opera with mime, acrobatics and lavish costumes. For information, call (212) 931-7630. The Chinese Music Ensemble, 149 Canal Street, Tel. (212) 925-6110, is a group of musicians that gives regular concerts of traditional Chinese music. The Chinese American Arts Council, 45 Canal Street, Tel. 931-7630, publishes a calendar of events that serves as a guide to what's happening in Chinatown. There's a big celebration on Chinese New Year, with fireworks and huge paper lions snaking through the streets of Chinatown. There are also a number of festivals featuring Chinese music and dance sponsored by the Chinese American Arts Council. Call (212) 931-7630 for complete information.

For a much more complete look at New York's Chinese community, a book called *The Complete Guide to Ethnic New York* is worth picking up. It's by Zelda Stern, published by St. Martin's Press.

Los Angeles

The history of Los Angeles is similar in many ways to the other cities of California. A dusty little pueblo near some old Spanish missions is suddenly transformed into a boom town when gold is discovered. For Los Angeles it was the dazzling riches of the Mother Lode in the Sierra foothills. Discovery here had the same effect it had had in the north. Settlers began pouring in from all over. But, unlike San Francisco, Seattle, and Vancouver, there was really no city to speak of when the settlers arrived in the Los Angeles basin. So, the city grew in a different way. It was built as a kind of conglomerate of small communities. L.A. still has that kind of layout—lots of communities and very little central city. The Chinese that came to Los Angeles staked out their neighborhood near the center of what is now downtown, just off North Broadway near College Street. But in Los Angeles, Chinatown doesn't seem so much like a city within a city. The "mixed-bag" nature of the Los Angeles area seems to accommodate easily every community and somehow make all of them appear to be part of a cohesive whole.

Chinatown in Los Angeles is a collection of curio shops, restaurants, businesses and tourist entertainments strung along the "Street of the Golden Palace." There are many very fine tea houses, a food mall, and a famous restaurant called "Hong Kong" that features Chinese entertainment nightly. There are wonderful values in the silk and brocade markets, and you'll find lovely lacquerware and jade items as well. Don't expect the excitement of the San Francisco or New York Chinatowns. This one is not really worthy of an extended visit. But you'll see a wide selection of authentic Chinese goods, and the nightlife here can be surprisingly lively!

Vancouver

There's an old legend in Vancouver, British Columbia, that tells of some stray Chinese adventurers actually arriving in North Vancouver a thousand years before Columbus set sail for the new world. The legend may be fanciful, but just as the Chinese were some of the first on the scene in San Francisco, they were also very early in Vancouver. Chinese settlers came to Vancouver in Canada for much the same reasons they came to the cities of the United States. They came to work, to be free, and to make a fortune. Vancouver proved to be a particularly hospitable environment and many stayed. Today, the Chinatown in Vancouver is the second largest Chinatown in North America.

Like Chinatowns in the United States, Vancouver's Chinatown is located in the heart of the downtown district. Its main commercial avenue is West Pender. The concentration of Chinese establishments is between Carrall and Gore streets on Pender. There are interesting Chinese establishments on East Pender, too. In 1913, Sam Kee built what is generally thought to be the world's narrowest office building. It's located at East Pender and Carrall and is now used as a retail store.

This Chinatown, much like the one in San Francisco, has close ties to the Republic of China (Taiwan), and reveres its founder, Dr. Sun Yat-Sen. During Dr. Sun Yat-Sen's campaign for revolution in China, he visited Vancouver and stayed briefly in the historic Chinese Freemasons Building. Now a park is being developed adjacent to the Freemasons Building—a park dedicated to Dr. Sun Yat-Sen. It's scheduled to be completed this year and will extend south to Keefer Street.

Be sure to visit the Chinese Cultural Center Shopping Arcade at 10 East Pender. There you'll find an interesting array of Chinese arts and crafts as well as imported products from Taiwan and the PRC. If you can plan your visit around the time of the Chinese lunar New Year (late January or February) you'll be treated to one of the best celebrations this side of Hong Kong. There are parades, firecrackers, and lion dancers, plus lots of good food and music.

For more information about visiting cities with Chinatowns, write:

San Francisco Convention & Visitors
 Bureau
1390 Market Street
San Francisco, California 94102

New York Convention & Visitors Bureau
2 Columbus Circle
New York, New York 10019

Seattle-King County Convention and
 Visitors Bureau
1815 Seventh Avenue
Seattle, Washington 98101

Greater Los Angeles Visitors and
 Convention Bureau
505 South Flower Street
Los Angeles, California 90071

Greater Vancouver Convention &
 Visitors Bureau
#1625-1055 W. Georgia Street
P.O. Box 1142 Royal Centre
Vancouver, B.C. V6E 4C8
Canada